Endless Income

Endless Income

50 Secrets to a Happier, Richer Life

Ted Bauman

2nd edition

BANYAN HILL

Banyan Hill Publishing
P.O. Box 8378
Delray Beach, FL 33482
Tel.: 866-584-4096
Email: https://banyanhill.com/contact-us
Web: https://banyanhill.com

ISBN: 978-0-578-73809-3

Notice: this publication is designed to provide accurate and authoritative information in regard to the subject matter covered. It is sold and distributed with the understanding that the authors, publisher and seller are not engaged in rendering legal, accounting or other professional advice or services. If legal or other expert assistance is required, the services of a competent professional adviser should be sought.

The information and recommendations contained in this publication have been compiled from sources considered reliable. Employees, officers and directors of Banyan Hill do not receive fees or commissions for any recommendations of services or products in this publication. Investment and other recommendations carry inherent risks. As no investment recommendation can be guaranteed, Banyan Hill takes no responsibility for any loss or inconvenience if one chooses to accept them.

Banyan Hill advocates full compliance with applicable tax and financial reporting laws. U.S. law requires income taxes to be paid on all worldwide income wherever a U.S. person (citizen or resident alien) may live or have a residence. Each U.S. person who has a financial interest in, or signature authority over bank, securities, or other financial accounts in a foreign country that exceeds $10,000 in aggregate value, must report that fact on his or her federal income tax return, IRS form 1040. An additional report must be filed by April 15th of each year on an information return (FinCEN form 114) with the U.S. Treasury. IRS form 8938 also may be due on April 15th annually, depending on the total value of foreign assets. Willful noncompliance may result in criminal prosecution. You should consult a qualified attorney or accountant to ensure that you know, understand and comply with these and any other reporting requirements.

AUTHOR BIO

Ted Bauman

Ted Bauman joined Banyan Hill Publishing in 2013. As an expat who has traveled to over 60 countries and lived in the Republic of South Africa for 25 years, Ted specializes in asset protection and international migration. He is the editor of *Bauman Daily*, *The Bauman Letter*, *Alpha Stock Alert* and *10X Project*. Born in Washington, D.C. and raised on Maryland's Eastern Shore, Ted migrated to South Africa as a young man. He graduated from the University of Cape Town with postgraduate degrees in Economics and History.

During his 25-year career in South Africa, Ted served a variety of executive roles in the South African nonprofit sector, primarily as a fund manager for low-cost housing projects. During the 2000s, he worked as a consultant, researching and writing extensively on financial, housing and urban planning issues for clients as diverse as the United Nations, the South African government, and European grant-making agencies. He also traveled extensively, largely in Africa, Asia and Europe.

In 2008, Ted returned to the U.S., where he served as Director of International Housing Programs for Habitat for Humanity International, based in Atlanta, Georgia. During that time, he extended his travels to Latin America and the Caribbean. He continued to research and write on a variety of topics related to international development. In 2013, Ted left Habitat to work full-time as a researcher and writer. Ted has been published in a variety of international journals, including the *Journal of Microfinance*, *Small Enterprise Development, and Environment and Urbanization*, as well as the South African press, including the *Cape Times*, *New Internationalist*, *Cape Argus*, and *Mail and Guardian*.

TABLE OF CONTENTS

INTRODUCTION

Why do people think the way they do? Sometimes the answer is obvious. People raised in strict cultural environments often end up with similar beliefs as their parents. Those who experience profound personal dislocations are usually permanently affected.

In my case, an unusual combination of factors made me what I am. I was born into a conservative American family with strong beliefs about personal liberty and the dangers of statism. Then I ran off to Africa and experienced firsthand (a) the revolutionary overthrow of an oppressive government and (b) the rise and ultimate corruption of another.

During my years in South Africa, I developed the conviction that true freedom isn't something to be purchased. It does not result from wealth. Nor should it depend on handouts from the government.

Instead, freedom comes from a never-ending struggle by individuals and groups to define and pursue their own interests within broader society. Those interests consider the interests of others. They are not exclusive or oppressive. Freedom means coordinating with others for everyone's best interest.

But freedom never comes from politicians — at least, not from them alone. Voting will never secure freedom. Voting is important. So is speaking your mind to influence others. But freedom also requires a willingness to take direct personal action.

The strategies in this book are examples of that kind of personal action. In every case, I identify a solution to a problem, or an opportunity. These strategies are legal. But they are often buried deep in bureaucratic regulations or case law. Sometimes they are even deliberately obscured by those who stand to benefit financially or politically if you don't know about them. Other times people ignore them because they assume they are only for the rich and powerful.

Creating an asset protection trust in the state of Nevada, for example, is an inexpensive and powerful way to ensure that your assets — no matter how large or small — are protected from legal challenges. I don't mean that you can get away with crime; I mean that if you are sued, or faced with a difficult divorce, or a business partnership goes sour, whatever you vest in the trust is safe.

Similarly, the tax optimization strategies I discuss aren't illegal. Nor are they unethical. But they are often restricted to wealthy clients of wealthy tax attorneys because those attorneys like to pretend that they are difficult to implement. They aren't, and I show you how to do it.

Opportunities like self-directed individual retirement arrangements (IRAs) are little-known because the retirement-saving industry vastly prefers it that way. They tell scary stories about what can happen if you do something wrong with your IRA, then take your money and invest it in weakly performing stocks and charge you high fees. It's true IRA mistakes can be costly, but I tell you how to avoid them — without charging you an arm and a leg.

These three examples have something in common: People are often afraid to try them. They think they will get into trouble, or that they are too expensive, or too complex and risky.

That illustrates another thing about freedom: It means overcoming those fears. The best way to do that is to consult someone who truly cares about you and your prosperity. Someone who does what he does not just for a job, but as a personal mission.

I'm that someone. I know you will benefit from this book, and from the strategies for freedom and prosperity contained in it. And you should know that when you do, I will be very happy indeed!

Kind regards,

Ted Bauman
Editor, *The Bauman Letter*

INCOME

The freewheeling '80s churned out a bevy of movies about how a little guy with grit, intelligence, and a little cash could make it rich investing on Wall Street. But there's far more to smart investing than just scooping up the hottest names trading at the moment. In this section, you'll learn about several types of assets that pay out a steady stream of income, how to get paid by your country treasury, and a critical way to slash fees that are eating away at your returns. Punch your ticket now to beating Wall Street with its own tricks.

INCOME SECRET NO. 1:

Turbocharge Your Portfolio With High-Yielding, High-Performing REITs

You've heard the adage, "It takes money to make money."

While that's not necessarily true, it doesn't take a degree in economics to realize that the more money you already have and invest, the more additional income you can generate.

Trouble is, nowadays, you won't get rich any time soon relying on interest-bearing certificates of deposit (CDs), savings and money market accounts and dividend-paying stocks.

Currently, interest rates are near their all-time lows. At best, savings accounts only offer 2% or less annual interest, which means $100,000 will earn about $2,000 per year. The current inflation rate is 1.7%, so you're only .3% ahead of the game — and that's before taxes.

Same goes for the top money market accounts and CDs, the latter of which requires that you keep your money in your account for one, two or up to five years to avoid a penalty.

As for dividend-paying stocks, the average yield on various sectors range from less than 2% to just under 5%. Not bad, but not as impressive as another alternative — one that can generate two times, three times or even *five times* as much income on your investment...

I'm talking about real estate investment trusts (REITs).

A REIT is a company that owns, operates or finances income-producing real estate and offers investors the opportunity to not only own a share of the properties in its portfolio, but also access dividend-based income.

These companies don't pay corporate income tax. To enjoy that status, they must pay out at least 90% of their net income as dividends.

Keys to the Real Estate Kingdom

There are two types of REITS:

Equity REITs are the riskier type of REIT. And I typically don't recommend investing in them. **Equity REITs** represent the majority of REITs. They own or operate income-producing real estate. When people talk about REITs, this is generally the type they are referring to.

REITs tend to focus on specific sectors of properties, such as retail or shopping centers, hotels and resorts, or health care and hospitals.

So you may be wondering ... What makes them such a lucrative asset compared to other investment opportunities?

Well, for one thing, consider recent dividend yields on some of the top publicly-traded REITs:

- AGNC Investment Corp (AGNC) — 11.53%

- Iron Mountain Inc. (IRM) — 9.37%

- Innovative Industrial Properties Inc. (IIPR) — 4.89%

- Ventas Inc. (VTR) — 8.93%

- Vornado Realty Trust (VNO) — 6.92%

- St. Green Realty Corp. (SLG) — 8.03%

- Medical Properties Trust Inc. (MPW) — 5.78%

Another key advantage of REITS is their dividend growth rate. Unlike bonds, they can raise their payouts each year, thereby keeping shareholders ahead of the inflation rate.

And, not only do REITs historically deliver competitive total returns based on high and steady dividend income and long-term capital appreciation, they also have outperformed leading U.S. bonds over extended periods.

What's more, the FTSE NAREIT Composite Index which tracks U.S. equity and mortgage REITs has absolutely crushed the S&P 500 since the turn of the century:

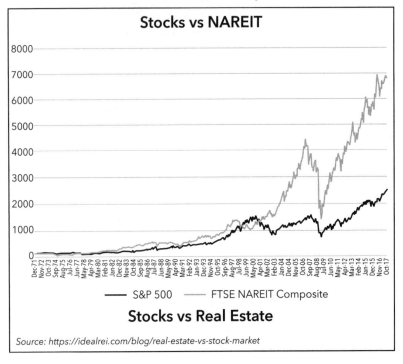

Source: https://idealrei.com/blog/real-estate-vs-stock-market

What to Look for When Assessing a REIT

Of course, not all REITs are created equal. So before investing in one, you need to look at some key fundamentals...

REITs are total-return investments, meaning they provide high dividend yields with moderate long-term capital appreciation, so you should focus on those companies that have historically provided both.

Unlike traditional real estate, many REITs trade on stock exchanges. Those that do, provide diversification and liquidity because you're not locked in long term.

Instead of using its payout ratio (as you would as a dividend investor) to assess a REIT, concentrate on its funds from operations (FFOs) since depreciation tends to overstate a decline in property value. FFO is the net income minus the sale of property in a given year and the depreciation. Take the dividend per share and divide it by the FFO per share. The higher the yield, the better when comparing with other REITs.

Seek out companies that have a lengthy history or at least one with an experienced management team.

Also, worth noting: The Tax Cuts and Job Act (TCJA) affords significant tax savings to REIT shareholders, allowing you to deduct up to 20% of your ordinary REIT dividends with the rest of the income taxed at your marginal rate. So, instead of the 39.6% top income tax rate of 2017 distributions, investor's taxable rate is now 29.6% resulting in after-tax savings of 25.3%.

My recommendation? Consider investing in a REIT exchange-traded fund (ETF) or mutual fund, leaving the research and portfolio selection to the professionals.

To learn more about REITs, visit: https://banyanhill.com/archives/weekly-podcast-heres-why-reits-are-the-way-to-go-for-income-growth.

Also, read Income Secret No. 2 to find out how you can become a "lazy landlord" and collect rent without buying or managing a single piece of real estate.

INCOME SECRET NO. 2:

Become a "Lazy Landlord" and Collect Rent Without Buying or Managing a Single Piece of Real Estate

Wouldn't it be nice to invest in real estate and derive a steady income without having to lift a finger and actually manage the property?

Well, you can — and you don't need to put up millions of dollars of your own money to do it. The trick is to use crowdfunding sites to invest in real estate investment trusts (REITs) and, in the process, generate a substantial amount of income.

As stated in Income Secret No. 1, a REIT is a company that owns, and often operates, income-producing real estate. There are many types of commercial real estate owned by REITs, including office and apartment buildings, hotels, hospitals, shopping centers, warehouses — even timberlands. Other REITs are focused on financing real estate.

But REITs aren't you're only option...

There is also real estate crowdfunding.

You may already be familiar with "crowdfunding" sites, such as GoFundMe.com, but did you know there are sites also used for real estate?

With crowdfunding sites such as FundRise.com or RealtyMogul.com, your annualized yield could be as high as 11%.

Real estate crowdfunding provides you with the ability to individually select the properties you wish to invest in. You can be more selective on a project-by-project basis and build yourself a custom portfolio that is to your specific investment objectives.

In addition, real estate crowdfunding affords you the opportunity to invest in certain real estate markets that were previously off limits, such as commercial real estate.

Plus, crowdfunding doesn't require a large minimum investment. You can own a stake in a major real estate project without having to invest a large amount of money. Being able to invest small amounts of money in real estate deals, you can diversify your ownership in multiple properties. That allows you to build a more diversified portfolio with minimized risk exposure. For example, instead of investing $250,000 in one property, you can invest $50,000 in five different projects.

Another important consideration: Investments in real estate crowdfunding campaigns are not publicly traded. Therefore, they are not subject to market-to-market valuations from minute to minute. This means the value of your real estate crowdfunded investments doesn't fluctuate. That's why crowdfunded REIT investments provide a safe haven from market volatility.

To further explore this opportunity to become a "lazy landlord" while boosting your income, here are four of the top real estate crowdfunding sites worth looking into:

- Fundrise
  (https://investorjunkie.com/44325/fundrise-review)
- LendingHome
  (https://investorjunkie.com/48088/lendinghome-review)
- Patch of Land
  (https://investorjunkie.com/47907/patch-land-review)
- Realty Mogul
  (https://investorjunkie.com/reviews/realty-mogul/)

INCOME SECRET NO. 3:

Score Double-Digit Dividends Investing in Emerging Companies

While we're on the subject of dividends, another less than widely known source of income derived from shrewd investments are Business Development Companies, or BDCs.

They're a form of unregistered closed-end investment companies that finance small- and mid-sized businesses, as well as distressed companies. A BDC helps the small- and medium-sized firms grow in the initial stages of their development or — in the case of distressed businesses — helps them regain their financial footing.

Now, you might be wondering why the average investor would want to invest in a BDC, given that their use of leverage and targeting small or distressed companies makes them high-risk.

The answer is that they offer some very attractive dividend yields — anywhere from 9% to 11% among the top 10 BDCs — and some capital appreciation potential as well.

BDCs are set up similarly to closed-end investment funds. They are either listed, nonlisted or private. But many are public companies whose shares trade on major stock exchanges and are open to retail investors. As of May 2019, there were approximately 49 publicly-traded BDCs.

The Whys and Hows of BDCs

Business Development Companies were created by the U.S. Congress back in 1980 as a means of fueling job growth and assisting emerging businesses in raising funds. As such, BDCs are closely involved in providing their portfolio companies — both private and small public firms with low trading volumes — with advice about their operations. They offer permanent capital to these businesses using a wide variety of sources, such as equity, debt and hybrid financial instruments.

To qualify as a BDC, a company must meet specific standards:

- It must be registered in compliance with Section 54 of the Investment Company Act of 1940.

- It must be a domestic company whose class of securities is registered with the Securities and Exchange Commission (SEC).

- It must invest at least 70% of its assets in private or public U.S. firms with market values of less than US$250 million.

- The BDC must provide managerial assistance to the companies in its portfolio.

If BDCs sound a lot like venture capital funds, that's because they are. However, there are some key differences.

Venture capital funds are available mostly to large institutions and wealthy individuals through private placements, while BDCs allow smaller, non-accredited investors to invest in them, and by extension, in small-growth companies.

Whereas venture capital funds keep a limited number of investors and must meet certain asset-related tests to avoid being classified as regulated investment companies, BDC shares are typically traded on stock exchanges and are constantly available as investments for the public.

The Advantages of BDCs

So, what are the advantages and disadvantages of investing in BDCs?

They provide exposure to debt and equity investments in predominantly private companies that are typically closed to investments.

Also, since BDCs are regulated investment companies (RICs), they must distribute over 90% of their profits to shareholder, like REITs. Because of their RIC status, they don't pay corporate income tax on profits before they distribute them to shareholders.

That's why BDCs can offer above-average dividend yields. Investors who receive dividends from BDCs pay taxes on them at their tax rate for ordinary income. Distribution of net investment income and net realized capital gains are made quarterly.

On top of that, BDCs can diversify your portfolio with securities that can display substantially different returns from stocks and bonds. And since they trade on public exchanges, they provide a certain amount of liquidity and transparency. You have the flexibility of entering or exiting the investment whenever you desire.

Shareholders in publicly traded BDCs receive Form 1099-DIV and are not required to file Schedule K-1 (Partner's Share of Income, Deductions, Credits, etc.) Form, which keeps things simple.

To learn more about BDCs, visit https://www.dividend.com/how-to-invest/everything-you-wanted-to-know-about-bdcs/.

INCOME SECRET NO. 4:

Garner High Yields and Built-In Liquidity With Affordable BDC "Baby Bonds"

Skittish about the potential risk of investing a good portion of your investable assets in a Business Development Company (BDC), but still looking to take advantage yield as high as 14%, as well as some liquidity?

You can have skin in the game with an affordable alternative — or, if you will, an "offspring" of BDCs — known as "baby bonds." They are issued in small denominations and, like BDCs, offer high yields but with lower risk.

> **Baby bond:** A fixed income security issued in small-dollar denominations, with a par value of less than $1,000. The small denominations enhance the attraction of baby bonds to average retail investors.
>
> — Investopedia

BDCs have been offering these baby bonds to individual investors at enticing yields currently ranging from about 6% to 7.5%, depending on the credit rating of the issuer and maturity of the bond.

Investment grade baby bonds have yields at the low end of the range, while non-investment grade ones are at the higher end for similar maturities. That compares favorably with yields on junk bonds, which are relatively similar, though the bonds are all non-investment grade.

"Investment grade" simply means that a bond issuer has a relatively low chance of defaulting on its debt obligation. "Non-investment grade" means that chances of default start to increase further. These measures refer to the "credit quality" of the bond issuer in question.

So how exactly should investors evaluate the safety and quality of BDC baby bonds? You can start by looking at the credit quality of the parent company who issued the baby bonds. Many BDC's carry credit ratings from one of the major U.S. rating agencies. The big three agencies include Standard & Poor's (S&P), Moody's and Fitch Ratings. Analysts at these firms deploy a strict set of criteria when evaluating the creditworthiness of any company, or the likelihood that you'll be paid your interest and principal on time. They take a variety of financial metrics and business end market conditions into consideration.

For example, at the time of this publication, the BDC company Main Street Capital Corp. was rated "BBB" by S&P, with a stable outlook. By S&P's guidelines, that rating qualifies as investment grade.

But, it's important to also know that not all BDC's are rated, so as always, it pays to do your own homework.

Since BDC baby bonds are debt securities, you should be most concerned about receiving your interest payments and principal at the maturity of the bond. Therefore, you should focus on the ability of the parent BDC to generate sufficient profits to pay debtholders.

Given their structure, BDC's already carry relatively high levels of debt. (Don't forget, you are a creditor as a baby bond-holder!). So you should focus on the BDC's interest coverage ratios.

Interest coverage simply measures how much operating profits a company generates relative to debt payments being made. A higher ratio is better because it indicates a BDC has more operating profits to make interest payments.

And since we are talking about BDC's, their operating profits are essentially the income they collect from their investment portfolio. So we should look at the ratio of investment income to interest expense. At a minimum, I prefer a ratio of two or higher.

But the better quality BDC's will tend to have an interest coverage ratio close to three or better. Simply put, a higher ratio means our interest payment is safer should business conditions deteriorate.

Aside from their yield benefits, baby bonds offer a number of other clear and compelling advantages. With par values as low as $25, they are more accessible to investors and come with built-in liquidity. Usually listed on either the Nasdaq or New York Stock Exchange, they can be bought and sold just like a normal stock.

Though liquid, investors should still use limit orders. That's because BDC's and their baby bonds can have large price swings, especially during periods of volatility. While a market order will execute immediately at the prevailing price, a limit order is all about getting the price you want.

But overall, baby bonds tend to exhibit lower volatility than their BDC parents. Unlike the stocks of their issuers, which typically fluctuate more in price, baby bonds generally have a greater likelihood of returning principal, plus interest, provided the bonds are held to maturity. Maturity can range from 10 to 30 years, with most in the 10- to 15-year range.

What exactly do I mean by lower volatility? The chart below is a great example of the price ups and downs among baby bonds and BDC's in general. This compares an index of each from the start of 2017 through the end of 2019. The gray line is an index of BDC's, while the black line is an index of BDC baby bonds. While the BDC index is ahead at the end of 2019, it took a much wilder ride to get there!

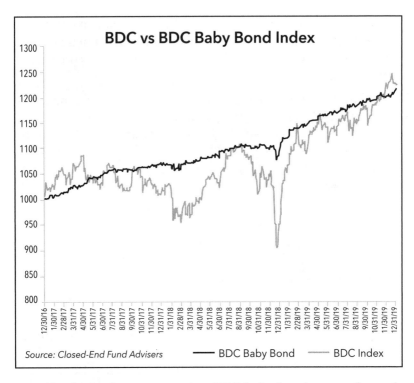

BDC vs BDC Baby Bond Index

Source: Closed-End Fund Advisers ——— BDC Baby Bond ········· BDC Index

Here's the important point: BDC baby bonds are safer and less volatile, because of senior liquidation preference to equity shareholders. That means a BDC must first meet its obligations to baby bond investors before stock shareholders in the BDC receive their dividend payments.

But there are also a few nuances to understanding your overall yield and income potential when investing in BDC baby bonds.

For example, baby bonds trade with accrued interest in their price. As a result, investors can use a key metric called the "effective yield" to evaluate and compare baby bonds. That's because the effective yield reflects current price less the accrued interest.

It's also important to note that many BDC baby bonds are "callable," which means the parent BDC issuer can exercise an option to redeem the bonds before reaching maturity. In many cases, this is done when a bond issue can be redeemed and re-issued at lower interest rates, saving the parent BDC on interest costs.

To this end, you can evaluate BDC baby bond issues with a metric called "yield to worst." Sounds bad, but this measure takes into account the yield you would experience should the BDC issuer "call" and redeem the baby bond at the earliest possible date. In other words, this represents a worst-case scenario of the yield received should the bond be called at the earliest possible date.

Baby bonds provide an alternative way of gaining exposure to BDCs — especially for investors who have lower tolerance for volatility or who need greater assurance of principal protection.

Nevertheless, caution is advised when investing in baby bonds as yields may not meet your expectations should you need to sell your shares prematurely. Shareholders are required to own the baby bond one trading day before the ex-dividend date to be eligible for a full quarter of interest.

That aside, BDC baby bonds offer investors overall portfolio diversification, minimal price volatility, permanent equity capital, and relatively safe and stable yields.

For more information about BDC baby bonds, visit https://seekingalpha.com/article/4292897-balancing-portfolio-bdc-baby-bonds.

INCOME SECRET NO. 5:

The One Asset Class Paying Out a Steady Income Stream

Retirement is supposed to be a time of leisure and relaxation. It's supposed to be a worry-free time where you travel, learn new things, enjoy hobbies and spend time with loved ones.

But thanks to years of ultra-low interest rates, retirement has become a frantic search for income to make all those dreams a reality.

Over the past three decades, the investment environment has changed — and not for the better — when it comes to those on a fixed income.

Interest rates have fallen sharply due to economic weakness and turmoil. The Federal Reserve has kept rates at bargain-basement levels year after year in an attempt to keep the market alive, while leaving those dependent on income out in the cold.

You may have forgotten exactly how far we've fallen:

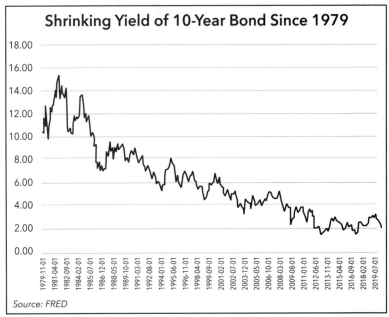

Source: FRED

In September 1981, the 10-year government bond yielded an average 15.32%.

By September 1990, the yield was down to 8.89%.

In September 2000, it was at 5.80%.

And today ... the 10-year bond yields a mere 0.55% (at the time of writing this).

If you had invested $100,000 at a yield of 15.32%, you would have earned $15,320 in a year. That was more than the median annual salary of $11,669 in 1981 and would have made for a nice retirement.

Then using recent rates, $100,000 invested at a yield of 0.55% gets only $550 per year. That is a frightening prospect for retirement income.

However, you can still find much higher yields — yields that are closer to what we saw in 2000, 1990 ... and even 1981. But you need to consider a different type of asset.

These assets are master limited partnerships (MLPs), and they are different from the stocks that you've likely already traded in your brokerage accounts and 401(k)s.

There are currently 568 MLP's slated to pay $34.6 billion over the next year to investors.

A company can operate tax-free if it becomes an MLP.

To meet the requirements, a company must:

- Generate 90% of its revenue from the production, processing, storage and transportation of natural resources, commodities or real estate in the U.S.

- Pay out lucrative checks to all shareholders.

You can trade MLPs on major exchanges. You can purchase them just as easily as shares of a company or an exchange-traded fund (ETF). That makes investing in an MLP very easy.

When it comes to an MLP, instead of shares of a company, you are typically buying "units."

So instead of being a shareholder, you're a "unit holder" of an MLP.

And where a company pays you a dividend, an MLP pays a "distribution." Just a small change in language, but the concept is similar.

The key difference comes in the treatment of their payouts to investors.

As an MLP investor, you have to pay taxes on 10% to 20% of the cash you collect. Taxes on the remaining 80% to 90% are deferred until you sell your units.

With an MLP, every time you receive a check, a portion of your initial investment is returned to you. As a result, the IRS does not consider these MLP payments as "taxable income," but rather a "return of capital." The IRS doesn't tax most of your quarterly income checks until you sell your units.

This sounds complicated, but it's really not.

Ordinary dividends must be filed on Form 1099-DIV (https://www.irs.gov/pub/irs-pdf/f1099div.pdf). Distributions from an MLP must be filed on Form K-1 (https://www.irs.gov/pub/irs-pdf/i1041sk1.pdf). This means that your taxes are going to require a little more time for preparation, but the upside is that the payments you receive for investing in MLPs should more than make up for the added tax headache.

How much more? Let's take a look at what the market has to offer right now and how we can beat it with not only great-yielding MLPs, but also units that are set to rise in value over time.

As of July 2020, the S&P 500 Index has a pathetic yield of just 1.82%. Utilities, which have long been seen as the go-to for income, are paying dividends ranging mostly between 2%-4%.

And as I mentioned earlier, the U.S. 10-year note is yielding only 0.55%.

So far, we're still lagging behind even the average yield of the 10-year bond in the early 2000s.

We can do better.

The average yield of 128 high-yield, tax-advantaged MLPs is 8.9%. That matches Treasury yields we haven't seen since 1990!

Check into adding MLPs to your trading portfolio and start earning a steady stream of income.

INCOME SECRET NO. 6:

Take the Fast Lane to Higher Yields With These Corporate Dividend Growers

Would you prefer higher yields than those paltry interest rates currently offered by banks and other financial institutions?

Plenty of high-profile and blue-chip companies offer dividends on their publicly traded stocks. At first glance, their 3%, 4%, 5% or higher annual yields might sound like a pretty good deal.

But here's the thing — these dividends are subject to change. Some, if not most, of the companies issuing them may not stand the test of time and may be forced to cut or eliminate their dividend payouts, depending on their earnings or unforeseen economic circumstances.

When evaluating dividend stocks as potential investments, one of the most important factors to consider is their history of steadily increasing dividend payouts over a period of at least several years.

This is how we identify corporate dividend growers that, added to your portfolio, can be a significant source of *consistent, increased* net income over the long-term — especially if you are soon-to-be or already retired.

Harnessing the Power of Dividend Growers

Think about it: Traditional pensions are practically a thing of the past, and Social Security alone won't support the lifestyle you desire. And even if you have a substantial balance in a 401(k) or other retirement plans, it may not outlast your retirement. At age 70, you'll be required to not only start withdrawing your money, but also pay taxes on it if it was previously tax-deferred.

However, buying and holding a corporate dividend grower can definitely pick up the slack, providing you with quarterly supplemental income.

To be clear, we're not talking about investing in stocks that currently offer the highest dividend yields. Your focus should be on companies that have been increasing their dividends at least once per year for at least the past 25 years.

The 10 top companies that have been doing so for *over 50 years or more* include:

Company Name	Stock Symbol	No. of Years	Dividend Yield	Current Price	Annual Dividend
American States Water	AWR	65	1.68%	$79.85	$1.3400
Dover Corp.	DOV	64	1.79%	$110.50	$1.9800
Northwest Natural Gas	NWN	64	3.56%	$54.36	$1.9100
Genuine Parts	GPC	63	3.36%	$94.07	$3.1600
Emerson Electric	EMR	63	2.93%	$69.11	$2.0000
Procter & Gamble	PG	63	2.38%	$134.62	$3.1628
3M	MMM	61	3.77%	$163.84	$5.8800
Cincinnati Financial	CINF	59	2.88%	$83.42	$2.4000
Johnson & Johnson	JNJ	57	2.74%	$149.00	$4.0400
Lowe's	LOW	57	1.46%	$155.52	$2.2000

Source: Dividend.com

These are among an elite group of dividend growers often referred to as "dividend aristocrats."

How to Spot a True Dividend Grower

Besides its historical track record, how do you tell whether a company is an enduring dividend aristocrat — and therefore worthy of your long-term investment — or merely a short-lived success story?

One of the best litmus tests is its dividend payout ratio — the proportion of the company's earnings allocated to paying dividends. Since it is based on the total amount of dividend distributions paid to shareholders relative to total earnings or net income, a low dividend ratio indicates a company has enough earnings to support future dividend distributions or rising dividend payouts, whereas a high payout ratio indicates a company is providing most of its earnings as dividends and could find it necessary to reduce — or eliminate — dividend distributions as a result of a financial setback.

Take pharmaceutical giant Johnson & Johnson, for example. Over 13 years, it's median payout ratio was just 0.54, lower than 84% of the 410 companies in the drug manufacturer industry.

In 38 years (1966-2008), Johnson & Johnson grew to such a degree that it increased its payout. If you had bought JNJ stock in the early 1970s, the dividend yield between then and 2004 on your initial shares would have grown about 12% annually, with the earnings from your dividends alone resulting in a 48% annual return on your shares.

Calculating Dividend Growth

Another way to gauge the income-generating power of a particular stock is by its dividend growth rate.

The dividend growth rate is the annualized percentage rate of growth of a stock's dividend over a length of time. If a company has a history of strong dividend growth, it could indicate likely dividend growth in the future and signal long-term profitability.

You can calculate and compare the dividend growth rate for any period with the following formula:

Dividend Growth = Year X Dividend/(Year Y Dividend) — 1

Using this formula as of 2019, here's Johnson & Johnson's growth in dividend payment to shareholders over the following time frames:

1 Year — 5.9%

3 Year — 19.0%

5 Year — 35.9%

Conclusion

As you can see as a savvy investor, the true value of a dividend stock is measured over time — not by a short-term gain.

Those with a history of steady dividend growth — in addition to healthy balance sheets and demonstrated financial strength — can richly reward your patience with a perpetual income stream that only keeps increasing as the years go by.

INCOME SECRET NO. 7:

Triple Your Dividend Income With a Few Nearly Forgotten "High-Class" Stocks

So ... how much is that "hot" new common stock paying you in dividends on a quarterly basis? Two percent? One percent? How about 0% — because it doesn't even offer its shareholders a dividend?

Maybe it's time to start investing in preferred stock shares. They offer dividends of 6% to 7% on average.

Not only that, but they're safer than common shares of stock, which is another reason they're popular among retirees who want to boost or stabilize their cash flow.

What's the difference between a preferred stock and a common stock since both have the potential to appreciate in price?

A preferred stock is a class of ownership in a corporation that has a higher claim on its assets and earnings than a common stock. Generally, preferred stocks have a dividend that must be paid out before dividends to common stock shareholders. They also yield more than common stocks and can be paid on a monthly (or quarterly) basis. These dividends can be fixed or set in terms of a benchmark interest rate.

The finer details of each preferred stock depend on the type of share. For example, adjustable-rate shares specify certain factors that influence their dividend yield, while participating shares can pay additional dividends that are determined by the company's profits.

Preferred stocks are also classified as either perpetual or callable. Perpetual shares have no stated maturity date, while those with a call date may be redeemed by the authorizing company at a future date. Those are considered a risk and thereby generally pay a slightly higher yield than perpetual shares.

In addition to the income they generate, "called" preferred stocks provide the opportunity for capital appreciation. The risk, however, is that they will eventually be called, at which point the investor will have to replace the yield and expected income with another holding.

Since preferred stocks with a call date may be redeemed at face value (usually $25), it can be advantageous to pay as close to par value as possible (also generally $25).

Dividends from preferred stocks are usually labeled as either cumulative or noncumulative. Cumulative dividends are those that must be paid by the company (or at least accrued until the company can pay), whereas noncumulative dividends can be withheld from shareholders based on the company's profitability. That being the case, you may think it best to consider only cumulative dividends. However, they aren't as popular as noncumulative versions, so in order to truly diversify your portfolio, you may want to incorporate both.

One caveat: Preferred yields can rise into double digits or languish on the lower end of the scale. While that makes preferred stocks with higher yields more desirable, they usually come with far more risk in terms of the company's credit rating, corporate fundamentals, tax eligibility, industry market conditions and bid-ask price.

Therefore, it would be wise to balance yields with these factors when considering which preferred stocks to choose. For example, a corporate credit rating dictates the rate at which a company can borrow. So you may want to consider investment grade companies that carry ratings of AAA, AA, A or BBB. They may pay lower rates than those rated BB or lower, but what you sacrifice in a lower yield, you'll gain in added investment safety.

Two helpful sites to broaden your understanding of the benefits of using preferred stocks to boost your retirement income are QuantumOnline.com and PreferredStockChannel.com.

INCOME SECRET NO. 8:

Get Paid $2,500 a Month From Your County Treasury

There's tax-free income hiding in plain sight.

Nearly every town across America offers it.

Multimillionaires collect it whenever they can. But most working-class families still haven't taken advantage of it.

In case you haven't guessed, I'm talking about municipal bonds. The interest you receive from them is exempt from federal tax.

But that's not all. If you live in the state in which they're issued, they're also exempt from state and local tax.

Plus, the tax exemption prevents the income you earn from boosting you up into a higher tax bracket ... which is one of the reasons millionaires absolutely love their munis.

Yet most middle-class investors overlook municipal bonds and, in doing so, are missing out on a great opportunity to generate additional income.

For example: $500,000 in savings placed into a tax-free municipal bond that yields 6% would generate $30,000 per year ... which amounts to $2,500 per month in interest income.

Not bad, eh? And having the benefit of being exempt from state income tax in addition to being exempt from paying federal taxes increases the taxable-equivalent yield. That's why the higher a state's income tax, the more likely state residents will buy their state's bonds, while states without an income tax are forced to offer higher yields to attract both in-state and out-of-state buyers.

Those states that have no personal income tax include: Alaska, Florida, Nevada, South Dakota, Texas, Washington and Wyoming. As such, they offer slightly higher yields to offset the fact that their bonds offer no local tax benefit to their own citizens.

Elsewhere, the rules vary. For example, New York State's municipal bonds are exempt from city and state income taxes. So, interest from municipal bonds issued in New York may be triple tax-exempt from city, state and federal income taxes.

Meanwhile, Utah doesn't tax its own bonds ... but it also doesn't tax bonds issued in states that don't tax Utah bonds. To put it another way, if a particular state doesn't collect taxes on Utah's bonds, Utah doesn't collect interest on that state's bonds. So, Utah residents are free to buy bonds from states with no income taxes such as Texas, Florida or Washington and avoid paying Utah state income taxes on the interest.

Among the states that tax in-state bonds are Oklahoma, Utah, Iowa, Wisconsin and Illinois.

For most other states, only interest from bonds issued within the state is exempt from that state's income taxes. So, if you invest in bonds from other states, it's likely that you'll have to pay tax on the interest from those bonds.

And what about residents of Washington, D.C.? The district doesn't tax in-state or out-of-state municipal bonds, so they can buy bonds from anywhere and not pay state or district income taxes on the interest.

Regardless of whether or not your state taxes the interest on municipal bonds, most of your tax savings are going to come from not having to pay federal income taxes. So, when it comes to dealing with state taxation, the best strategy is to diversify your municipal bond portfolio across multiple states.

INCOME SECRET NO. 9:

Supercharge Your Savings With Accounts That Pay You 22 Times More Interest

As we all know, standard savings accounts have been offering paltry interest rates for some time now. And by paltry, I mean next to nothing. In fact, the current national average is a measly 0.06%.

But that doesn't mean you can't generate extra income from savings accounts or that you should scratch them off your list of investment options. It just means you need to find the right kind of savings account available at some of the most reputable and recognized banks in the nation.

Here's why: High yield online savings accounts from banks such as Barclays, CIT, Goldman Sachs, Synchrony and many more offer up to 1.3% annual percentage yield (APY) — as of this writing — versus the national average of 0.06% for standard savings accounts.

Do the math: 1.3% divided by 0.06% equals about 22. So that's as much as 22 times more in interest you could be accumulating with an online savings account.

Plus, besides offering much higher interest rates than the average savings account, the best of these online banks offers other perks, such as no minimum balance, ATM access and/or free checking.

Here is just a small sampling of some of the highest-yielding online savings accounts (Note: rates can fluctuate, so check the individual bank websites for the latest APYs):

- Synchrony Bank — This one offers 1.05% APY with no minimum balance, no monthly fee and it'll even throw in an ATM card. While most internet-only banks require electronic funds transfer that can take a few days, having ATM access means quicker access to your money.

- Marcus by Goldman Sachs USA — Along with a 1.30% APY, this account requires no minimum balance, and there are no transaction fees. You can deposit funds by check or by electronic or wire transfer, and access funds via electronic or wire transfer.

- American Express National Bank — With a personal savings account, you can earn a variable 1.30% APY with no minimum balance and without any fees. Plus, the FDIC insures your deposits up to $250,000.

- Barclays Bank — With more than 300 years of history, Barclays is as dependable a bank as they come. It offers a 1.60% APY for its online saving account with no minimum balance or monthly fees.

- Ally Bank — Not only does Ally offer a 1.25% APY with no minimum balance required, but you can get a free checking account with no minimum balance that provides easy access to your funds.

- CIT Bank — This savings account comes with a 1.25% APY and interest compounds daily. In addition, there are no monthly maintenance fees.

- Popular Direct — You'll need a minimum of $5,000 to open this account and you'll have to maintain a $500 balance to avoid a $4 monthly service fee, but that's because it pays a whopping (by today's standards) 1.70 % APY that, over time, could generate the most interest income of comparable online savings accounts.

Just about anyone can open an online savings account and rake in hundreds, if not thousands of more dollars each year in interest compared to your average neighborhood savings bank. Which, frankly, is why I'm amazed that more retirees aren't taking advantage of them.

To keep abreast of the best offers (which are subject to change on a monthly basis), type "Best Online Savings Accounts" in your search engine.

INCOME SECRET NO. 10:

Ramp Up Your Retirement Fund With This Surprisingly Simple Move

Many of us dream of retiring early — say, at 50 years old instead of 65. But all too often, it's just that — a wishful fantasy — because we simply don't have the savings or retirement income needed to sustain us for the next 20, 30 or 40 years.

Nevertheless, when William was just 38, and his wife Nancy was just 33, they did just that: they retired.

No, they weren't high-powered CEOs raking in seven-figure salaries. And they didn't win the lottery. They were your ordinary middle-class couple living in Seattle, Washington.

And yet, thanks in large part to a surprisingly simple move, William and Nancy turned a modest nest egg into a $1 million fortune ... and are on track to make $3 million in investments over the next 30 years while millions of other Americans are still struggling just to get by.

What's their "secret"?

Three words: low-cost income funds. They saved as much as they could and focused on investing in low-cost income funds rather than ordinary mutual funds. Today, 100% of their savings are in these funds because of what William read from billionaire investor Warren Buffett and Jack Bogle, founder of the Vanguard Group, on low-fee and diversification benefits.

In fact, William and Nancy invested the bulk of Nancy's money in one simple exchange-traded fund (ETF) — the Vanguard S&P 500 Index Fund. And in 2015, she made $172,500 in interest and dividend income. Basically, investing in no-cost or low-cost ETFs allows you to slash your fees from an average 4.25% to 0.25%, which makes a huge difference in your total return on investment when you factor in reinvested dividends.

An ETF is a marketable security that tracks an index, a commodity, bonds or a basket of assets. Unlike mutual funds, an ETF trades like a common stock on a stock exchange and experiences price changes throughout the day as it's bought and sold.

The Vanguard S&P 500 Index tracks the S&P 500 Index and is a low-cost fund started by Jack Bogle in the 1970s. As you can see in the chart below, the Vanguard S&P 500 Index Fund returned over 200% from 2011 to 2019:

Vanguard 500 Index Investor Total Return Price % Change

Source: Refinitiv

With returns like that, combined with low-maintenance fees, it's easy to see how William and Nancy were able to amass their fortune and watch it grow, enabling them to retire at an age when others are just starting to take retirement saving seriously.

Warren Buffett is such a true believer in the power of investing in low-cost ETFs like the Vanguard S&P 500 Index Fund that his estate plan specifies that if his wife outlives him, 90% of her inheritance should be put into the same ETF.

It's amazing to think that earning an extra $172,500 per year while you just sit back and watch your investment income soar could be so effortless. Yet you too can ramp up your retirement fund with this unusual "hands-off" approach to automatic income and possibly retire happily ever after much sooner than you originally planned.

INCOME SECRET NO. 11:

Increase Your Brokerage Statement $3,120 Each Year by Firing Your "Robo" Stock Adviser

Welcome to the "robo" age — complete with robocars, robocalls, robochefs, roboworkers and ... yes, robo stock advisers.

What, you may ask, is a robo stock adviser? It's an automated electronic system that provides financial advice or investment management online with little human intervention. A robo-adviser provides digital financial advice that is based on algorithms executed with software that automatically allocates, manages and optimizes your assets.

These automated advisers have soared in popularity in recent years, mostly because they make investing easier. In fact, there are well over 100 robo-advisery services that have the capability to allocate your assets in many different investment products, such as stocks, bonds, commodities, futures and real estate. The funds are often directed toward exchange-traded fund (ETF) portfolios, and you can choose between offerings with active management styles or passive asset allocation techniques.

Of course, as we all know, there's no such thing as a free lunch ... or a free robo-adviser. While they do offer competitively low fees compared to human, professionally managed investment assistance, robo-advisers like Asset Builder, Betterment, Wealthfront and others can charge up to 0.50% in their fees alone.

That may seem fairly reasonable, but you could save as much as $3,120 per year simply by ditching your robo-adviser and instead putting your money into low-fee stock and bond index funds — much like robo-advisers often do anyway.

Here's an example furnished by self-made millionaire and wealth management adviser Chris Reining...

Let's say you sign up with a robo-advisery service, deposit $3,000 in the account and set up an additional $300 investment every month. Assuming you earn an annual return of 10%, your investment would be worth $70,893.

However ... don't forget there's a fee to have the service invest your money in an index fund. Let's say it's only 0.25%. You need to subtract that fee from the return to calculate what you're actually making. So now it's 9.75%. At that rate of return, your investments are worth $69,825 — so, you've already lost about $1,000 in fees. But it doesn't stop there.

Keep in mind that the robo-advisery service isn't paying the index funds fees for you. So, you have to pay those as well to the average tune of 0.16%. That boosts the total fees to 0.41% and lowers your return to 9.59%. Now your investment is worth $69,150.

No big deal? Then, consider this:

Let's say your goal is to save $1 million in order to generate $40,000 in passive income every year. You realize that to reach that goal, you would have to invest a lot more money. So you start out investing the same $3,000 ... only now you're investing an additional $3,000 every month.

Following that strategy, you're going to end up with $1.2 million within 15 years. But how much will you pay your ro-bo-adviser in total fees on that $1.2 million? The answer is $3,720 per year.

Now, had you invested your $1.2 million directly with the stock index fund with a fee of 0.04% and a bond index fund with a fee of 0.05%, the index fund would only be skimming off about $600 per year, putting the extra $3,120 in your pocket.

If you're living on $40,000 a year, can you really afford to pay an additional $3,120 (7.8% of your passive income) in fees?

It simply comes down to this: While robo-advisers charge lower fees than most financial advisers, they charge higher fees than if you simply invest in an index fund yourself. And over time, those fees can make a huge difference in your nest egg.

INCOME SECRET NO. 12:

Become an Early Investor ... With as Little as $500 ... With Peer-to-Peer Lending

Maybe you've always wanted to invest in a startup company or a venture capital opportunity, but that brass ring always seemed to be just out of reach because you simply didn't have enough funds to take the plunge ... or the amount needed was too much to finance on a credit card ... or the amount was too low for banks and angel investors to get the return they wanted.

But now anyone can become an early investor ... with as little as $500 ... and collect a steady stream of income every month.

The key is peer-to-peer (P2P) lending. It's a method of debt financing that enables you to borrow (or lend) money without using an official financial institution as an intermediary.

In other words, it removes the middleman. It's a form of crowdfunding that involves borrowing money from your peers, including other businesspeople and investors who are interested in relatively small financing amounts.

Peer-to-peer lending offers several benefits:

- No collateral is required.
- Lower interest rates are available, depending on your credit score, loan amount and loan term.
- You can repay the loan early without prepayment penalties.
- You can get faster approval.
- There's no paperwork besides a few online forms and a digital signature.

Also, you can continue using your P2P lending connection to tap additional funds once you borrow and repay the initial loan.

You can obtain P2P through sites, such as LendingClub.com and Prosper.com.

Launched in 2006, Prosper was the first P2P lending company, followed in 2007 by LendingClub, which became the world's largest P2P lending platform.

Today, these are the two preeminent choices for peer-to-peer investors. Both offer good deals for early investors, but have different conditions.

Here's a comparison:

	LendingClub	Prosper
Promotions	Get up to 100,000 United Miles when investing	None
Fees	1%/year	1%/year
Minimum Deposit	1,000 (taxable); $5,500 (IRAs)	$25
Loan Term	3 or 5 years	3 or 5 years
Loan Amount	$1k-$40k consumer, $5k-50k auto, $5k-$500k business	$2k-$35k consumer
Accredited Investor	No (unless in Kentucky)	No
Note Types	Unsecured Consumer Debt, Auto Refinancing and Business Loans	Unsecured Consumer Debt
IRA Account	Yes	Yes

Source: Investorjunkie.com

The first thing you need to do before becoming a P2P investor is find out whether peer-to-peer lending is available in your state. Although LendingClub and Prosper are regulated by the Securities and Exchange Commission (SEC), they are still subject to the laws of individual states regarding the solicitation of investors.

Currently, LendingClub is available to new investors in all U.S. states and the District of Columbia with the exception of Alaska, New Mexico, North Carolina, Ohio and Pennsylvania.

However, the LendingClub trading platform FOLIOFN — where investors trade in existing loans — is available to investors in each of these states except Ohio.

Prosper is currently available for new investors in most states, including D.C., with the exception of Alabama, Arizona, Arkansas, Iowa, Kansas, Kentucky, Maryland, Massachusetts, Nebraska, New Jersey, New Mexico, North Carolina, North Dakota, Ohio, Oklahoma, Pennsylvania and Vermont. However, it doesn't allow any additional states on its trading platform.

In terms of interest charged to borrowers, LendingClub offers an annual percentage rate, or APR, ranging from about 6% to 28% based on factors, such as the borrower's FICO score, number of recent credit inquiries, length of credit history, total number of open credit accounts and revolving credit. Most borrowers tend to pay a higher interest rate for higher loan amounts and for 60-month loan terms versus 36 months.

Prosper offers slightly higher rates ranging from 6% to 34%, but also allows borrowers with lower credit scores on their platform. These rates change regularly, so be sure to check with both sites.

For more information on P2P lending offered by these and other companies, visit https://www.goodfinancialcents.com/peer-to-peer-lending.

INCOME SECRET NO. 13:

Dividends: To Reinvest or Not to Reinvest?

A while back, somebody asked me whether or not it made sense to reinvest dividends. My initial response was: "Well, it's up to you. It depends on your investment strategy."

Things are a little bit more complicated than that when it comes to dividend-paying companies. So, let's review some of the variables to consider.

Generally speaking, the first thing to ask yourself when you consider reinvesting dividends is whether or not you need the cash. Commonly, people who are older and living off the proceeds of their investments will take their dividends as payouts if they have big enough stakes in those companies. That gives them an extra source of income they can use to sustain themselves in retirement.

Younger people, on the other hand, typically reinvest dividends because they're trying to build up a stake in a company until retirement, or until they want to take the dividends.

That allows them to take advantage of something called compounding. Compounding is something that most people are aware of when it comes to interest. Essentially, it's the same phenomenon when it comes to dividend reinvestment.

What's happening is that you're taking the dividend generated from an investment and using it to purchase more of that investment. That means the next time the dividend is paid, it'll be paid on a larger investment, which means the dividend will be bigger. If you keep doing that over time, eventually you will have a much more valuable stock than you would have if you didn't reinvest the one you originally bought.

Let's look at a graph that shows the powers of dividend compounding.

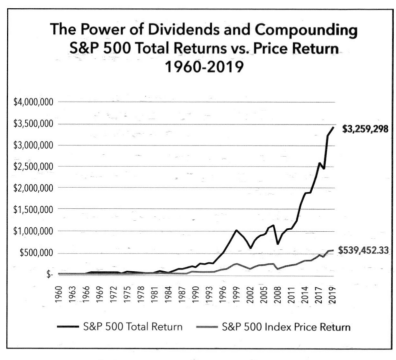

The Power of Dividends and Compounding S&P 500 Total Returns vs. Price Return 1960-2019

This graph shows what would happen if you invested $10,000 in 1960 until the end of 2019. No question, reinvesting the dividends would be the best bet. If you didn't reinvest the dividends, you'd end up with a total of just under $540,000. However, if you reinvested the dividends in the S&P 500 index, you would have ended up with more than $3.2 million.

But remember, 1960 to 2019 is a long time just to let an investment sit. And if you are already in retirement, that's out of the question. So, that makes things more complicated. Theoretically, it's good for a young person to buy dividend-paying stocks earlier in their investment career and let them sit, if they can.

Let's look at another chart that shows the example of compounding.

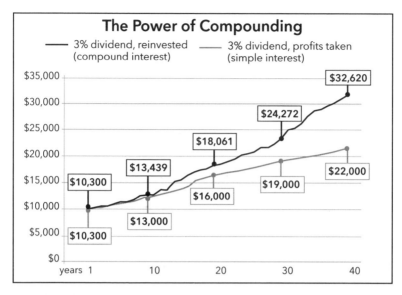

This shows an example of a 3% dividend compounded over time, and it shows you what happens to $10,000 over 40 years. Mathematically, you can follow how the reinvestment of the dividend leads to a higher outcome (more than $10,000 by the end of the period for that particular investment versus if you took the dividends as they were paid out). Now, another way to look at it is to think about different types of companies and how their dividend performance should influence your decision-making.

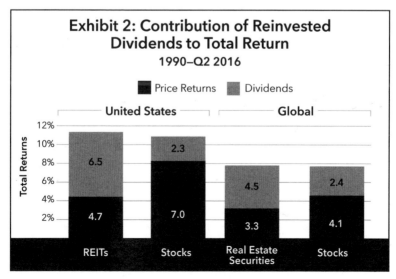

This chart shows the average returns to stocks and real estate securities, like REITs, since 1990, both in the United States and globally. What we're looking at is how much is contributed to the increase in value of those assets based on reinvestment of dividends.

Now, as you can see when it comes to REITs, 6.5% out of the total growth of that asset — in other words, on average, 11% growth every year — comes from reinvesting dividends. Whereas for the stock market, reinvesting dividends in stocks gives you about 2.3% of your total gain. The majority of the gain you get in the stock market, not in REITs per se, is coming from stock price appreciation. So that's another factor to consider.

If the payout is so high for a REIT, and if you had the time to let it run, letting a REIT with a high dividend run could end up being a good strategy — even if you only have 10 or so years to wait — because so much of their potential appreciation comes from the dividend reinvestment and compounding. But again, it comes down to your personal needs and your personal strategy.

4 Reasons Not to Reinvest

Now, there are times when it makes sense not to continue to reinvest dividends. I'm going to give you some examples of why you might or might not. Even if your strategy is to take dividends, while you might want to override that choice or vise-versa — if your strategy is to reinvest, why you might want to override it and take cash instead.

First, as I've mentioned, if your goal is to generate income for yourself, then obviously you're going to take dividends.

But the second issue to consider is whether or not the company is becoming overvalued. If you think about it, reinvesting in a company that is reaching an excessive valuation means you're basically buying more stock at a very expensive price point. If you have a company that is trading at 30- or 40-times earnings (P/E ratio), that's an expensive company. And if it's not one of these high-flying growth stocks — technology stocks like 5G or something like that — then at that point, maybe it doesn't make sense to reinvest the dividends. The chances are that the company might come down in value, which means the value of the extra stock you buy with those dividends is also going to come down.

So, yes, in that case, I think there are scenarios where I might want to say: "Hey, right now this company is overvalued," so I recommend you don't reinvest your dividends because you'd be getting them at too dear a price.

A third consideration is that sometimes it makes more sense to take the dividends you get from your investments and reinvest them into other stocks. In other words, dividends generate cash you can use to buy other positions. This is particularly the case within your retirement portfolio. If you have a conventional IRA, your dividend payments are released back into the IRA and not taxed yet because you haven't withdrawn them. You can then reinvest those dividends into other companies that maybe have more rapid price appreciation potential than does the current dividend-paying company.

So, in that case, yes, again, it would make sense not to take the dividend and reinvest it, but to redeploy the dividend instead of buying a company that has the potential for greater price appreciation, which increases your overall return.

The fourth scenario is one where you don't think that the dividend is sustainable — the company's business model and its long-term trajectory suggest it might be cutting its dividend in the future. Why would you want to buy more stock of a company that's going to be cutting its dividend? In that kind of scenario, again, you would say: "Yep, it's not a good idea to reinvest these dividends. I should just take the money while it's good and use it for something else."

The Bottom Line on Reinvesting Dividends

Reinvesting your dividends can be a lucrative option if you are a retiree, provided you have other sources of short-term income. It certainly is one of the easiest ways to grow a portfolio, regardless of your age. However, it's not the best strategy for everyone. You should carefully examine your financial situation and long-range needs before choosing this investment option.

ASSET PROTECTION

I f you want to enjoy endless income, you need to protect it. Government surveillance, militarized police, a national debt spiraling out of control ... these are the very real threats facing you and your assets in America today. Without an effective asset protection strategy in place, you might find yourself a victim of wealth confiscation by the government with no legal recourse. That's why you should prepare today.

INCOME SECRET NO. 14:

The Low-Cost Maneuver to Defeat Disaster ... Trust Me

Do you like horror stories? Good ... because the world of asset protection is full of them. Here's a doozy.

It involves a couple I met via an ex-colleague, just as I was transitioning from the nonprofit world to writing about sovereignty and asset protection.

Belinda and Ryan were at that stage in life where everything is starting to come together ... just bought a home, student loans paid off, careers looking good, bun in the oven. Nice folks.

When I met them, though, they were pale with stress and worry.

Besides their new Atlanta home, Belinda and Ryan also owned a couple of inherited properties, one on the East Coast and one in the Rockies. They were also passive co-owners of a thriving business, managed by Belinda's brother. Belinda's dad, who had started the business, had left Belinda a fair chunk of money, which was doing nothing in particular in a bank account except serving as collateral for a loan they'd taken out to renovate their new house.

Those renovations included construction of a new retaining wall at the back of their house, which overlooked a wooded stream — common in Atlanta. A few days after a torrential downpour, which caused the stream to swell a bit more than usual, the partially completed retaining wall collapsed on a workman, killing him instantly.

Unbeknownst to them, the contractor they'd hired — at the recommendation of their architect — had no business liability insurance. Belinda and Ryan were therefore personally responsible for restitution to the man's family.

When I met them, they faced a multimillion-dollar lawsuit that would force them to sell almost everything they owned ... including their new house and their share of the business, which meant liquidating it entirely, drawing Belinda's brother into the turmoil and straining the family.

Two sadder faces I will likely never see. Almost there ... now, nothing. But the really sad thing is that it didn't have to be like that.

A simple, quick, low-cost legal maneuver would have put the bulk of their assets out of reach of that lawsuit. Their real estate, their business and their bank balances would have been safe. They'd have had to pay something, but their legal shield would have led to a quick and more reasonable settlement amount.

Nobody knows where lightning may strike. But strike it does, thousands of times a day, all over the country. Sometimes it does real damage. The odds of a lawsuit like the one against Belinda and Ryan, however, are far greater than those of a lightning strike.

The U.S. has 80% of the world's lawyers. They file over 15 million tort suits in U.S. courts every year. Fifty-five percent of those are found in favor of the plaintiff. You have a 1 in 5 chance of being sued in any given year, unless you're in medical practice, a business owner or a landlord, in which case it's much higher.

But what if "you" and "your assets" can't be sued at the same time? A potential plaintiff can only claim what you own personally. If most of "your" assets aren't actually "yours," you're not much of a target.

For a few thousand dollars, you can make that happen ... and protect yourself from Belinda and Ryan's fate.

In Trusts We Trust ... Up to a Point

The Anglo-American legal tradition is rich in mechanisms that protect personal assets so that people can focus on wealth building instead of wealth defense. There are lots of ways to reduce the risk of personal loss, thereby increasing the attractiveness of innovative business activity.

One of these mechanisms is the trust. The concept of a "trust" is fundamentally very simple: One person holds legal title to an asset for another. If I transfer the title of the family business to you and say, "Hold this business for the benefit of my family," then a trust has been created.

The basic trust has four components:

1. The person who creates the trust (the "settlor" or "grantor").

2. The trust itself and its assets.

3. The person who controls the trust and its assets ("trustee").

4. Those who are to receive the benefits of those assets ("beneficiaries").

The concept of the trust has expanded greatly over the centuries. Large financial institutions often hold billions of dollars in trusts for families all over the world. There are now many types of trusts: revocable and irrevocable trusts, grantor trusts, qualified trusts, lead trusts, life insurance and annuity trusts, unit trusts and even the bizarre "intentionally defective trust."

An asset protection trust (APT) is a trust that protects the trust assets from potential future creditors and liabilities of the beneficiaries. That is, as long as the assets are in a properly formed trust, they are not the personal property of the beneficiaries, and therefore not subject to claims arising from the beneficiaries' debts, including those generated from lawsuits like the one against Belinda and Ryan.

Unlike a traditional revocable living trust, an APT must be an irrevocable trust. This is critical, because a creditor can come after any assets over which you have control.

A revocable living trust, by design, is one in which you have control over the assets. You can terminate the trust, withdraw funds and so on. A creditor who is awarded a claim against you would have the same ability to withdraw trust assets or funds to pay the claim. Your assets are not protected at all.

But in a traditional irrevocable trust, you relinquish any right to the assets and have no control over them. If you don't have control and can't benefit from or withdraw the assets, your creditors can't either. Your assets are safe.

Traditionally, this is achieved in a trust through inclusion of a "spendthrift provision" in an irrevocable trust that prohibits creditors from making claims against a beneficiary's interest in the trust, and prevents the beneficiaries from transferring or pledging their interests in the trust to someone else, such as a creditor. Even if you wanted to settle with a creditor, the provisions of the irrevocable trust wouldn't permit it.

This "spendthrift provision" protection, however, is generally unavailable to the creator of the trust — the "settlor" who donates its initial assets. If you establish a trust of which you are also a beneficiary — a so-called "self-settled trust" — it is generally ignored for purposes of the creator's/beneficiary's debts and liabilities, and your assets are unprotected. In other words, the only way trust assets could be protected from your potential creditors as creator of the trust is for you, as the settlor, to give up complete control of and benefit from the trust and its assets. That means, for example, that you couldn't put the family home into such a trust and live in it, or profit from a business held in trust.

So, it seems you face a choice of a trust where you can't access the assets at all or one where you can, but they aren't protected from creditors. Clearly, what's needed is a way to put assets into an irrevocable trust so creditors can't access them, but still be a beneficiary of the trust's assets — say, your house, investment accounts or shares in a family business.

This is where the domestic asset protection trust (DAPT) comes in. A DAPT allows the trust creator, the settlor, to be a discretionary beneficiary, and yet the trust assets are still protected from the settlor's creditors. That's why, in the past, in order to obtain such protections, U.S. citizens often looked to offshore jurisdictions that permit spendthrift trusts that also allow the settlor to be a beneficiary, and thereby be protected from creditors.

Do the Nevada 2-Step

In 1999, the Nevada Legislature amended its trust statute to permit self-settled, first-party spendthrift trusts, commonly referred to as a Nevada asset protection trust (NAPT). Under this law, as long as the settlors strictly comply with statutory requirements, they can name themselves as beneficiaries of their own trusts and enjoy the same creditor protection as third-party beneficiaries of the trust. Problem solved.

It is important to remember that an NAPT is an irrevocable trust. Once a traditional irrevocable trust is established, the settlor cannot take back the assets and terminate the trust, or even change how they are distributed — you can't change your mind later.

But Nevada law allows you, as the settlor, to keep the ability to change where the trust assets are ultimately distributed — "the power of appointment." That means you can change who the final beneficiaries are, or how the assets are distributed.

There's more. With a traditional trust, a single trustee is responsible for making distributions from the trust, taking care of all administrative matters (such as filing tax returns and bookkeeping) and overseeing investment and management of the trust assets.

That means giving up control to someone else, even if you are one of the beneficiaries of the trust. You couldn't run your own business or manage your investment portfolio, for example.

But another unique feature of the NAPT is that the powers and duties of the trustee can be allocated to more than one trustee. As a result, you, as the settlor, can also serve as a trustee of the trust.

This is important because Nevada law restricts the settlor from being the sole trustee or having the power to make distributions to himself. The settlor can only serve as a trustee of the trust with the authority to invest and manage the trust assets. Someone else — a second trustee — has to make any distributions that benefit the settlor, such as allowing him or her to live in a property or receive profits from a business held in trust.

With this in mind, Nevada law requires that if a non-Nevada resident is establishing an NAPT, one of the trustees must be a resident of Nevada — the trustee who takes care of the general administrative tasks and makes any distributions to the settlor/trustee/beneficiary.

The only limitation is that this second, Nevada-based trustee cannot be required by the terms of the trust to make distributions to the settlor. While this seems like a limitation, it is outweighed by the benefits of the powers and controls you as the settlor, can retain while still having creditor protection.

Timing Is Everything

When it comes to investing, we all know that timing is critical. The same is true for asset protection trusts.

When you first hear about them, APTs sound almost magical. With the wave of a hand (OK, the stroke of a pen), your assets are legally no longer yours — but you can keep using them as if they were!

This is sort of magical, but there's an important caveat: The trick doesn't work if you are aware of an impending claim against you.

Let's say Belinda and Ryan called a lawyer and set up an APT the day after the accident that killed the workman happened. They knew what was coming, so they moved to protect their wealth.

Nothing would stop them from setting up such an APT, but for the purposes of any lawsuit arising from the workman's death, it would be useless. That's because the transfer of assets to their new APT would be regarded as a "fraudulent conveyance."

A fraudulent conveyance is a transfer of an asset with the intent to hinder, delay or defraud a creditor. Just like you can't buy insurance after an accident has happened, you can't transfer assets to an APT and have them protected by it once you know they will be pursued by a creditor — even if the lawsuit hasn't even been filed yet.

This is where the NAPT is unquestionably the best of its kind in the U.S.

Specifically, under Nevada law, if a creditor was the creditor of the settlor (at the time the settlor made the transfer to an NAPT), the creditor must commence an action to challenge the transfer within (a) two years after the transfer, or (b) six months after the creditor discovers — or reasonably should have discovered — the transfer.

A creditor who was not a creditor of the settlor at the time the settlor made the transfer to an NAPT must commence an action to challenge the transfer within two years of the transfer. If a creditor does not bring a claim against the settlor within the prescribed period, the claim is barred.

This two-year statute of limitations on fraudulent conveyance for NAPTs is one of the shortest in the country. Note that the act that starts the statute of limitations running is the transfer of assets from the settlor to the NAPT. Therefore, each time assets are transferred to the NAPT, a new transfer has occurred, and the statute will begin to run on a claim against that specific asset.

Even if the statute of limitations does not bar the claim, the creditor is required to show that the transfer was a fraudulent conveyance. This may be difficult for the creditor to prove, especially if the creditor's claim arose after the transfer of assets to an NAPT.

7 Additional Benefits

In 2009, the Nevada legislature passed important changes affecting NAPTs. These include some critical enhancements:

- The trustee of an NAPT can "decant" or transfer the trust property to a second trust with different provisions, without first obtaining court approval.

- "Directed trusts" are allowed, which permit the delegation of the trustee's investment powers over the trust's assets to a third-party investment adviser.

- "Trust protectors" are allowed. These are non-trustees who have certain discretionary powers over an otherwise irrevocable trust.

- No "exception creditors" are allowed. Previously, divorcing spouses' claims against an NAPT were not included in the trust protections. Now they are. Here's what that means for you — in addition to some pre-existing benefits of the NAPT:

Decanting

"Decanting" a trust is when the trustee distributes the trust's assets into a different trust with different terms for one or more of the same beneficiaries of the original trust. In most cases, this second trust is brand-new. Traditionally, this requires the permission of a judge, since it could easily be used to defeat the purpose of the original trust.

Nevada has traditionally been one of the most innovative states when it comes to decanting. In 2015, Nevada legislators approved SB484, which essentially gives an NAPT trustee a "do-over" to make changes to trust terms that traditionally would not have been permitted without a judge's permission.

Most importantly, it is now possible to decant an NAPT to remove a mandatory income distribution under the terms of the original NAPT. This creates two opportunities.

First, it allows a trustee — which, remember, can be the settlor, i.e., you — to decant trust assets that were subject to a mandatory income distribution under the original NAPT to a new trust where they are not. For example, if the original NAPT called for trust-investment income to be directed to a child or spouse who has become alienated from the settlor, the investments that generate this income can be decanted to a new trust that does not contain such a provision.

Second, if an NAPT is designed to direct all income to one particular beneficiary, there is no ability to shift income to the lower federal and state income tax brackets of other trust beneficiaries, or to retain income in the trust for taxes that the beneficiary must pay if receiving the distribution. Decanting income-producing assets to a second trust overcomes this by changing the terms of distributions.

Investment Advisers

As I often recommend in the case of offshore trusts and limited liability companies (LLCs), an investment adviser can play an important role in maximizing the investment returns of your assets.

If you're lucky, the Nevada-based trustee for your NAPT can do this. But in most cases — especially where the settlor, as second trustee, has investment expertise — it's too much to expect the trustee to handle this. In such cases, Nevada law allows you to appoint an investment adviser who is authorized under the terms of the trust to advise the trustees on investment decisions. This could easily be someone with whom you already work and in whom you have established trust.

The Trust Protector

The requirement that one trustee of an NAPT be a Nevada-based person is central to the legislature's intentions, which was to make the state a center of business incorporation and associated services. But, as with any relationship with a potential stranger, you can never be entirely certain that you'll always see eye-to-eye ... or that the trustee won't abuse his position to enrich himself through excessive fees, etc.

To deal with this, Nevada trust law allows an innovation that originally appeared in offshore APTs — the "trust protector," or often just "protector." The idea behind the protector is to have somebody who can watch over the trustee, and terminate the trustee for any misconduct.

Nevada law incorporates all the experience of offshore APTs in this regard. Originally, the only power the protector had was to fire the trustee. But as offshore APTs evolved, protectors were sometimes given additional powers, such as to appoint the successor trustee if one was fired. This creates a theoretical threat: If the protector has the power to both fire and appoint a trustee, the protector might appoint herself as the trustee. Thus, offshore APTs further evolved to prohibit a protector from being the trustee or appointing somebody close to the protector.

All trusts should have a protector — even if you are the trustee and beneficiary of your own trust. This seems odd: You get to control and use the trust assets freely while you are alive, so why would you need a protector?

The problem is that you will eventually die, and whoever you have appointed as the successor trustee in your trust document will become the acting trustee. It's this trustee you have to worry about — with you gone, this new trustee could potentially abuse the trust for fees, leaving the beneficiaries with no recourse except to engage in expensive litigation. With a protector, the misbehaving trustee can be fired.

No Exceptions!

All other U.S. states provide for some type of "exception creditors," typically as divorcing spouses or pre-existing tort claims. Essentially, this means that in such jurisdictions, even if you have made it past the statute of limitations and there are no fraudulent conveyance issues, the exception creditor could still get at the trust's assets.

Nevada is the only U.S. jurisdiction that does not allow exception creditors. This has made NAPTs an alternative to prenuptial agreements. By agreeing to put assets in an NAPT, prospective spouses are essentially agreeing to protect those assets from lawsuits, asset division or other claims in the event of a divorce. By acting before marriage, you're basically stashing away a "nest egg" and setting aside a certain amount of your assets to be protected in the event the relationship unexpectedly terminates — notwithstanding your hope and expectations to the contrary.

This is nice, but NAPT planning related to marriage shouldn't wait until right before a divorce — or even during a marriage. That's because establishing an NAPT might be regarded as a fraudulent transfer, a breach of a fiduciary duty owed by one spouse to the other.

Taxation

Because the settlor retains powers and controls in an NAPT, the trust is treated as a "grantor trust" for tax purposes. This means that all income and losses of the trust pass-through and are reported by the settlor on his or her tax return; there are no additional taxes; and you retain any personal tax deductions.

Similarly, because transfers into an NAPT are not regarded as a "completed" gift, there are no gift tax implications — unless you design it so that transfers to the trust are treated as completed gifts and therefore excluded from your estate.

The values of the NAPT assets, however, are included in the settlor's estate for estate tax purposes ... unless you adopt the next nifty trick.

Dynasty Trusts

A dynasty trust is a trust designed to avoid or minimize estate taxes on wealth transfers to subsequent generations. By holding assets in the trust and making well-defined distributions to each generation, the entire wealth of the trust is not subject to estate taxes with the passage of each generation.

Dynasty trusts avoid the generation-skipping transfer tax that occurs when traditional trusts attempt to bypass transferring all assets to spouses or children — for example, reserving property assets to one's great-great-great-great grandchildren, to be held in trust for them, but not fully owned, by the intervening generations.

In most cases, the common law rule against "perpetuities" forbids any legal instrument — contracts, wills, trusts and so on — from tying up property for too long a time beyond the lives of people living when the instrument was written. (Charitable remainder trusts are excepted.) For example, the head of a family might stipulate in a trust document that assets be used in a certain way forever, preventing a spouse or heirs from accessing them after his death.

The common-law tradition is that any heritable "interest" must vest to heirs no later than 21 years after the death of the last identifiable individual living at the time the interest was created. A 2005 Nevada law, however, explicitly allowed for dynasty trusts that can last for 365 years — thus permitting skipping many generations for estate tax purposes.

Although this was challenged, the Nevada Supreme Court ruled in March 2015, in the case of *Bullion Monarch Mining Inc. v. Barrick Goldstrike Mines Inc.*, that the 365-year perpetuities law is the law in Nevada.

Combining an NAPT With a Limited Liability Company

The limited liability company (LLC) format provides an excellent form of protection, especially for real estate holdings. There's nothing stopping you from creating an LLC to hold certain assets under an NAPT — and plenty of advantages to doing so.

Here's why. All states permit personal creditors of an LLC member (i.e., owner) to obtain a "charging order" from a court against the debtor-owner's "membership interest" — i.e., their proceeds from the LLC's operation, such as rental income from properties owned by it. But most states' charging orders only give creditors the debtor-member's "financial rights." A creditor with a charging order doesn't get to participate in LLC management, so they can't order a distribution of cash or liquidation of assets.

So, if the LLC members direct the LLC manager not to make a distribution to the debtor-member, or refuse to sell the real estate in question, the creditor is stuck. Moreover, because a creditor with a charging order has the debtor-member's "financial rights," the IRS could hold the creditor responsible for taxes on the debtor-member's share of LLC profits — regardless of whether or not any profit distributions are made! That makes lawsuits against assets owned by a properly constituted LLC very unattractive indeed.

The problem is that many states allow alternative remedies for creditors beyond the charging order. Such remedies are known as "piercing the veil" since they allow the creditor or litigant to get directly at the LLC's members. Not Nevada. Charging order protection is the exclusive remedy for the creditor of a member of a Nevada LLC. Nevada also allows single-member LLCs, which receive the same protection from charging orders and multimember LLCs. That means the trustee of your NAPT could also be the sole member of an LLC owned by the trust, in which you could hold rental properties, for example. This LLC will protect the other assets held by it from any claims or liabilities arising from other assets owned by it.

How an NAPT Could Have Helped Belinda and Ryan

If Belinda and Ryan had placed their home, other properties, business interests and inherited cash assets in an NAPT, they would have been insulated from the lawsuit brought by the workman's family.

The spendthrift provision inherent in the nature of the irrevocable NAPT would have prevented either of them from agreeing to attachment of assets in trust, even if they wanted to do so.

Of course, this would have entailed some careful planning. For example, Belinda and Ryan's own home and inherited bank accounts would need to be owned directly by the NAPT, which would insulate them from liquidation (as would Georgia's homestead exemption for personal residences).

Their other two inherited properties should be in an LLC owned by the trust, set up specifically as a "series" LLC, which insulates each property for liabilities arising from the other. Their shares in the family business managed by their brother could have been in a separate trust-owned LLC.

Having an NAPT doesn't mean Belinda and Ryan could dispense with liability insurance on their home, however.

After all, the legal fees to defend against the lawsuit would need to be paid, and without insurance, any award to the plaintiff would require liquidating assets not owned by the trust, like vehicles, furniture and other personal items.

A Special Deal on the NAPT

The NAPT is a great vehicle for domestic asset protection. It can do almost everything that an offshore APT can do at a fraction of the cost.

This makes the NAPT ideal for folks who want a low-cost, quick, easily manageable route to strong domestic asset protection. And as an exclusive for my readers, I've managed to secure a great deal on getting one set up.

My good friend, attorney Josh Bennett, will set up a properly constituted NAPT for an all-inclusive cost of $12,500. He will help with the first-year setup and registration costs, including drafting the trust documents, appointing a Nevada-based trustee and completing all the required paperwork.

Now, you will find offers for rough-and-ready NAPTs on the internet. Don't do it. As should be clear from what I've shared with you here, it is critical to have an experienced, qualified attorney draft the specific trust agreement and other documents that you need to address your particular needs. You're not going to get that off the internet.

Instead, I strongly encourage you to contact Josh to get started on your personal asset protection plan right away ... after all, you can never know if and when the lightning bolt that struck Belinda and Ryan will strike you.

Contact:

Josh N. Bennett, Esq.
440 North Andrews Avenue
Fort Lauderdale, FL 33301
Tel.: (954) 779-1661
Mobile: (786) 202-5674
Email: josh@joshbennett.com
Website: www.joshbennett.com

INCOME SECRET NO. 15:

Protect Yourself and Your Business(es) by Forming an LLC or Series LLCs

It's one thing to accumulate wealth. It's another to protect and keep your hard-earned assets.

One false move — be it an ill-advised financial decision or simply a careless act, breach, or negligence — and you could lose everything you've worked so hard to create and build over the years.

That's the challenge facing entrepreneurs who start their own businesses; how to protect themselves and their budding enterprise from certain legal liability risks, especially in today's highly litigious environment.

One of the best ways to avoid personal liability is by forming a limited liability company (LLC). Recognized by all U.S. states, an LLC is a form of business ownership that provides protection for its owners (referred to as "members") from the following risks:

- **Personal liability from your LLC's debts** — With an LLC, you don't personally guarantee or promise to pay its debts, so you're not personally liable for the company's debts. Although creditors can go after the LLC's bank accounts and other property to settle a debt, they cannot touch your personal property (bank accounts, home, car). At best, they can only demand that you personally guarantee any business loans, credit cards or other extensions of credit to your LLC.

- **Personal liability for actions by the LLC's co-owners and employees** — An LLC protects its owners from personal liability for any wrongdoing committed by any co-owners or employees of the LLC during the course of business. Of course, if the LLC is found liable for the negligence or wrongdoing of its owner or employee, the LLC's money or property can be taken by creditors to satisfy a judgment against the LLC. But the LLC owners are not personally liable for the debt. While the owner or employee who committed the act might be personally liable for their actions, a co-owner who was not involved in the act or wrongdoing isn't.

- **Personal liability for your own actions related to the business** — Here's where there is an exception to the limited liability afforded by forming an LLC. You remain personally liable for any negligence, malpractice or wrongdoing committed during the course of business, such as: personally and directly injuring someone due to negligence during the course of business; failing to deposit taxes withheld from employees' wages; intentionally engaging in fraudulent, illegal or reckless activity during the course of business that harms the firm or any individual; or using the LLC for personal gain, instead of treating it as a separate legal entity. If found in violation of these rules, both your assets and the LLC's assets could be confiscated by creditors to satisfy the judgement. To guard against such action, it is advisable that you carry liability insurance when forming an LLC.

- **Liability for other members' personal debts** — Your LLC's assets cannot be taken by creditors of an LLC's owner to satisfy personal debts against the owner. Nevertheless, instead of taking property directly, there are other ways creditors can try to collect from someone with an ownership interest in your LLC. These measures vary from state to state, but may include getting a court order that forces the LLC to pay the creditor all the money due by the LLC owner/debtor; foreclosing on the owner/debtor's LLC ownership interest; or getting a court to order the LLC to be dissolved.

If considering forming an LLC, be sure to check out the state's laws in which your business is located as they may differ from one jurisdiction to another.

Although not a corporation, an LLC provides the same liability protection as a corporation since it is separate from its members. If there are several members, the LLC may be taxed as a partnership, with its profits passing through to the partners according to their share of the business.

The Pros and Cons of LLCs

As with any form of ownership, there are advantages and disadvantages to limited liability companies.

On the plus side, LLCs:

- Limit liability for managers and members.

- Enable flexible management.

- Are taxed as a partnership (if there are several members), allowing profits to pass-through to the partners according to their share of the business and taxing profits at their personal tax level, thus avoiding double taxation.

- Provide good privacy protection.

- Are a premier vehicle for holding appreciating assets (real estate, stock portfolios, intellectual property, etc.).

- Provide exceptional flexibility in the ability to allocate profits and losses to members in varying amounts.

On the negative side, LLCs:

- Are charged extra fees in some states, including California.

- Restrict professional groups (i.e. doctors or dentists) from operating as LLCs in certain states.

- Allow income splitting, but unlike an S Corp, all income may be subject to payroll or self-employment taxes.

- Require consent of membership for each and every transfer of membership interests.

- Reduce asset protection for single member LLCs or (in many states) do not honor asset protection for LLCs with a single owner.

Again, check your state's laws pertaining to forming an LLC to be sure it's the right strategy for your business.

What If I Own More Than One Company?

If you own several companies and want to limit your personal liability, you might want to consider a series limited liability company (SLLC, aka series LLC). This is a form of a limited liability company that provides protection across your multiple "series" against liabilities arising from the other series.

Put another way, the series LLC is like a master LLC that has separate divisions, similar to an S-corporation with several subsidiaries (or "cells"). Each cell LLC has assets that are separate from the others, while the master or umbrella LLC controls all the LLCs in the series.

The benefits of series LLCs include:

- **Reduced startup costs** — The process only requires one filing fee and your attorney can set up both the parent company and cells at less cost than setting up multiple LLCs.

- **Protection of assets** — Each cell's assets are protected from judgments against the assets of other cells.

- **Less administration** — You're free to set up as many LLCs as you wish, provided they are separate and are administered separately. This allows you to save on administrative time and cost.

- **Less complex structure** — A series LLC is not as complex in terms of taxes, structure, and records as a corporation with subsidiaries.

- **Lower sales taxes** — Depending on which state your parent LLC is located, the rent paid by one cell in the series may not be subject to sales tax. Only the parent LLC needs to be registered with the state, resulting in fewer legal costs and registration fees, as well as only one annual or biennial fee required for the series (assuming all LLCs in the series are registered in the same state).

- **A single tax return is necessary.** This should be filed by the parent LLC, but it must include financial information on all the cell LLCs.

Conclusion

Despite their many advantages, forming an LLC or series LLCs can be a complex task for an inexperienced or small business owner. It often requires the expertise of a seasoned and qualified attorney.

One that my father Bob Bauman and I have worked with for many years and would readily recommend is Josh Bennett, who specializes in tax and corporate rules. He can be reached as follows:

Josh N. Bennett, Esq. PA 4
40 North Andrews Avenue
Fort Lauderdale, FL 33301
Tel.: (954) 779-1661
Mobile: (786) 202-5674
Email: josh@joshbennett.com
Website: www.joshbennett.com

INCOME SECRET NO. 16:

How to Protect Your Assets From Probate With an Irrevocable Trust

Benjamin Franklin was right when he coined the phrase, *"In this world nothing can be said to be certain, except death and taxes."*

It's not enough to protect your hard-earned assets throughout your life, you also have to shield them from a potential threat after you've passed on.

That threat is called "probate" — and unless you prepare for it, your heirs may be in for an unpleasant and unrewarding surprise.

The Probate Trap

Probate is a compulsory legal process often triggered when someone with considerable net worth dies. It inventories your assets, ensures that all your debts are settled and distributes what's left to the heirs designated in your will. Sounds fairly uncomplicated and inconsequential, but often that's hardly the case.

That's because if you don't leave behind a will, each state has its own rules defining who is entitled to receive your property, and how much.

Not only can this intestate probate process be drawn out, but while your estate is being settled, your heirs receive nothing — in some cases, not even access to your life insurance proceeds. There are minimum periods during which creditors are allowed to respond and your estate cannot be distributed.

Also, probate can be costly. There are attorney's fees, executor's fees, court filing fees and other costs set as a percentage of the value of your estate. In some states, attorneys are allowed to charge hourly fees, subject to court approval of their "reasonableness."

Bottom line: If you don't have one, create a will.

There's also the issue of federal taxes.

The Potential Tax Consequences of Probate

The Internal Revenue Service (IRS) doesn't miss a beat when it comes to probate inheritance. It taxes a decedent's right to pass property to beneficiaries, based on the value of the estate and subject to certain thresholds. Thankfully, your estate, rather than your beneficiaries, pay the taxes, but it can still deprive your heirs of a sizable portion of the assets.

Let's define probate assets. They are those that require court intervention to be legally passed from the decedent to a new owner, typically including anything held solely in your name since assets that are jointly held usually transfer automatically to the other owner. That means that retirement benefits and life insurance policies that pass directly to beneficiaries are not subject to probate. The exception to the rule, however, is when the named beneficiary on a policy or retirement plan is the decedent's estate. Any asset that is payable to the state is considered a probate asset and possibly subject to probate tax.

The same is true of income the decedent earned before death that was not included on the estate's income tax return by the executor of the estate. In that case, your heirs would be responsible for claiming this income on their own returns, including the interest earned before and after the date of death.

Then there's the matter of capital gains from the sale of an inherited asset. If the amount is in excess of the asset's tax basis, your heirs will owe a tax. Say, for example, a member of your family inherits your home valued at $1 million and sells it for $1.5 million. They would owe capital gains tax on $500,000.

And it's not just the federal government that wants a slice of your probated assets. Several states — including Iowa, Kentucky, Maryland, Nebraska, New Jersey and Pennsylvania — tax beneficiaries of inherited assets (although some exempt surviving spouses). Though the exact amount varies by state, it is typically a percentage of the estate's value.

Is a Will Enough?

It's not just the size of your estate that matters … it's also what is contained in your will that's critical. If you have more than a bank account, home and a few personal possessions, a will is crucial to ensure some control over how those assets are handled after you're gone. If you own a business, for example, and your heirs can't agree on whether to keep it up and running or sell it, a probate judge can order it sold so it can be divided according to state law. Same goes for ownership of properties in more than one country or if you have various investments, or a collection of valuable items.

Here's the rule: If the value of your and your spouse's estate is more than the combined gift/estate tax exemption — currently $10.8 million ($5.43 million x 2) — then you'll need more than just a will. You'll need to transfer some of your assets out of your estate while still making them available to your heirs.

For example, if you have long-term investments with un-realized capital gains, the appreciation on those investments from the date of purchase will be considered income for estate tax purposes, even if they aren't actually liquidated. You might want to give your heirs a head's up to liquidate something else — perhaps, the family house — as a way to avoid having to pay unnecessary taxes or having to sell valuable stock.

Also, be aware that the death benefit of a multimillion-dollar life insurance policy will be included in the value of your estate. Combined with your property, investments and other assets, this could put your total assets into estate tax territory and create a burden for your heirs.

If you have long-term investments with unrealized capital gains, for example, the appreciation of those investments from the date of purchase will be considered income for estate tax purposes upon your death — even if they aren't actually liq-uidated. That could mean your heirs would have to liquidate another asset — like the family house — to avoid having to sell valuable stock.

In such a case, you would benefit from an irrevocable trust, which enables your heirs to receive certain assets (either before or at the time of your death). Those assets are excluded from the calculation of your estate. Such a trust could even be the beneficiary of your life insurance policy, keeping it, as well, out of your estate and out of probate, since trust assets aren't yours.

In the U.S., there is a difference between revocable and irrevocable trusts. A revocable trust is one you, as the grantor of the trust assets, can terminate. That means that, for all intents and purposes, those assets remain "yours" and they do not enjoy asset-protection features. An irrevocable trust, on the other hand, is permanent — once you transfer assets into it, you cannot undo it. If your living trust is irrevocable, and depending on how it is structured, it should enjoy the basic asset-protection features of any trust.

Benefits of an Irrevocable Trust

There are numerous advantages to placing your assets in an irrevocable trust. For one thing, your assets are protected from liability because the trust is a separate entity from yourself. By employing this strategy, your gifts to your heirs remain intact, even if someone sues you and wins.

Also, an irrevocable trust enables you to avoid taxation. Since you no longer own the assets placed in the trust, their value is not taxable to your estate when you die. There is one exception, though, worth noting. If you transfer ownership of your life insurance policy to the trust and die within three years, the IRS treats the transfer as if it never happened and the policy's death benefit is included in your estate. However, you can side-step this scenario by having your trust purchase a policy instead of transferring one into it. In that case, you would just fund the premiums by making monthly payments to the trust.

Best of all, you bypass the probate process when you die by placing your assets in an irrevocable trust. Also, the total amount of your holdings in the trust are not a matter of public record, as they would be in a last will and testament.

An irrevocable trust is a sound way to protect your assets, as well as the financial security of those you will one day leave behind. To set one up, first consult with your financial adviser.

INCOME SECRET NO. 17:

The One Form You Need to Keep the IRS' Hands Off Your IRA Beneficiary Money

Who gets what when you pass away — and how?

It should be a simple enough process, right?

If you have a will, then that settles that. Or if you don't, then a probate court decides.

You'd think so. But it's more complicated than that.

You're free to leave your possessions and assets to whomever you wish. But there's one claimant who gets something from many of us, whether we want it to or not ... the IRS. And if you don't plan properly, the taxman will get more than he should ... leaving your heirs with less.

You didn't work your whole life to provide for the spendthrifts in Washington ... so don't let them take more from your true heirs than they should.

A perfect example is what could happen with your individual retirement account (IRA) if you aren't careful.

An IRA is a dual-purpose vehicle. We think of it as a tax-advantage retirement savings account. But it also serves as an ideal way to leave money to your heirs.

It's simple to leave an IRA to your spouse or children. Inheriting one is the complicated part. That's why it's critical that you and your heirs understand the IRS rules to minimize the tax burden.

The Importance of Listing Your Beneficiaries

The rules governing inheritance of IRAs are different for spouses and non-spouses, like your children or grandchildren. But they have one thing in common: An IRA isn't part of your estate. It passes directly to the beneficiaries.

That means your will doesn't determine who gets your IRA money when you're gone. Instead, you must make that choice separately on a "beneficiary form" provided by your IRA custodian. No matter what your will might say, *that form* determines who gets what.

So, if you're planning on leaving IRA money to your heirs, it's critical that you name them on the account's beneficiary form, in the order of your preference. There are two reasons for that.

First, for non-spouse IRA heirs, being named on the form allows them to stretch out distributions from the IRA over their own lifetimes. That allows them to take small distributions every year. That way, they don't jump into a higher tax bracket.

But if you don't list any beneficiaries by name, the IRA distributions can't be stretched out, and the tax shelter is lost. Your heirs will have to pay tax on the *entire distribution*. Nearly 40% of an IRA could be lost to taxes if the heir cashes it out in one go.

Second, if your first choice of beneficiary dies before you or doesn't want to take the IRA, listing other beneficiaries in order creates a sequence of "contingent beneficiaries."

Keeping Your IRA Benefit All in the Family

A surviving spouse can choose to take an inherited IRA as their own or remain a beneficiary. But for non-spouse beneficiaries — such as a child — the rules are very different.

First, a non-spouse beneficiary must rename the account to include both the beneficiary's name and the decedent's name. For example, the account could be renamed as "Joe Bloggs (deceased March 1, 2020) for the benefit of Mary Bloggs."

Second, a non-spouse heir can't roll the money into their own IRA. Instead, required minimum distributions must be taken by December 31 each year, starting in the year after the original owner died. Your beneficiaries won't pay an early-withdrawal penalty on the distributions, but they will pay income tax on required minimum distributions (RMDs) from inherited traditional IRAs. (Roth IRAs are tax-free.) If an heir misses an RMD, they will be hit with a 50% penalty for each year missed.

Finally, if your heir — say, your child — decides to pass on the IRA to one of your grandchildren, they can only do so if your original beneficiary form lists those grandchildren as contingent beneficiaries.

Important Note: Previously, those who inherited an IRA could stretch out the required minimum distributions over their lifetime, thus allowing them to continue reaping the benefits of tax-advantaged investment gains. However, under the SECURE (Setting Every Community Up for Retirement Enhancement) Act, which took effect on January 1, 2020, those who inherit a Roth or traditional IRA from someone who dies — with the exception of a surviving spouse, minor children, or people with disabilities — must now take the money out and pay any taxes due within 10 years of the death of the retirement account owner.

One Form to Rule Them All

Whatever you do, don't forget to update the IRS beneficiary form if and whenever your life changes so that your money doesn't unintentionally end up in the wrong hands.

For example: If you divorce and never update your form to remove your ex-wife's name as the sole primary beneficiary, she will get the money at your death even if your will says the money should go to your new spouse.

And adding your children as contingent beneficiaries will allow them to pass on your IRA to their own children. That's another reason to keep that form up to date.

The humble IRA beneficiary form appears as one piece of paperwork among many when you establish an IRA for the first time. As you can see, it's anything but ... so take your time, follow the rules and keep your money in the family ... and out of the clutches of the IRS.

INCOME SECRET NO. 18:

Shield Your Homegrown Assets With an Offshore Trust

Looking for one of the savviest ways to protect your assets from creditors, lawsuits, legal judgments, an unstable economy, and/or overzealous tax collectors? Then look beyond borders and consider setting up an offshore trust.

If you think offshore trusts are strictly for the one-percenters — the wealthiest of the wealthy — think again. Anyone can benefit from the returns derived from an offshore trust so long as the individual resides offshore (not in the same jurisdiction as where the offshore trust is located). Also, practically any type of asset can be transferred to offshore trust assets. That includes cash, securities, real estate, art, gold or even one's businesses.

An offshore trust—just like any other trust — is a contract or private legal agreement. It's similar to an onshore trust in that both involve a settlor or a grantor who transfers the trust property or assets to the trustee for the benefit of any individual or group called beneficiaries. The trustee is the person or corporate body that ensures that the wishes of the settlor are carried out and that the beneficiaries' interests are protected.

In a sense, an offshore trust is a living will in that it applies before and after the death of the settlor and it can be revoked by order of the settlor. However, an offshore trust is much more than that, offering numerous benefits that include:

- **Asset protection** — An offshore trust creates a means of transferring your assets to the name of a trustee as a way to protect them against future litigation or other issues that can lead to — the seizure of your assets, unstable economic conditions, or legal judgments, such as divorce or bankruptcy.

- **Strategic tax planning** — Offshore jurisdiction assures an efficient tax structure for your assets, as well as a low to zero taxation rate.

- **Probate protection** — Since the trust is outside your country of residence, any associated expenses and delays due to probate are avoided.

- **Asset confidentiality** — Here in the United States, you are mandated by law to declare your assets and liabilities to the government. However, you can have absolute financial privacy — as well as better returns and the aforementioned tax savings — by transferring your assets to an offshore trust. Just bear in mind that your offshore assets will still be under the law of the foreign country in which they are located.

- **The preservation of your family assets** — An offshore trust enables the settlor to pass on trust assets via precise allocations as per agreement.

- **The avoidance of excessive taxes levied on property sales and investments** — You can sell personal and corporate assets without having to contend with capital gains or corporation taxes.

Choosing the Offshore Trust That Meets Your Needs

If you are planning to take advantage of these offshore trust benefits, the first step you need to take is conducting a comprehensive financial review of your assets and determining which trust structure best fits your needs. Examples include:

- **A bare trust**, which provides the beneficiary with the right to access the income and assets of the trust.

- **A fixed trust**, in which the settlor creates a predetermined condition on how the beneficiary will obtain the assets of the trust. For example, setting up a trust for a child accessible only when he or she reaches the age of 18.

- **A discretionary trust**, in which the settlor sets certain criteria for the trustee's discretion on how assets will be invested on behalf of the beneficiary.

The next step is to determine who your beneficiaries are, and deciding the purpose of the trust and which of your assets will be included in it. Then it's a matter of creating a trust deed or a written document containing these details and having your attorney review the document.

Last, but not least, you'll need to choose a trustee to finalize and complete the process. Your financial adviser can help you find the most reputable offshore trust company to ensure that you maximize your offshore trust benefits.

Cost Considerations

When you transfer your assets to an offshore trust, it will involve certain costs. So, you'll want to weigh the benefits against the actual costs involved before taking the plunge. However, if you are residing in a country that imposes high taxes on income and investments, a foreign trust fund that offers less or zero taxation — along with confidentiality — is undoubtedly a much better option.

While there is no minimum amount required to be invested in an offshore trust, there are fees for such things as opening a bank account, communication, advice and other administrative tasks, which is why most trust companies recommend maintaining at least $25,000 in assets in the trust.

Also, if you receive dividends from your offshore trust, the country from which the payment is made may impose a withholding tax on the payment as it leaves the country. However, if a double tax treaty exists between your country of residence and the country where the offshore trust is held, the tax could be reduced, or you may be allowed to claim a portion — or all — the withheld money.

Choosing the Right Jurisdiction

Investing in an offshore trust in a tax-free or low-tax jurisdiction will increase your opportunity for greater returns. That's why more and more people are transferring their assets to offshore trust assets. However, there are several factors you should consider before you transfer to a particular jurisdiction, such as:

- Whether it's a low- or no-tax jurisdiction. Ideally, the income earned by your offshore trust assets should not be subject to taxation.

- Whether it has favorable trust laws. Not every foreign country recognizes offshore trusts or allows this type of financial arrangement. This is why you need to make sure that the jurisdiction you choose allows for flexible offshore trusts that provide both privacy and maximum asset protection.

- Whether the country that offers your offshore trust has a stable political and economic system. If not, your assets may be vulnerable to the whims and dictates of a rogue government.

- Whether the chosen jurisdiction assures total confidentiality in regard to the details of your trust.

- Whether you maintain the ability to easily transfer your funds in and out of the country without any interference or restrictions from local authorities. With exchange controls, you must have the ability to easily move your funds in and out of a foreign country without interference or restriction from the authorities.

There are several countries that meet these criteria and are considered to be the best places to keep one's assets. These include:

- Switzerland
- Republic of Uruguay
- Republic of Panama
- The Cook Islands
- Federation of Saint Kitts & Nevis

Whichever of these jurisdictions is best for you will depend not only on your investment objectives, but also on such factors as the size of your trust, the assets you intend to place into the trust, your risk level of litigation and the reputation of the banks located there.

Making the Most of the Offshore Solution

With the right trustee, jurisdiction and management, your offshore trust could prove to be one of the shrewdest financial decisions you ever make in terms of preserving, protecting, and potentially growing your assets. If you have any questions about offshore trusts or need guidance on which assets can and should be transferred from your country of residence to its offshore haven, speak with your financial adviser.

INCOME SECRET NO. 19:

Keep Your Gold Safe Offshore

These days, money in the bank just isn't safe.

Wealth taxes have been a target ever since the International Monetary Fund (IMF) put a stop to the idea of a mass "bail-in" back in November 2013. They've already been imposed in Cyprus. Four European countries — Spain, France, Switzerland, and Belgium — have it. And it is a subject of debate among progressive 2020 Democratic candidates as a means of reducing government debt and redistributing wealth.

A bail-in — or wealth tax — is a statutory procedure to seize a portion of private wealth and it could be imposed on your net worth—including your shareholdings and fixed assets, such as real estate. However, this would pose liquidity problems for many people, not to mention enforcement problems for governments.

A more likely scenario is a levy on bank balances, as was the case in Cyprus. Banks would simply be instructed to deduct a certain percentage of the balance — say, 10% — of each savings, checking or deposit account and transfer it to the government or central bank.

There's only one sure way to keep this nightmare scenario from happening to you. You've got to convert some of your portfolio into physical assets that are hard to track, value and attach … and aren't reportable to Uncle Sam.

But let's be clear. You won't be *hiding* your wealth. You're just taking advantage of legal provisions that allow you to keep your wealth in forms and places that aren't subject to offshore reporting requirements. Perfectly legal strategies include:

- Keeping cash, in U.S. dollars and select foreign currencies, in a home safe and/or in secure private storage.

- Investing in tangible assets, such as rare collectible stamps, gemstones and other nonmonetary stores of value.

• Investing in a "dirt bank" of foreign land holdings.

• Creating offshore and onshore legal holding structures that make it difficult for a creditor (including the IRS) to attach your wealth, putting you at the "back of the queue" for wealth confiscation.

• Accumulating gold or other precious metals in bullion form, whether coins or bars.

Gold is one of the best countercyclical assets around and tends to appreciate in value just when it is needed most — in a crisis. And owning actual *bullion* is far better than owning a gold ETF or shares in a mining company — neither of which would be worth anything in a real crisis.

There's also the question of how much of it to keep. Whether you invest in Good Delivery gold ingots — the ultrafine "four nines" 400 troy-ounce bars you see in the movies — or smaller bars and wafers of the metal, the question of *storage* arises immediately.

Your Golden Options

I don't have to tell you that gold is one of the most popular targets for thieves. Secure storage goes with the territory. Broadly, you have three options for secure storage:

1. **Bank safe-deposit boxes** are ubiquitous and easy to obtain, at least in the U.S. To get one in a foreign bank, however, you have to open an account, and that isn't easy in this age of the Foreign Account Tax Compliance Act (FATCA), a 2010 U.S. federal law which requires foreign financial institutions to report on the foreign assets held by U.S. account holders and subject to withholding payments.

   Safe-deposit boxes are nowhere near as safe as specialized vaults, and they are significantly more expensive. Banks can and do open safe-deposit boxes under court order — even in foreign countries, although not as easily as in the U.S.

2. **A home safe** is much better than the proverbial mattress for home storage. But anything less than a built-in and bolted-down safe with the highest security rating, accompanied by top-level security and alarm systems, is likely to be less safe than a safe-deposit box and is not the place to keep your core gold holdings. It's also more expensive per unit of stored gold value.

3. **Private vault companies** exist worldwide. If you have physical gold in your Individual Retirement Arrangement (IRA), it's almost certainly in one of them in the U.S., as per IRS requirements. Private vault companies abide by rigorous standards that are audited regularly by third parties. Their operations are bonded and insured, usually by top-drawer firms such as Lloyd's of London.

   They provide storage arrangements on a strictly private basis, in which you and your legal designee have exclusive access to the storage unit. The vault company has no ownership or other financial interest in what's in your vault and, in most cases, doesn't even know what it is. Paradoxically, despite all of this, private vaults are often less expensive than safe-deposit boxes.

Of the three choices, I vote for the private vault company option hands down.

Plus, there's another critical question: Where to keep it? Here in the U.S. or offshore?

Longtime readers of *The Bauman Letter* know I don't trust the U.S. government to abide by the Constitution, or even by its own laws.

Nor do I trust most U.S. banks. Most will do anything the government tells them to do to stay out of trouble. Many are financially unsound, and I certainly wouldn't want to keep my core gold holdings with them — especially since the contents of safe-deposit boxes aren't covered by Federal Deposit Insurance Corporation (FDIC) depositor insurance.

I also extend that caution to most U.S. storage companies. It's not that I don't trust them. It's just that no matter how principled and honest they are, they are located inside a country where government thinks it can do anything it wants and almost always gets away with it.

The Offshore Option

If the feds come to take your gold, they will get it, regardless of where it is inside the U.S. That leaves offshore storage.

Some people immediately envision a complex process of setting up a storage relationship in person in some expensive foreign city where they don't speak English, buying and transporting gold bullion, and having to deal with legal and reporting hassles every step of the way.

It *can* be like that if you try to do it yourself. But it needn't be.

In fact, there are ways you can acquire and store gold overseas without getting up from your computer — except for the occasional trip to the postbox to receive and send some documents.

Before we get to a great option I've discovered, allow me to point out some things you need to think about before you even start looking at a specific company — choosing the right country.

- **The Legal Environment**: U.S. banks routinely accede to any demand made by the feds. You want to keep your gold in a country that still respects the rule of law and has asset-friendly laws on its books.

- **Import Duties:** You don't want to do storage business in a country that imposes import duties on gold brought into their country. Most "good" countries don't, as long as it's "fine" (pure) metal.

- **VAT on Gold Purchases:** Some foreign countries levy value added taxes (VAT) on bullion purchases. But some countries don't for fine metal. You want to store yours in one of those places — even if it's gold you acquired elsewhere — because VAT will influence the price you get if you decide to sell it down the road.

- **Taxes on Sales and Transfers:** Most countries impose taxes on profits from the sale of bullion, either as capital gains or as ordinary income. Unlike stocks, which produce a stream of income, gold bullion is usually owned in anticipation of a future time when it will be sold in exchange for currency. That makes it an asset subject to capital gains. Look for the lowest-tax jurisdiction possible.

Of course, there are many other things to consider, such as long-term stability and the likelihood of cooperation with the U.S. government in any future financial crisis. We'll address that in a bit.

Destination: New Zealand

Auckland, NZ is home to a firm I discovered that meets all of my criteria for secure offshore gold storage for U.S. clients. That firm is New Zealand Vault (NZV). Established in 1931, it's New Zealand's oldest vault business. Its vaults are "Treasure Grade," which means they're on a par with those used by major banks and reserve banks, and guarded 24/7. It's also insured by Lloyd's of London.

Best of all, NZV is privately owned and independent of the banking sector and government. Its corporate finances aren't mixed up with other business lines, so there are no counterparties involved. NZV's management are all ex-senior executives from the banking industry.

NZV is highly concerned about client privacy. It has a low-key web presence and doesn't do a lot of advertising, preferring word of mouth.

Partnering with NZV is Grant Thornton, a global accountancy firm that acts on behalf of its offshore client. When you do business with NZV, Grant Thornton is essentially an extension of you as the client — it acts on your behalf, not NZV's. If you like, you never need to go to New Zealand at all.

An NZV safe-deposit box can only be opened with two keys — one for the client and one for NZV. Both keys are required in order to open the safe-deposit box. NZV cannot access the client's safe-deposit box without the client's key, and the client cannot access it without NZV's key.

If you choose not to go to New Zealand personally, Grant Thornton will keep your key in safe custody and undertake all this for you. But that's not all. A Grant Thornton representative will also personally deposit your bullion into your box, whether its purchased via NZV or shipped in, and confirm in writing that it's securely stored as agreed. They'll hold the key to your box in the safe custody of their own NZV box, and control access to your box to ensure that it's only ever opened when you request and authorize it.

Of course, as the primary box holder you can nominate other people to have access to your safe-deposit box, such as an attorney or trustee. In the event of the death of a sole hirer of a safe-deposit box, the safe-deposit box will not be accessible by anyone other than the legal personal representative appointed by the hirer's estate.

For Your Peace of Mind

Earlier, I explained why it's important to consider the country as well as the vault company. What about New Zealand? Here's what you need to know:

- **The Legal Environment:** New Zealand is rooted in the same legal system as the U.S. and the United Kingdom. The great difference is that New Zealand is a vibrant democracy and the government simply cannot get away with the sorts of things we see here in the U.S. The rule of law is sound and property rights are respected. Note, however, that like any other country, New Zealand has a process by which a court can order a search of a safe-deposit box.

It is very rare for this to happen and can only be done after a case has been argued in New Zealand in front of a local judge. Foreign judgements are not automatically honored. New Zealand is ranked No. 1 in personal freedom by *Forbes*.

- **Import Duties:** There are no import duties on gold bullion brought into the country.

- **VAT on Gold Purchases:** There is no VAT charged on sales of investment grade "fine" bullion.

- **Taxes on Sales and Transfers:** New Zealand taxes locally sourced income. The maximum rate is 33%. There is currently no long-term capital gains tax on bullion sales. However, even if one is eventually implemented, New Zealand has a double tax agreement with the U.S., which means that you will receive a U.S. tax credit for any profits from the sale of your bullion inside New Zealand.

Of course, gold bullion stored in a private NZV box is not reportable to U.S. authorities under FATCA or the Report of Foreign Bank and Financial Accounts (FBAR).

Opening an NZV Account

Opening a safe-deposit box and depositing your bullion at NZV is simple and can be done from your own home. Here's how it works:

- **Step 1:** Complete NZV's online registration here: www.nzvaultbullion.com/NZVB_OpenAccount.aspx

- **Step 2:** Make a credit card payment through NXV's secure online-payment engine.

- **Step 3:** Obtain a copy of each of the following forms of ID and have them authorized as a true copy by a notary:

  1. In order to comply with the New Zealand Anti-Money Laundering and Countering Terrorism Act 2009, NZV requires one primary form of ID issued by state or federal government that has your photograph, full name, signature and date of birth, such as a driver's license or passport; and

  2. One secondary form of ID such as a utility account or bank statement which is no more than three months old and has your current residential address on it.

• **Step 4:** Post your notarized identification documents to NZV.

Accounts can also be created in the name of limited liability companies (LLCs), trusts and other vehicles, both U.S. and non-U.S. In this case, the documentation will reflect the details of the director or trustee.

What It Costs

NZV stores offshore clients' gold in its vault in the North Island city of Wellington. The annual cost (in USD) is $695 for a box that can hold up to 10kg. This price includes the services provided by the Grant Thornton auditor, who unpacks the bullion, checks it, places it in the customer's box and holds the customer key. For more information, visit https://www.nzvaultbullion.com.

NZV can also arrange for the insurance of the contents of the safety deposit box. The Insurance fee is 0.25% of the total value held per annum. Alternatively, you could have your own insurer cover the contents of your box.

Getting Your Gold Into an NZV Box

U.S. clients can ship existing gold holdings to NZV with the assistance of Grant Thornton in the U.S. As always, top-tier secure companies are used, like Brink's.

But what if you don't have any gold to send?

NZV is a fully accredited broker in gold, silver and palladium bullion in both coin and bar form. Gold comes in various sizes, from 1-ounce wafers to kilogram bars. Bullion coins include 1-ounce Australian Philharmonics and Kangaroos, and Canadian Maple Leafs. All metals are quoted in U.S. dollars.

If you wish to purchase gold through NZV to add to your box, send the required funds via wire transfer to their Bank of New Zealand account.

Alternatively, if you take advantage of theft assistance in opening your own NZV account, you can use that to pay for gold. If you plan to make regular purchases, that's the best bet, since it'll save on wire-transfer fees.

NZV can also sell your gold for a small brokerage fee.

Is It Legal?

There is no legal obstacle to buying gold overseas. Ditto for buying it here in the U.S. and sending it abroad. And there's certainly nothing illegal about storing it privately.

The fundamental reason is that *gold bullion isn't money*. That means it isn't subject to the sorts of reporting requirements of actual currency.

If you bring into or send out of the U.S. "negotiable monetary instruments" (i.e. currency from any country, endorsed personal checks, traveler's checks, non-collectible gold coins, securities or stocks in bearer form) valued at $10,000 or more, a "Report of International Transportation of Currency or Monetary Instruments" form FinCEN 105 must be submitted to U.S. Customs and Border Protection. If you don't and they find out about it, they will take it away from you … permanently.

Bullion gold, on the other hand, is a "commodity" like any other. It isn't currency. When it comes to reporting to Uncle Sam, $10,000 worth of gold is no different from $10,000 worth of corn, car tires or paintings.

That means you can ship it in and out of the U.S. without being obliged to tell anyone.

Getting Started

There are many reasons to own gold. Ten percent of your portfolio should be long-term gold holdings and NZV is an ideal place to keep it and, if need be, acquire it.

If you'd like to pursue this great opportunity, contact them as follows:

New Zealand Vault Limited
P.O. Box 10206
Wellington 6143
New Zealand
Web: http://www.nzvault.com
Email: support@nzvault.com
Tel: +64-4-499-9333

(Please phone after 1 p.m. on the West Coast and after 4 p.m. on the East Coast. During U.S. daylight savings, New Zealand is 16 hours ahead of the East Coat and 19 hours ahead of the West Coast.)

INCOME SECRET NO. 20:

3 Ways to Avoid This Devastating Privacy Mistake

In 2016, Mr. and Mrs. Connors, a retired couple in Georgia, logged into their individual retirement account (IRA) to find a balance of only a few dollars. That balance should have been more than $500,000.

Frantic calls to the IRA custodian ensured. The Connors' password had been changed. So, too, had the secret questions used to validate their identity in the case of a forgotten password. The couple was in the frustrating and stressful position of being refused access to their own account information by their IRA custodian.

The Connors finally managed to get through to a senior account manager. He told them they'd received written instructions to liquidate their IRA and mail a check to an address that had been registered on their account a few weeks before. The letter in question bore Mr. Connors' signature.

For confirmation, the IRA custodian called the telephone number on the account — which had also been changed. The person who answered the phone confirmed he was Mr. Connors and that the request to disburse the funds was correct.

The IRA custodian did as the letter requested — all the money was gone. And since the letter had specified that no tax should be withheld, the Connors were on the hook to the IRS for income tax on the entire transaction ... which had put them into the highest tax bracket for the year!

How could this happen? Better yet, how can you keep it from happening to you?

The Threat Is Real

Eventually the Connors managed to convince the IRA custodian that they had been defrauded. Investigations by the Georgia state police revealed that a young man living near Atlanta had perpetrated the fraud. Here's how he did it...

First, he combed through free online databases, containing information about residential property in Georgia. He cross-referenced this with other online databases that allowed him to identify the names and ages of the titleholders. From there, he whittled the list down to the Connors as a likely target.

The fraudster then began to intercept the Connors' mail. He didn't do this physically. He simply went to the United States Postal Service website and registered for a service called "Informed Delivery" that sends a digital picture of mail to be delivered every day. From these, the fraudster was able to identify the Connors' IRA custodian.

He then did a Google search that led to a blog post on a community website on Yahoo Groups that included Mr. Connors' email address. The Connors' Yahoo email account had been hacked in 2013 (along with roughly three billion other email accounts), but Yahoo had yet to announce this fact publicly.

The fraudster was then able to obtain the password for the Connors' Yahoo email address from a hacker's community on the dark web for a few dollars. After logging into the Connors' Yahoo email account, he found an attachment that included Mr. Connors' scanned signature. He was able to clean it up and make it appear nearly original when printed.

Then, assuming correctly that the Yahoo email password was probably reused, the fraudster was able to log in to the Connors' IRA website. That's when he changed the password, security questions and responses. He also changed the mailing address and phone number.

From there, it was a simple matter of composing a fake letter and sending it to the IRA custodian. He waited a few months after making the address change to send it to allay any suspicion.

In the end, the thief that stole the Connors' retirement money was caught. Luckily, they got most of their retirement funds back. But imagine the anguish they went through in the process. Unfortunately, most victims of fraudsters aren't so lucky.

What happened to the Connors could easily happen to anyone — including you. The only way you can protect yourself is to invest a little money and time into simple techniques that would make what happened to the Connors impossible.

Forget Email ... It's Time for "MeMail"

The risks we face in the digital world come from data harvested from us by American companies. We didn't choose these risks. They happened because of decisions made by these companies in their pursuit of profit.

However, there are ways to minimize these risks. The most important is to limit the type and amount of information you give out. The second most important is to do business only with companies that have solid privacy policies and date protection systems.

Despite these risks, millions of Americans continue to use the "free" services of email providers like Google and Yahoo. The risk their corporate practices pose to us is, in effect, the "price" of these services. But for most people, this risk remains abstract until something happens to them.

This is completely unnecessary ... and given the potential costs, fundamentally uneconomical. It is far less expensive to pay for a secure email service than it is to face the risks of a free one.

There are plenty of secure email services. These companies provide an email address, secure encrypted servers, multifactor authentication and other services that preserve your digital privacy and security. They charge a fee for it. It usually works out to $10-$15 a month.

But we need a way to sift through these options.

The first thing to do, sadly, is to eliminate those based in the United States. That's because the Patriot Act allows the government to force any company to hand over any information in its possession. That includes private information about its customers. When they are told to do so, these companies are forbidden to inform the customers in question.

This is why my recommendation for private secure email is a company called **ProtonMail** (https://protonmail.com). Because it is based in Switzerland, its operations are protected by that country's extremely strict privacy laws. Unlike the U.S., where the FBI can simply issue a secret "National Security Letter" to get any information it wants, Switzerland requires a full presentation of the facts to an independent judge, who must then issue an order that can be appealed. They rarely do.

It's not just the company's headquarters that are based in Switzerland, however. The servers where it stores customer data are inside deep caverns carved into the Swiss Alps. They were originally designed to protect from nuclear fallout.

But neither Swiss law nor bomb-proof caverns are enough to protect your privacy. That's why ProtonMail's technical design is so important.

ProtonMail uses multiple levels of encryption. They are as follows:

- ProtonMail allows you to encrypt the directories on your computer's disk where your email is stored. That makes it inaccessible to anyone without the passcode.

- Your emails are separately encrypted on ProtonMail's servers. Nobody — including ProtonMail itself — can read them without your individual passcode.

- ProtonMail will never allow a third party to access your email account unless you have provided them access right. Those rights involve a special recovery code that is sent by encrypted email to the people whom you designate as your digital "heirs."

- ProtonMail gives you several options that increase email security by addressing risks on the recipient's end. You can set a special password that the recipient must enter to open and read an email sent to them. You can opt to have the recipient's copy of an email self-destruct after a certain period. You can also prevent it from being printed, screen copied or otherwise stored.

- Finally, ProtonMail offers a virtual private network (VPN) service that you can add to your package.

And here's why you need a VPN...

Free Wi-Wi seems to be everywhere these days. Airports, restaurants, hotels — they provide free or low-cost Wi-Fi, and they're all terribly insecure.

This insecurity isn't necessarily the Wi-Fi provider's problem. Even if the Wi-Fi infrastructure is secure, the problem is that a public Wi-Fi system, like those we use when we travel, is child's play to hack. A hacker with the right software on a cell phone or laptop can see all the Wi-Fi connections around him and tap into yours with a click of a button. He'd be able to see any sites you visit or any information you submit online, like your username and password combinations. He'd be able to read your emails.

That's because public Wi-Fi networks, by their very nature, are not encrypted. But a VPN turns an unsecured public network into a secure private network by encrypting all the data sent and received from a connected device, ensuring that all browsing and email activity is safe and private.

A VPN isn't just for public Wi-Fi, however. It's also essential when you're at home or work. That's because most major internet service providers (ISPs), like Comcast and AT&T, routinely monitor their customer's online activity. Once again, this is part of their efforts to compile data from which they can profit — even though you already paid for their service.

A VPN renders your ISP blind. As its name suggests, a VPN is about privacy. It creates a closed system of communication between you and the VPN provider. It's called a virtual network because there is no dedicated infrastructure involved. Instead, a VPN creates a virtual "tunnel" whose walls are built out of high-level encryption. Everything that travels through this VPN tunnel is inaccessible to anyone outside of it.

A VPN does more than just protect your online activity from outside snooping. Any time you log onto the internet, the network assigns the device you're using something called an IP address. It's a unique identifier for your device, which distinguishes it from all the other devices connected to the internet.

Your IP address is public information. It's designed to reveal your geographical location. But VPN routes your Internet traffic through the VPN's encrypted tunnel. Instead of your own IP address, your traffic now reaches the internet from the location of the VPN's server. Many VPN providers allow you to select from a variety of servers located around the world.

There are many VPN providers out there. The criteria for choosing amongst them are straightforward.

First, they must use high-quality encryption.

Second, their infrastructure must be adequate, so encryption doesn't slow down your use of the internet.

Third, they must adhere to a strict policy of not retaining any record of your internet activity on their own servers.

Finally, they should be easy to use and work on all your devices, including your home computer, laptops and cell phones.

Here are three recommendations:

1. **Use the VPN that comes with ProtonMail.** Besides the fact that it can be bundled with the email service I recommend, ProtonVPN uses OpenVPN (UDP/TCP) protocol, with AES-356 encryption. As TheBestVPN.com says: "This is bank-grade, state-of-the-art encryption standards. Put it this way: If you are going to suffer a hack, it won't be because they broke through this encryption. Because it's never been done."

2. **Combine a VPN with your password manager.** A password manager is essentially a software package that stores all your various passwords. It allows you to insert them automatically into any website when you log in. It's protected by a master password and by secure encryption, both on your device and on their servers

   I recommend a password manager called DashLane. It's robust, secure and easy to use. And the most recent version includes a VPN service.

3. **Invest in a high-quality, full-service VPN.** ProtonVPN and DashLane's VPN are very good products, and they have the advantage of coming paired with other essential privacy tools. But if you're looking for something with an established track record and loads of features, consider **NordVPN.**

It has a vast network of servers, located in more than 60 countries. That investment in infrastructure means that NordVPN is typically faster than most other VPN services. That's especially important if you want to have a VPN running when you're doing something like watching a streaming service over your home's Wi-Fi or internet connection.

Triple-Play Protection

Secure private email, a VPN and a password manager are absolutely essential in today's digital world. But don't take my word for it. Imagine yourself in the Connors' position — and the role that these techniques would have played.

By far the greatest role would be reserved for secure private email. In the Connors' case, it was their use of the highly insecure Yahoo mail system that allowed the fraudster to conduct his nefarious scheme.

Using a secure email like ProtonMail wouldn't have prevented the fraudster from learning the Connors' email address of they had shared it in an insecure online forum. But the robust encrypted password system used by ProtonMail would have prevented him from getting onto their email account. That would've stopped him from getting Mr. Connors' signature.

A password manager like DashLane would have nullified the key element in the fraud process: the fact that the Connors' Yahoo email password was the same as for their IRA custodian.

What about the VPN? The hack that almost left the Connors destitute was characterized primarily by what we call "social engineering." The hacker exploited the failures of both the Connors and the employees at the IRA custodian to perpetrate his fraud. By contrast, he never had to resort to hacking the Connors' unencrypted communications.

But that sort of old-fashioned fraud is rapidly becoming the least of your concerns. The thing to fear is the guy or gal sitting at a table near you in the airport cafeteria, or on the same Wi-Fi-equipped flight as you, or even down the aisle from you at the big box store.

That kind of fraudster can do far more damage than the guy who almost got the Connors ... and there are millions of them.

Secure email, a good password manager, a VPN ... that's all it takes to avoid the fate that almost befell Mr. and Mrs. Connors.

Ultimately, digital security is every bit as important as financial security in today's world, and it's a lot less complex and difficult to achieve.

INCOME SECRET NO. 21:

10 Ways to Beat Phone Scammers

"A pestilence."

"Deserving of a fate worse than death."

"A curse on all their houses."

Those were some of the comments regarding an article I wrote about the scammers responsible for the epidemic of scam phone calls. To recap:

- By mid-2019, half of all U.S. phone calls will be scams. Ninety percent of those calls will appear to come from local numbers.

- The government is more concerned with deregulating the telecoms sector than with addressing the problem. And with our monopoly-protected telecoms, providers feel little market pressure to address it.

As with so many other problems in today's world, this means the solution is entirely up to you — and to people like me, whose job it is to help you find and implement it.

So, here are 10 ways you can fight back against the "scum of the earth" ... phone scammers.

Technology Always Has a Dark Side

According to the Federal Trade Commission, in 2019, scammers extracted a reported $1.9 billion from Americans ... and 74% of the time, fraud began with a phone call.

These days, in addition to your landline or mobile phone, you can also initiate a call from an app such as Skype, WhatsApp and Facebook Messenger, among others. These methods use "voice over internet protocol," or VoIP.

Unlike traditional networks, VoIP calls are difficult to detect. That's because they are blended in with all the other internet traffic flowing around the globe.

Telemarketers use sophisticated VoIP programs. They auto-dial millions of numbers a minute. They usually dial randomly, using fake caller ID information. Occasionally, they dial lists of actual numbers hacked from poorly protected business databases.

Ultimately, these VoIP calls are routed through conventional mobile or landline networks. But because they originated using VoIP, it's difficult (but not impossible) to identify the actual caller, including their real phone number and physical location.

If a scam VoIP call is answered, it is routed to a live telemarketer or to a phone tree, and the scam begins:

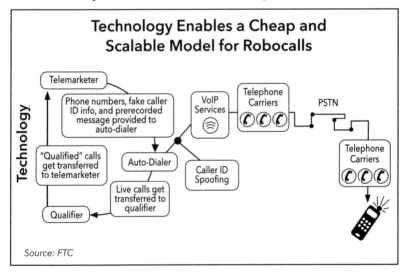

Technology Enables a Cheap and Scalable Model for Robocalls

Source: FTC

Now, most scam calls using VoIP aren't encrypted, since this would increase the cost and complexity for the scammer.

The U.S. government's spy agencies have the technology to trace unencrypted VoIP calls. The same technology is available to U.S. telecoms companies. However, they are reluctant to use it because it would require investment and ongoing expense on their part.

That's why the problem is yours to solve.

How to Defend Yourself From Phone Scammers

There are three broad ways to combat scam calls. The first is technological.

I've been using a service called Nomorobo for a couple of years now. It maintains a list of known scam callers and blocks them on both landline and mobile phones.

Other apps do the same thing, including TrueCaller, RoboKiller, Hiya, Mr. Number, CallBlocker, TrapCall and YouMail (which I have also used for about a year).

Most major phone companies offer similar blockers, although they are far less effective.

Unfortunately, these apps suffer from a fatal flaw. They can block calls only from numbers reported by their users.

But since scam callers can switch fake caller IDs in milliseconds, there is no way these apps can possibly keep up.

To make matters worse, many of these caller IDs belong to legitimate customers, whose calls are also blocked by these apps.

Change Your Phone Habits

The second approach involves changing the way you use your phone.

Here are 10 ways to defeat phone scammers (admittedly, some of these do involve technology):

1. **Do not register on the Federal Trade Commission's Do Not Call List.** Scammers will never abide by the list, and there is a suspicion in tech circles that the list has been hacked by scammers.

2. **Never give your actual phone number to companies who ask for it, unless it is absolutely necessary.** You know how cashiers will often ask you for your email and phone number when you buy something at a store? Or when hotel employees ask you for a number where they

can contact you during your stay? Don't do it. Given the appalling lack of data security in the U.S. corporate sector, that number is highly likely to end up stolen by a scammer.

3. **Create a disposable second number to give out instead.** VoIP applications like Skype have long allowed subscribers to create a telephone number that rings only on that app. If the number is compromised, you can simply change it. The same technique works on other platforms, such as Google Voice, Sideline and Line2. Also, these apps are VoIP-based, and the companies that provide them have incentive to invest in identifying and blocking scam VoIP calls.

4. **Do not answer calls without caller ID information.** This includes calls marked "Private Number," "Invalid Caller ID," "Anonymous Caller" and so on. If it's a legitimate call, let the caller leave a message. The flipside of this, of course, is that you should not set your own phone to hide your caller ID. People like me will ignore your calls.

5. **Do not answer calls from unknown numbers.** This is the most unfortunate aspect of the scam call pestilence, but there is no way around it. Again, if it's a legitimate call, the caller will leave a message and you can return it.

6. **Save important contact numbers on your phone's address book so that the name will appear when you're called.** Of course, there is a possibility that a scammer might try to call you from a saved number, but the likelihood is miniscule (for now).

7. **Buy a landline phone that prevents calls from unsaved numbers from ringing.** I helped one of my relatives set up such a system. It's a bit of a pain, since you must save important numbers into the system up front, or else they won't ring. I helped my relative get around this by telling her to keep the phone with her for a couple of weeks, so she could see the caller ID of incoming calls. She could choose to answer them and add the number to the system's address book.

8. **Educate yourself about common scams.** Scams, like the Social Security cons, rely on one thing that rarely happens in real life. If there is really a problem with your Social Security, IRS or other government agency, those institutions would send you a letter asking you to contact them. They would never call you and ask to start solving a problem on the phone. The same goes for scams involving infected computer software. Microsoft would never call anyone to inform them of a software issue. All such calls are scams.

9. **Adopt one of the aforementioned apps.** Nomorobo, TrueCaller, RoboKiller, Hiya, Mr. Number, CallBlocker, TrapCall or YouMail.

10. **Make an issue of it.** The final way is to make an issue of this problem. As I've stressed repeatedly, effective blocking technologies do exist that could dramatically limit the amount of scam robocalls infesting U.S. phone networks.

The only thing that prevents it is our monopolistic telecoms sector. Big Telecoms know people aren't going to give up their phones, even if 90% of their calls are scams. What other options do they have? It's not like they have a wide choice of service providers.

When systemic problems like this happen, it's up to our representatives in Congress to get busy and do something about it … like passing laws forcing telecoms companies to address the issue.

After all, an effective national barrier to scam robocalls is a wall every American would support.

INCOME SECRET NO. 22:

How to Avoid Costly Scams

The U.S. Fraud Enforcement Task Force estimates that Americans lose $8 to $10 billion in securities, commodities and investment scams every year.

The FINRA Investor Education Foundation surveyed 2,400 U.S. adults age 40 or older and asked them whether someone had ever intentionally given them false information to encourage them to make an investment. The survey found that 84% of respondents had been solicited to participate in a fraudulent investment scam under this definition.

But although 11% of respondents lost money this way, only 4% admitted to being a victim of fraud when asked directly — an under-reporting rate of over 40%, reflecting people's shame when they have been scammed.

Even though investment scams are widespread, many Americans are vulnerable because they don't know the telltale signs.

For example, many lack an understanding of reasonable returns on investments, leaving them vulnerable to fraudulent pitches promising unrealistic or guaranteed returns. In fact, over 40% found an annual return of 110% for investment to be reasonable. Similarly, 43% found "full guaranteed" investments to make perfect sense. Both are highly improbable and are commonplace in pitches by scammers.

The FINRA Foundation's survey found that investment scams were equally likely to come from inside the U.S. as from abroad, despite the common assumption that they are largely the work of foreigners.

- Sixty-four percent of those surveyed had been invited to an "educational" investment sales pitch conducted inside the U.S.

- Sixty-seven percent of respondents said they had received an email from another country offering a large amount of money in exchange for an initial deposit or fee.

- Thirty-six percent had received a letter stating they had won a lottery in another country, including a sample cashier's check as an advance payment.

- Thirty percent had received recommendations to purchase a penny stock.

- Twenty-four percent had been cold called by a stranger offering an investment opportunity.

- Eighteen percent had been asked to participate in an investment that offered a commission for referring other investors.

Eighteen percent had been asked to participate in an investment that offered a commission for referring other investors.

But here's the scariest stat of them all: Nearly 60% of people in the FINRA survey who had been scammed were introduced to the scheme by word-of-mouth — friends, professional contacts or casual acquaintances in social settings.

Those people weren't necessarily solicited to join the scam — most of them voluntarily pursued on their own after having heard about it. And that's the danger: Our excitement gets the better of us.

Scams 101

When we refer to "scams," we're not talking about "hacking." The latter is when someone obtains and uses sensitive information about you without your knowledge or consent.

For example, when someone sends you an email that sounds legitimate. The email contains a link, which then compromises your computer remotely if you click it. That's hacking.

Another common type is when your financial details are compromised by a third-party hack. It's happened to numerous major retailers over the last several years.

Scams are different from hacking. They require your willing participation — and therefore, that you believe they aren't a scam — at least at first.

There are two broad types of scams.

One is what I call an "active" scam, when someone pursues you using techniques such as email or phone solicitation. They've somehow identified you as a likely mark — perhaps because you were in a data source stolen by a hacker.

These are the easiest scams to detect and avoid. An example of an active scam is fake debt collection. A scammer will call you claiming you owe money and threatening dire consequences if you don't pay up.

The technique uses fear to convince you to hand over information, which is then used to defraud you. Most people don't fall for this sort of thing easily.

The other type of scam is "passive." That's when a scammer sets up a website and waits for people to find it and sign up.

These are the most dangerous kinds of scams, because they rely on your own initiative and reflect an underlying need on your part — a need for increased yield, for example.

I'll describe both of these types of scams below, along with others.

Are You a Mark?

The first thing you need to assess is your likelihood of being targeted by scammers or falling for a "passive scam." That means being honest with yourself.

It's hard to talk about the likelihood of becoming a fraud victim without sounding like I'm insulting your intelligence. But the truth is that successful scams aren't about intelligence. They're about emotion, which is the enemy of sound investing. The same goes for susceptibility to fraud.

In this time of extremely low yields on traditional and fixed-income investments, many people are especially desperate to find opportunities to earn extra income. But the same impulse to find the "hidden yield" that leads people to follow sound advice can easily lead to disaster at the hands of a scammer.

The desire for yield is especially strong amongst retirees. They have a number of characteristics that lead scammers to target them:

- They're most likely to have a "nest egg," to own their home and/or to have excellent credit.

- People who grew up in the 1930s, 1940s and 1950s were generally raised to be polite and trusting. Scammers exploit these traits.

- Older people may not report a scam because they're ashamed at having been conned. That's especially true if they're concerned that relatives may think the victim no longer has the capacity to manage their own financial affairs.

- Older fraud victims may not be able to supply detailed information to investigators. In addition, many people don't realize or admit they've been scammed until months after contact with a scammer.

Of course, older people are by no means the only ones at risk of falling for a scam. Indeed, adults of all ages have been known to fall for them ... in some cases, with disastrous results.

Common Passive Scams

Passive scams require that you seek them out. They rely on internet searches, online ad, word-of-mouth and other low-key ways to gather potential victims. They always prey on people's desire to get "something for nothing." These include:

- **Binary Options Scams** — A binary option is a type of contract in which the payout depends on the outcome of a yes/no proposition related to a stock or index. It usually says that the price of a share in a specific company will be over or under a certain amount at a specific time. It might also specify that the price of gold or another commodity will be above or below a specific amount at a particular date and time.

Unlike conventional options, the buyer of a binary option doesn't have the right to purchase or sell the underlying asset or trade the option itself. Instead, the buyer gets a fixed payout if he guesses the option correctly, and nothing if he is wrong.

Binary options scams are usually internet-based and involve extremely short -term options periods. It's nothing more than pure gambling — like rolling dice. Nobody can predict the specific value of a stock over a short period. The short option period is designed to get you hooked so you'll keep trying for hours at a time, just like a slot machine.

The typical binary options scam will ask for a deposit of around $250 to open your "trading account." If you seem like an active "trader," the scammers will contact you to ask that you invest more, in return for which you'll get access to a "special" trading algorithm.

You can "trade" for months on these sites, accumulating what appears to be a large net position. But if you ask to have funds transferred to you, you won't hear from them again.

You can usually identify such scams by looking out for the following:

o They claim to be registered with a financial authority in an unusual place, like a Pacific Islands country.

o They will claim a physical address that sounds legitimate — say, in Canada — but will actually have phone numbers from somewhere else, like a Central American country and phone operators will have foreign accents.

o Their websites will be flashy but poorly designed, with many broken links and poor English usage.

o When you do an internet search for them, they will appear as paid advertisements at the top of the results list.

• **Ponzi Scheme**s — These promise high financial returns or dividends not available through traditional investments.

Instead of investing victims' funds, however, the scheme pays "dividends" to initial investors using the funds of subsequent investors.

A Ponzi scheme generally falls apart when the scammer flees with all the proceeds or when a sufficient number of new investors cannot be found to allow the continued payment of "dividends."

Here are some telltale signs of a Ponzi scheme:

o It will claim to produce exaggerated earnings, but typically won't tell you what the underlying investments are.

o The scheme will emphasize secrecy and may be available only via someone who is already invested in it.

o You will be encouraged to leave your investments in place for long periods, where they will generate impressive paper gains. But any attempt to draw out funds will be strongly discouraged via penalties and fees.

• **Pyramid Schemes** — Also known as "franchise fraud" or "chain referral schemes," pyramid schemes are marketing and investment frauds in which an individual is offered a distributorship or franchise to market a particular product.

Any profit you earn, however, comes not from the sale of the product, but from the sale of new distributorships. At the heart of each pyramid scheme is typically a claim that new participants can recoup their original investments by inducing two or more prospects to make the same investment.

As in Ponzi schemes, the money collected from newer victims is paid to earlier victims to provide a veneer of legitimacy.

Promoters fail to tell prospective participants that it is mathematically impossible for such a scheme to work. Some participants drop out, while others recoup their original investments and then drop out.

Emphasis on selling franchises rather than the product eventually leads to a point where the supply of potential investors is exhausted, and the pyramid collapses.

• **Pump and Dump** — This involves creating artificial buying pressure for a specific security — generally a low-trading, high-volume stock in the over-the-counter securities market. Typically, high trading volume is generated by inducing unwitting investors to purchase shares of the security through false or deceptive sales practices and/or public information releases.

Artificially increasing the trading volume of such a stock has the effect of increasing its price (i.e. the "pump"). The stock is then quickly sold off into the inflated market by the scammers (i.e. the "dump").

Traditional pump-and-dump schemes rely entirely on the willingness of investors to buy a specific stock. They are typically characterized by:

o "Little-known" companies that are touted as the "next big thing."

o High-pressure sales pitches.

o Research and information that tends to refer back to itself, i.e. web link to the analysis of the stock that refers to other sources also provided by the scammers.

o Stocks that trade on unusual exchanges, often in smaller foreign countries.

• **Letter of Credit Fraud** — These occur when scammers offer a "letter of credit" or "bank guarantee" from a U.S. bank as an investment. You are promised huge gains — 100% to 200% annually.

Legitimate letters of credit are issued by banks to ensure payment for good in connection with international trade and are never sold or offered as investments. Such investment "opportunities" simply do not exist.

A similar scam involves "bank guarantees" that victims are told they can buy at a discount and sell quickly at a premium. By doing so several times, it is claimed, victims can enjoy exceptional returns. To make the scam more enticing, these "guarantees" are said to be issued by the world's "prime bank."

Legal documents associated with such schemes often require the victim to enter into nondisclosure and non-circumvention agreements, offer returns on investment in "a year and a day" and claim to use forms required by the International Chamber of Commerce (ICC).

While banks use instruments called "bank guarantees" in the same manner that U.S. banks use letters of credit to ensure payment for goods in international trade, such bank guarantees are never traded or sold on any kind of market.

The purpose of these frauds is to encourage the victim to send money to a foreign bank, where it then disappears.

Common Active Scams

Unlike passive scams, which you initiate by responding to something you see on the internet or hear about from a friend, active scams require the scammer to go after you, based on something that makes them think that you will be susceptible.

They are the hardest to avoid because they play to our emotions and desires. They include:

- **Advance Fee Scams** — An advance fee scam is when the victim pays money to someone in anticipation of receiving something of greater value — such as a loan, contract, investment or gift — and then receives little or nothing in return.

   The most common advance fee scam is the "Nigerian 419 scam," named after the section of that country's penal code that criminalizes them. It involves an email from someone, such as the widow of a prince or politician, who claims to have a large amount of money tied up somehow, which they can only access with your help. All you need to do is send them some money up front to get the process started.

A twist on advance fee scams involves securing financing arrangements to help you come up with the money needed to unlock the larger windfall.

Scammers require victims to sign contracts in which they agree to pay a "finder's fee" when they are introduced to the financing source. Once they have done so, victims learn that they are "ineligible" for financing.

• **Debt Collection Scams** — These often target older people and people who have had debt problems in the past. In both cases, they prey on the insecurity that comes from owing money in the aggressive, creditor-biased U.S. legal system.

Debt collection scams typically involve a call or email out of the blue demanding payment for some debt that you can't recall. It's designed to sound just plausible enough that you agree to cooperate to investigate it by supplying further personal information. In fact, one of the most common debt collection scams involves receiving a threatening phone call or fake email from the "IRS" demanding money owed. Scammers use the IRS name, logo or a fake website to try and steal money from unsuspecting taxpayers fearful enough to comply.

Many victims actually send money to scammers even though no debt exists. Even worse, however, is handing over credit card or bank account details to scammers, who then quickly drain them of everything available.

The most pernicious debt collection scams are based on old debts that have been resold on the collections market. An investor buys old credit card debt from a bank or other creditor for pennies on the dollar. They then pursue the debtor with extremely aggressive and threatening tactics, including calls at all hours to family, friends and employers. In many cases, these debts have actually been discharged and are no longer valid.

The critical thing is to obtain written verification of the debt in a form that will stand up to legal scrutiny. Asking for such evidence will often prompt the scammer to hang up and not contact you again.

• **Reverse Mortgage Scams** — Also known as home-equity conversion mortgages (HECMs), reverse mortgages create significant opportunities for scammers.

A legitimate HECM loan product is insured by the Federal Housing Administration. It enables eligible homeowners to access the equity in their homes by providing funds without incurring a monthly payment.

Eligible borrowers must be 62 years or older, occupy their property as their primary residence, and own their property or have a small mortgage balance.

Reverse mortgage scams steal the equity from the property of unsuspecting victims — usually senior citizens — or use them unwittingly as straw buyers in property-flipping scams.

Victims are often offered free homes, investment opportunities and foreclosure or refinance assistance. They are frequently targeted through local churches and investment seminars, as well as through television, radio, billboard and mailer advertisements.

General Tips for Avoiding Scams

So, what can you do to avoid falling for these scams? The general rule is simple: Rein in your emotions and be a skeptic. More specifically:

• Exercise due diligence. Do your homework before investing and take your time.

The biggest danger is the impulse to act quickly, which usually means acting irrationally.

• When in doubt, consult an unbiased third party, like your financial adviser. Google the heck out of the outfit involved, as well as any specific individuals mentioned. Type in the name of the company with "+scam" in the search field, to ensure you see any references to them.

- Independently verify the terms of the agreement into which you intend to enter, including the parties involved and the nature of the investment. Know whom you are dealing with, and always check all claimed affiliations, like financial regulatory agencies or business associations.

- Don't invest in anything you don't understand. Scammers rely on complex transactions and complex logic to "explain" fraudulent investment schemes.

- Be wary of business deals that require you to sign non-disclosure or non-circumvention agreements. If you are in doubt, have the terms reviewed by a competent attorney.

- Depending on the amount of money you plan on spending, you may even want to visit the business's location.

- Be wary of businesses that operate out of post office boxes and don't have a street address.

- Also be suspicious when dealing with anyone who doesn't have a direct telephone line and who is never in when you call, but always returns your calls later.

And, above all, be wary of any investment that promises extremely high yields. As the old saying goes: If an opportunity appears too good to be true, it probably is.

TAXES

No one likes paying taxes. Every year, it feels like the tax-man takes a bigger and bigger chunk out of your earnings. But there are some steps you can take right now to lower your tax obligation and keep more of your hard-earned dollars in your wallet. In fact, this section contains a tip that would help you to legally stop paying U.S. taxes completely. Improving the income in your life means taking control of your taxes.

INCOME SECRET NO. 23:

Stop Giving Interest-Free Loans to Uncle Sam

People love the idea of a tax refund. It's free money, a windfall.

Over 73% of taxpayers get a refund after they file. Then they spend it on new mattresses, car down payments or a vacation.

If you got a tiny refund, that's understandable; taxes are hard to predict in advance.

If you get a big one every year, however, then you are missing a chance to cut your taxes by lowering your tax withholding (this is the W-4 form at work) and instead putting that money into a 401(k) or individual retirement account (IRA).

It's a cliché, but it's true. By taking the refund, you essentially have loaned the government money all year interest-free.

The IRS doesn't hide this fact. For 2018 tax year, it reportedly refunded $277 billion to taxpayers, averaging $2,729.

Invested in a Treasury bill at 2%, that's $5.5 billion in free money we give to Uncle Sam for no reason except our fear of owing taxes.

Put another way, that's a whole year of car payments given up by the average taxpayer because thinking for five minutes about your likely tax bill for the year is too hard.

If you're getting a sizable refund every year, contact the accounting or human resources department of your employer to adjust the withholding on your W-4 form — now.

Put that money to work for you rather than as an interest-free loan to the government.

INCOME SECRET NO. 24:

Defer Capital Gains Tax With a Deferred Sales Trust

How do you avoid a big capital gains tax when selling an asset like real estate or a business?

It's an issue often faced by readers of *The Bauman Letter*, particularly those with insufficient funds for their impending retirement.

Let's analyze the situation — and a viable solution — by starting with a hypothetical example.

Malcolm and his wife Allie are 10 years from retirement. Like many of us, they've neglected to save enough to see them through. But they have some assets they could sell to top up their retirement kitty.

Allie's father dabbled in real estate on the northern California coastline back in the '60s and '70s. He purchased several plots over the years, which he left undeveloped ... they served as a store of value for the future. When Allie's father died 15 years ago, he left them to her and Malcolm.

In the years since Allie's father passed, the stretch of coastline in question developed rapidly, and property values rose accordingly. They decided to sell the plots to raise some cash for a retirement account.

Had they sold the plots when they inherited them, Malcolm and Allie would have faced no capital gains tax.

That's because the "basis" on which capital gain is calculated — the baseline value of the plots used to calculate the capital gain — was "stepped up" at the time of inheritance to their current market value, not what Allie's dad had paid for them.

Assuming they got a fair market price for the plots when they sold them upon inheritance, there would have been a trivial difference between this "stepped up basis" and the sales price — hence no capital gain and no tax.

But they hadn't sold them. Instead, they held them ... during which time the value of the plots had more than quadrupled.

That meant that capital gains tax on the sale of the plots would be calculated as the difference between the stepped-up basis at the time of inheritance and the sale value.

Malcolm and Allie were looking for a long-term capital gains tax hit of almost half a million dollars. To make matters worse, the capital gains tax had to be paid in the tax quarter following the sale of the plots.

That's money that could be put to a better use ... namely, funding their retirement.

Sneaky Devil: Capital Gains Tax

We pay long-term capital gains tax on the profit we make when we sell a capital asset we've held for a year or more. It's calculated by subtracting what you paid for the asset from the net selling price. In the case of inheritance, it's the difference between the stepped-up basis and market sale price.

The current federal long-term capital gains tax rate is typically 15% to 20%, depending on your marginal tax rate on ordinary income. Most states charge 5% to 10% on top of that (California is 13.3%), creating a total capital gains tax bill as high as 37%. Moreover, if you took any depreciation allowance on the asset, the cost basis used to calculate capital gain is lowered by that amount, thus increasing the taxable gain.

That isn't the end of the story, however. Capital gains are added to your adjusted gross income (AGI) in the year that you sell. That can have some serious tax consequences.

AGI is used to calculate the "floor" above which one can no longer take several itemized deductions on your income tax, such as medical expenses, or you could face limits on your total deduction.

Similarly, if your AGI is too high, you can no longer contribute to a Roth IRA. It can also trigger the dreaded alternative minimum tax (AMT), a tax that is triggered when taxpayers make more than the exemption and use many common itemized deductions.

For this reason, the "hidden" capital gains tax rate for a property sale is often much larger than the stated federal and state rates.

Fortunately, outright sale of the California properties wasn't Malcolm and Allie's only option.

Option One:
A 1031 Exchange

Under Section 1031 of the United States Internal Revenue Code, you may defer capital gains and related federal income tax liability (such as AGI effects) by "exchanging" one property for another. It's not actually an exchange … you can sell one property and use the proceeds to buy another.

The properties exchanged must be owned for use in a business or for investment and be "of the same nature or character," even if they differ in quality. Residential property doesn't qualify.

Under a 1031 exchange, the accumulated capital gain represented by the original property is "transferred" to the new property.

In Malcolm and Allie's case, for example, they could sell their dad's plots and use the money to buy another investment property. They'd pay no capital gains tax on the sale of the plots. Instead, when they eventually sold the new property, the transferred capital gain from the original property would be used to calculate their tax bill.

This would have been useful if, for example, they wanted to convert their equity in the California plot into a commercial rental property and live on the proceeds. Since Malcolm and Allie were determined to liquidate their property to fund their retirement through a more diverse set of investments, however, a 1031 exchange wasn't a good fit for them.

Option Two:
A Deferred Sales Trust

Capital gains tax is calculated based on income received in any tax from the sale of capital assets. If you defer receipt of this income, you also defer the payment of capital gains tax.

How can you defer income from the sale of a capital asset, such as real asset, a business or other personal property?

One route is an installment sale. Malcolm and Allie could sell the plots to a buyer who promises to pay them in installments, calculated as principal plus interest. Capital gains tax would be due on the total principal repaid in a tax year. That spreads out the capital gains tax over the length of the loan.

But it also puts Malcolm and Allie at risk of buyer default. In any case, most serious purchasers of developable property such as their California plots wouldn't be interested in such an arrangement.

A second option involves the transfer of title to the plots to a third party that can sell them — "giving" the property to the third party for nothing up front.

This third party, however, would promise to pay Malcolm and Allie the proceeds of its subsequent sale of the property in fixed installments.

Malcolm and Allie would then pay capital gains tax on the proceeds as they receive it, in smaller chunks. The timing of the installments is up to Malcolm and Allie — they could defer receiving the income indefinitely.

This third party, however, would have to be legally separate from Malcolm and Allie. It would need to be managed by someone unrelated to them who assumes a legal, fiduciary responsibility to pay them according to the agreement they reached when they transferred the property prior to sale.

There is only one structure that fits this bill: a trust.

The Western legal tradition has long recognized the trust as a mechanism to create legal distance between people and property. The concept is simple: One person holds legal title to an asset for the benefit of another.

If I transfer the title of my house to you and say, "Hold this house for the benefit of my heirs," then a trust has been created.

The basic trust has four components:

1. The person(s) who creates the trust (the "settlor" or "grantor").

2. The trust itself and its assets.

3. The person who controls the trust and its assets ("trustee").

4. Those who are to receive the benefits of those assets ("beneficiaries").

Large financial institutions often hold billions of dollars in trusts for families all over the world. There are many types of trusts: revocable and irrevocable trusts, grantor trusts, qualified trusts, lead trusts, life insurance and annuity trusts, unit trusts, and even the bizarre "intentionally defective trust."

The specific form of a trust that can accomplish Malcolm and Allie's goal (deferring capital gains taxes on the sale of their dad's California plots) is sometimes called a Deferred Sales Trust (DST). It's a marketing term, not a legal term.

What counts is the *relationship* established with the trust, not the name of the trust itself.

A DST relationship is a legal contract between you as the property owner and a third-party trust … one in which you have no management or beneficiary role. You can transfer real estate, personal property, a business or any other significant asset to the trust in exchange for its contractual promise to sell it on the market and pay you the proceeds over a predetermined period of time.

Note that if done correctly, there are no capital gains taxes for the trust on the sale of the asset, since the transfer of the property from the previous owner to the trust will have specified its current market value. Since the trust sells the property at the same value, it realizes no independent taxable gain on the sale.

The accompanying contractual promise between you and the trust to pay the proceeds of the sale over time is called a "self-directed note," because you control its terms.

You decide the parameters such as the starting date of disbursement of the sale proceeds and the number and timing of installments. This is how you can defer or space out capital gains tax liabilities to avoid short-term tax complications.

In Malcolm's and Allie's case, a DST could be structured specifically to accomplish their main goal in selling their California plots: to finance their retirement by deferring payments until they retire.

But there's more to it than that.

The primary role of any trust and its trustee(s) is to hold and manage assets on behalf of other people. When a DST sells an asset that has been transferred to it under an installment payment arrangement — such as Malcolm and Allie's California plots — the effect is to transform that real estate into cash, which continues to be the property of the trust.

Cash, of course, can be invested for profit. Since the cash from the sale of their California plots transferred to the DST, it is legally bound to be used to make scheduled installment payments to Malcolm and Allie. Any additional investment proceeds that arise from the trust's management of that cash in the interim can also be paid out to them.

That means that Malcolm and Allie — or anyone who is a grantor in a DST arrangement — can actually end up receiving *significantly more* than the proceeds of the property sale itself.

If well-invested by the trust, the sale proceeds can generate additional income that will be paid out of the grantor in the future. That additional investment-derived income won't be subject to capital gains tax, since it isn't part of the principal sales proceeds of the property. It will be treated as ordinary income for tax purposes.

In other words, the DST strategy has the potential to generate substantially more money over the long run than a direct, taxed sale. Because the taxes are deferred, the DST arrangement is able to leverage the entire amount of the sale proceeds to provide a larger cash flow through investment.

For example, after-tax proceeds of $800,000 from a $1 million sale invested at 6% generates $48,000 a year in investment income. In fact, $1 million of proceeds in a DST invested at 6% generates $60,000 a year — 25% more.

Done the right way, it's possible that a DST arrangement could generate enough to pay for the entire capital gains tax on the original property sale — especially when you take into account the effect of gradual inflation on the real value of the deferred capital gains tax.

Getting It Done

The first step in taking advantage of the DST strategy is to identify a suitable trust relationship. The entire strategy stands or falls on the quality of this relationship. That's because the main risk is that the IRS may deem the transaction to be invalid because the trust is regarded as a "sham trust" created specifically to avoid tax. That would leave you with a huge tax bill and possibly a tax penalty, as well.

The next step is to offer the asset to the trust as a grantor. This involves due diligence to determine its market value and assess whether the transaction is viable for all involved. If it is, you'll negotiate with the trust to reach terms regarding the disposition of the asset.

Next, the trust enters into an installment payment contract with you, as described above. The contract promises to make installment payments to you — and with appropriate estate planning, can even be structured to continue into future generations.

This payment contract is created before the property is sold and can be adjusted to match the exact sale price.

Note that the payment contract must specify an annual interest rate that the trust will pay to you in addition to the principal proceeds. It's as if you're "lending" the sale proceeds to the trust, after all.

To meet IRS criteria, the interest rate must be a "fair and arm's length" or "competitive" rate. It is possible to specify interest-only payments to you and defer principal payments until a later date, in which case they would be subject to ordinary income tax rates.

Summary of the Benefits

The primary advantage of a DST isn't to "avoid" tax. It's to defer it so you can put that money to work in the meantime.

In addition to creating a future income stream with the power potentially to negate capital gains taxes altogether, a DST helps to avoid being shoved into a higher tax bracket.

Installment payment agreements can also be designed to vary payments as needed. It is also possible to "refinance" a DST installment agreement to increase or decrease the payments or increase or decrease their frequency, at the absolute discretion of the trustee.

Finally, with proper estate planning techniques, a DST arrangement can extend beyond your own lifetime. Schedule installment note payments otherwise due to you can continue to be paid to your legal heirs pursuant to the note term that you have chosen.

Note that if you decide to cancel the whole deal after a few years and take the proceeds as a lump sum, this will be at the discretion of the trustee. In that case, you would immediately owe all the taxes, including all unpaid capital gains due from the original sale of the asset.

When Does a DST Make Sense?

Generally, a DST arrangement can work for you if the situation meets two criteria:

1. You wish to dispose of an asset that is sufficiently valuable and is worthwhile to incur some setup costs to avoid the adverse tax consequences of a windfall.

2. You are prepared to and/or positively interested in receiving the proceeds of an asset sale over time, and don't need

the cash for immediate needs. Another way of looking at it would be if you were going to invest the money you got from selling an asset rather than spend it right way, a DST might be a good option, since that is essentially what it allows.

Here are some specific instances where a DST could work out well:

- Liquidating real estate that has appreciated significantly since you acquired it.

- Selling a business that has significant value as an ongoing concern, when you don't plan to invest in another business.

- Selling inherited personal property, such as art collections, jewelry or precious metals.

- Converting equity in any asset into a stream of income that can be used to purchase annuities or insurance policies designed to provide future income, such as a whole life policy.

- Creating an estate plan that can provide for your heirs whilst simultaneously reducing the value of your taxable estate, thereby minimizing estate taxes.

As with any strategy involving taxes and the IRS, it is essential not to take a do-it-yourself approach. That includes relying on the persuasive hype of internet-based hucksters who see DSTs as a way to move more property to their own benefit as estate agents.

If you are truly interested in the DST option — for real estate of any other asset subject to capital gains tax — I recommend that you seek the advice of qualified and experienced tax counsel.

It may cost you a little more than a "turnkey" DST, but as always, it is money well spent. The IRS is a notoriously unsympathetic beast when it comes to levying fines, and it does not generally accept "But I was misinformed" as an excuse.

INCOME SECRET NO. 25:

Double Your Tax Break With a Spousal IRA

Proper planning for retirement not only gives you a nice nest egg on which to survive and enjoy your golden years, but it actually helps you lower tax burdens and save some money right now.

If you're already contributing to a 401(k), your next step is to open a traditional IRA immediately. You can always put money into an IRA, even if you have a workplace plan. The question is whether it's deductible, and that's a matter of your income level and how much you already put into your workplace plan.

For couples, the deduction for an IRA contribution begins to fade after a modified adjusted gross income (AGI) of $104,000 — if you are covered by retirement plans at work — and then you get a partial deduction if you earn more.

If you are not and your spouse is not contributing, the income limit is $124,000 or more. Pretty high. (Note: These amounts can change each year, so check the www.irs.gov website for updates.) If you have previous 401(k) plans, you can roll them over into an IRA to grow the balance and manage them more coherently.

With a traditional IRA, you can contribute up to $6,000 a year if you're under 50. The limit bumps up to $7,000 if you're older than 50. That's a nice deduction you can claim at the end of the year, if you're making under $104,000.

But what if you're the sole breadwinner, and your spouse is unemployed or underemployed?

It's the same. You can put money into his or her IRA up to the annual limit of $6,000 (add another $1,000 if your spouse is over 50).

Effectively, you get to double the IRA contribution as a couple even though only one of you earns a salary. This money comes off your joint taxable income and pushes you even further down in the tax brackets.

INCOME SECRET NO. 26:

Pocket Extra Income by Taking Advantage of President Trump's Favorite Tax Loophole (TAX)

For most of my working life, I've been a contractor.

No, I don't build or remodel houses.

I just wasn't directly employed by the people who paid me. Instead, I sold my services to them as a product.

Sometimes my relationship with my clients was at arm's length. I did contractual work at a per-piece rate. Other times, I received a regular retainer under long-term contracts.

No matter the format, this setup had several things in common:

1. I managed my financial affairs — and my taxes — as a business separate from my household. I had business income and expenses that were separate from my personal finances. My personal income was whatever was left over.

2. I was responsible for calculating and paying my own taxes on that "leftover" income. My clients didn't withhold anything or hand it over to the government. I did that myself, every quarter.

3. Nobody told me how, where or when to do my work. I always cooperated with my clients' reasonable requests, of course … but the final call was always mine.

The lifestyle had its pros and cons.

The main downside was that my income fluctuated.

I had to maintain a healthy reserve of cash to meet my personal expenses. I also had to manage my commercial reputation, which is quite different from workplace relationships.

But the pros outweighed the cons. I was — and, above all, felt — independent. I had more control over my income and work effort. My time was flexible.

I worked from home most of the time ... and no commute!

But the main advantage was the leverage being an independent contractor gave me over the taxman.

This "income secret" — prompted by the recent tax bill passed by Congress and signed by the president — will show you:

- How the new tax code creates huge advantages for self-employed, incorporated individuals.

- When it makes sense to set yourself up as a "business" ... even if you're currently an employee.

- Why you should get expert advice and where to seek that advice.

You see, the revised tax code — which was supposed to be fairer and simpler — in fact, creates several hacks that allow some people to pay less taxes than others doing the same work.

These hacks are hugely contentious in the tax community ... but they are now legal and far from simple.

My goal here is to give you an accessible summary of these new tax opportunities so you can decide whether they make sense for you.

As is the basis for my subscription service, *The Bauman Letter*, I want to show you how to take advantage of any opportunity to enhance your income and protect your wealth!

Pass-Through to Heaven

During halftime at a Georgia-Alabama national college championship game here in Atlanta (sorry, Dawgs!), I asked my pal Joey if he knew what a "pass-through" was.

He thought it had something to do with digestion. Nice try, Joey, but no cigar.

In U.S. tax parlance, a pass-through is any corporate entity that pays no corporate income tax. All a pass-through entity's profits "pass-through" to the owner(s), who pay income taxes on those profits as an individual. (Lawyers call them "disregarded entities" because they are ignored for tax purposes.)

This contrasts with C-corporations, that pay taxes directly on their own account, which is separate from their shareholders, who pay tax on dividends.

Pass-through entities (PTEs) include sole proprietorships, partnerships, limited liability companies (LLCs) and subchapter S-corporations.

Up until now, the owners of such businesses have paid taxes on their net income at individual rates.

But the tax law that went into effect on January 1, 2018, effectively lowers the tax rate on PTE income to well below the individual rate. This creates a big opportunity for you.

Not Quite the Same as the Old Boss

Those who drafted the new tax law had to change the way PTEs are handled.

The new top U.S. corporate tax rate — levied on shareholder-owned C-corporations — is 21%. If Congress had left the treatment of PTEs as it was, their owners would pay much more tax than C-corporations because the top five individual tax brackets are well above 21% — 22%, 24%, 32%, 35% and 37%.

Now, let's be clear: Many PTEs aren't small businesses owned by Main Street Americans who would be cruelly disadvantaged by paying more tax on their profits than corporate behemoths.

In fact, 70% of PTE equity is in multimillion-dollar businesses. PTE structures are especially common in finance and real estate. Almost all of President Trump's businesses, for example, are organized as LLCs. More than two-thirds of all U.S. PTE income goes to the top 1% of U.S. households by income.

Nevertheless, the average small businessperson would be enraged if they had to continue to pay taxes on their profits at individual rates while the corporate rate was slashed to 21%.

Congress' solution to this political problem creates an opportunity for significant tax savings for those of us who aren't multimillionnaires.

As I mentioned, until January 1, 2018, PTE income was taxed as personal income, up to 39.6%.

But the new rules grant a 20% deduction for "qualified business income" (QBI) … PTE owners can now simply deduct 20% of their businesses' income from their taxable income and pay no tax on it.

For many people, this results in a big tax cut compared to the previous pass-through system.

For example, let's say you are married filing jointly and employed as a senior electrician with an annual salary is $75,000. Under the new tax brackets, your tax will be $8,612, or 11.5%.

If you create a PTE, however, and pay yourself an annual salary of $12,000, your tax under the new system will be $7,100, or 9.5%.

This also creates a paradoxical situation for owners of PTEs. Under the new rules, if you're a PTE owner and you want to pay less tax, pay yourself the smallest possible salary (since it's taxed at individual rates) and push as much income as possible in the qualified business income category (so you can deduct 20% of it from your taxable income).

Instantly, "qualified business income" becomes hugely important. Just what is QBI?

QBI is "the net amount of items of income, gain, deduction and loss with respect to your trade or business." In other words, it's your business' profit … what's left after you've paid all your operating costs, including your own salary.

(Of course, if QBI is less than zero, it's treated as a loss from a qualified business in the following year and can be used to offset your taxes then.)

Under the new rules, in other words, the more business income you can shoehorn into QBI, the more you can save on tax, since 20% of that amount is now tax-free.

It gets even better.

You've probably heard that there is now a $10,000 cap on the deductibility of state and local income and property taxes. That's going to hurt folks who pay a lot of those taxes.

But PTEs can deduct the full amount of any state and local taxes they pay as a business expense. That home office makes a lot more sense now ... you'll be able to use it to reduce your nondeductible personal property taxes by shifting some of it to your business accounts.

Naturally, there are some catches.

First, QBI excludes passive income such as capital gains, dividends and interest income (unless the interest is received in connection with a lending business). You can't put your brokerage accounts into a PTE and get 20% of your returns tax-free.

Second, the new 20% QBI deduction phases out for individuals who make more than $157,500 a year — or $315,000 for joint filers — with an important exception, as I'll show you below.

Third, the QBI deduction is limited to PTEs that provide a "specified service trade or business."

If your PTE provides services in health, law, consulting, athletics, financial services, brokerage services or anything "principally relying on the reputation or skill of one or more of its employees or owners" (except, for some unfathomable reason, architects and engineers), you're not invited to the party.

The new tax law calls such excluded occupations "listed professions." Even if you are in one of them, however, if your taxable income is under $157,500 individual/$315,000 joint, then you can take the full 20% QBI deduction. After that, the deduction phases out through a complicated formula until you hit $207,500 individual/$415,000 joint, at which point you lose the deduction completely and the old rules apply ... you pay tax at the individual rate.

Finally, even if you exceed this income cap, you can take another form of QBI deduction depending on how many employees and/or how much capital your PTE has.

Simpler? Hah!

So much for filing your tax return on a postcard.

In this next section, I'm going to expand a bit on two typical types of PTEs. For simplicity, I'm going to call them the "Independent Professional" and the "Corker Rule" cases.

The Independent Professional

This version of the pass-through entities (PTE) tax break is aimed at people who have few employees — perhaps only themselves as a single employee — or a small partnership. It's limited by income to prevent high earners from declaring themselves "consultants" to escape taxes. The rationale is that if you are contributing mainly your labor and not much capital, and/or not creating many jobs, then you can access the deduction only if your income is below certain thresholds.

Here's how it works.

For people in nonlisted professions and for those in listed professions earning under the thresholds above: If your taxable income is below $157,500 individual/$315,000 joint, the tax-free portion of QBI for any PTE you own is simply 20%.

So, if your income is $100,000 and your QBI is $75,000, then your deduction is $15,000, or 20% of your QBI. You don't pay any tax on that income. Period.

As I explained above, you can continue to take a partial, pro-rated QBI deduction until you hit $207,500 individual/$415,000 joint taxable income.

The Corker Rule

All is not lost if you are above the threshold amounts, however. Two further types of PTEs can join the game:

- You have a multimillion-dollar LLC that has a dozen or so employees — say, a car dealership. You pull in a decent six-figure income, so you're above the $207,500 individual/$415,000 joint taxable income cap.

- You have an LLC with a lot of equity in real estate but few employees. Again, your taxable income is above the cap.

In both cases, you have the option of calculating your QBI deduction as the greater of:

1. 50% of W-2 wages paid by your PTE, including your own, or...

2. The sum of 25% of W-2 wages paid by your PTE plus 2.5% of the original, underappreciated value of all qualified property. Qualified property is physical property used to produce QBI available for use in your PTE at the end of the tax year. This includes all capital equipment ... and, significantly, real estate.

For example, let's assume your car dealership pays $250,000 in W-2 wages and owns a building worth $1 million.

- Under the first option, 50% of W-2 wages equals $125,000.

- Under the second option, 25% of W-2 wages plus 2.5% of unadjusted basis of your qualified property is $62,000 plus $25,000, which equals close to $90,000.

So, your best option is to use the first method and declare $125,000 of your QBI as nontaxable income.

In the second case, let's say you're a real estate mogul like President Trump or former Senator Bob Corker of Tennessee, after whom this rule is named. He changed his vote from a "nay" to a "yea" after this option was slipped into the bill at the last minute. You have few employees and a small W-2 wage bill of $50,000, but your PTE owns $50 million worth of hotels, office buildings, condos and so on.

- Under the first option, 50% of W-2 wages equals $25,000.

- Under the second option, 25% of W-2 wages plus 2.5% of unadjusted basis of your qualified property is $12,500 plus $1,250,000, which equals $1,262,500.

I'm sure I don't need to tell you which deduction you're going to take in that case.

The Corker Rule — which was clearly created to benefit multimillionaires, including the authors of the bill — creates an intriguing angle for us lesser mortals, and it's a biggie.

2019: Year of the Tax Lawyer

"All the profit-shifting shenanigans that multinationals engage in will now be relevant for domestic businesses."

That quote comes from a document called "The Games They Will Play," an evolving analysis of the new tax law by a group of top tax law professors.

The professors are right. The new tax treatment of PTEs is a windfall for lawyers who design and create LLCs, partnerships and S-corporations.

Remember that the new tax treatment of PTEs doesn't apply to "specified service trades or businesses." These "listed professionals" include doctors, lawyers, financial consultants, etc.

If they earn too much, these poor souls aren't allowed to take advantage of the 20% QBI deduction! Rats!

But the Corker Rule creates a new quiver of lawyerly tricks … and I predict it's going to generate a lot of traffic at state company registration offices around the country this year.

Here's why:

Assume you're a partner in a law firm called LawFirm LLC. You and your partners form SideCar LLC, contributing some capital and using it to buy and hold the building you currently rent. SideCar LLC rents the building back to LawFirm LLC at an above-market rate.

BOOM! You suddenly have qualified "Corker Rule" income in a real estate PTE! Before, you were shut out of the game because you practiced a listed profession. By splitting your business into parts, you save on tax.

All it took was some company formation work, and you're sending less to the IRS.

This is the same as the "transfer pricing" trick U.S. multinationals use to shift income from U.S. to foreign subsidiaries. Create a foreign subsidiary and transfer something of value that your business uses to it — say, Apple's patent on the iPhone — then have the subsidiary rent it back to you at an inflated cost.

That slashes your taxable income in a high- tax situation (Apple Inc., subject to U.S. corporate tax) and shifts income to a low-tax situation (Apple Cayman Islands Inc., paying little to no tax).

Now, under the new law, "listed professionals" can play the same game. Just split an existing PTE into an unqualified (high-tax) professional PTE and one or more qualified (low-tax) PTEs.

The low-tax PTEs then can charge fees to the high-tax professional PTE — for example, rent for office space, secretarial services, a medical practice's X-ray operation ... even interest on loans from one PTE to another. Those business-to-business payments reduce QBI for the disqualified PTE and shift it to the PTE that can use the 50% W-2 wage or Corker Rule deductions ... just like Apple does when it parks its patents in a foreign subsidiary in a low-tax jurisdiction.

Bam. Doctors and lawyers are now in the real estate business!

There are other ways to hack the new system. The tax professors who wrote "The Games They Will Play" say, "...borrow(ing) from the terminology of gerrymandering strategies, let's call them 'cracking' and 'packing.'"

- **Cracking.** The first strategy is to "crack" apart the revenue streams from an existing PTE, so as much income as possible can qualify for the deduction. The anecdote above referred to the real estate angle.

But "listed" professionals could also form separate service — providing PTEs nonlisted services — PTEs handling their accounting, document management, software, secretarial services and so on. Again, the game would be to overcharge the main PTE for these services and manipulate the two alternative QBI deduction methods to minimize taxes.

• **Packing.** The second strategy is to "pack" qualifying professional activities into a PTE to transform it into one that isn't primarily providing a "listed" service.

For example, real estate lawyers might both provide legal advice and manage real estate — mixing the businesses so that the IRS can't distinguish them to get the 20% PTE deduction for the whole operation.

Another route is for a "listed" professional simply to join a PTE that doesn't provide "listed" services. For example, a lawyer that becomes a partner in a PTE that does real estate development could take advantage of the exception for "architecture" or "engineering" PTEs.

Finally, the new treatment of PTEs creates an opportunity for employees of PTEs, too. For example, associates at law firms could band together into what the professors call "Associates LLC — a separate partnership paid to provide services to the original firm." Each associate might then qualify for the 20% QBI deduction.

Does It Make Sense?

I can hear you thinking: Wow, Ted, this is fascinating. But it seems like a lot of effort!

True. But for some of you, the time to act is now — you only get the new tax treatment once your PTE is up and running.

First, if you own a PTE in one of the so-called "listed professions" forbidden from taking advantage of the 20% PTE deduction — whether as a sole owner or partner — you should book an appointment with a tax lawyer ASAP. The hacks I described in the previous section are real, and they could save you a ton of money.

Second, if you are a nonlisted professional employee of a company — an engineer working for a power utility, for example, or a junior architect at a large practice — you should sit down with a tax adviser to see whether you'd be better off "quitting" your job and becoming a "consultant" to your old employer. If your current taxable income is less than $157,500 individual/$315,000 joint, you will save money on your taxes by going solo.

There is one caveat: Leaving permanent employment to become a PTE-based consultant means giving up corporate benefits such as medical, dental and 401(k). But there are a couple of reasons that might not be as big a problem as you might think.

1. Self-employed people can contribute up to 25% of their QBI into a SEP-IRA, traditional IRA or Roth IRA.

   On a SEP-IRA, the current annual cap is $56,000 a year; you're not limited to $5,500. That is a viable alternative to a 401(k) — especially since you can manage your IRA investments yourself, as I've described several times in *The Bauman Letter* reports about self-directed IRAs.

2. The Trump administration recently authorized the formation of independent health insurance associations, which are ideal for self-employed people. Once they are up and running, self-employed people will be able to form insurance pools with others in their situation — and benefit from the same risk-spreading actuarial dynamics that produce lower insurance premiums for corporate health plans.

3. When you're self-employed, you're going to find that you can book many "personal" expenses to your business accounts. Your home office, your PC and laptop, your phone, a portion of your utilities — anything that you use for work can be written off as a business cost, at least in part.

   That means that although your overall cash flow may be the same as a self-employed PTE owner as it was when you were an employee, you're going to still have access to many things that you need — and enjoy a lower overall tax burden since they are deductible business expenses.

And don't forget ... the new tax law eliminates all "miscellaneous deductions" — including the deduction for home office expenses for employees who work remotely.

That makes setting up as a PTE even more attractive, since all those expenses could be assigned to your business, reducing your taxable income and keeping you below the threshold to take the full 20% QBI deduction.

Conclusion

Though Republicans promised a simpler tax system, all these new loopholes are certain to keep the nation's CPAs and tax attorneys busy.

For many people, the opportunity to game the tax system this way will be irresistible. But if you're on the fence about it, consider this ... you may have no choice.

Consider existing partnerships, for example. Each partner will have to figure out their individual values for qualified business income and qualified property to calculate their tax-deductible QBI ... just to file their individual 1040s. They'll have to figure out their individual share of the unadjusted basis of the partnership's qualified property. Based on how the law is written, many tax experts think this includes everything from real estate to paperclips.

And they'll have to be able to document all of this to the IRS, if necessary.

So many of us are going to have to grapple with this new PTE tax regime even if we don't choose to take advantage of any new loopholes. The rules for PTEs — including the simplest LLCs and partnerships — have changed, and you're going to need help figuring them out.

It's not just an accounting issue, either. You're going to need advice.

Much of the actual practice of tax law is shaped by opinions issued by the IRS in the form of "private letters" and other rulings on how to interpret the tax code.

That code now has some radical new modifications. That means the IRS is going to spend the next few years reacting to the good-faith efforts of tax attorneys to interpret the new rules for their clients.

The IRS can't just throw the book at someone who adopts a particular strategy based on good-faith efforts to interpret the new law during the period when the IRS is trying to figure it all out.

That creates a window of opportunity for many of us ... one we should seize ... but with experienced expert advice.

To my mind, the most qualified tax attorney I know is Josh Bennett, who has worked with my father, Bob Bauman, and me for many years.

Whether you are based in Florida or not, he's a great place to start if you think any of this is going to apply to you this year — voluntarily or not:

Josh N. Bennett, Esq. PA
440 North Andrews Avenue
Fort Lauderdale, FL 33301
Tel.: (954) 779-1661
Mobile: (786) 202-5674
Email: josh@joshbennett.com
Website: www.joshbennett.com

INCOME SECRET NO. 27:

Collect Cash With a Property Tax "Circuit Breaker" Refund

When was the last time you paid your property tax, only to open your mailbox sometime later to find a $770 refund check inside?

If you did, it wasn't a fluke. It meant you were a part of a Circuit Breaker program, a little-known, special tax credit for homeowners and renters in at least 18 states and the District of Columbia.

Originally, this government initiative was intended to provide property tax relief for older homeowners and renters who met certain income and other requirements.

However, in many states (including Arizona, Maryland, Massachusetts, Michigan, New Jersey, Vermont, Wisconsin and West Virginia) homeowners of all ages are eligible for a Circuit Breaker refund — and in some state, renters too.

Here's how it works: Eligible property owners can claim a credit that is equal to the amount by which their property tax payments — including water and sewer charges — exceed 10% of their annual income.

Meanwhile, tenants can claim a credit of 25% if the rent they paid is more than 10% of their yearly income.

What's more, eligible taxpayers can file for the credit up to three years retroactively.

And that's not all — even people who don't typically file returns because they don't owe taxes can apply for the refund.

Massachusetts (along with Maine, Montana, New Mexico, Oklahoma, Rhode Island, D.C. and the aforementioned states) has a Circuit Breaker refund program. Out of the 86,000 taxpayers who took advantage of it in 2012, the average refund was $774.

Eligibility requirements may differ from state to state and are subject to change. However, recent rules in Massachusetts require that total income for single people could not exceed $60,000 ($75,000 for a head of the household) or $90,000 for a married couple. For homeowners, the assessed value of their primary residence could not be more than $808,000.

Some beneficiaries of the Circuit Breaker program use their refunds for necessities, such as food, medicine and utilities.

What would you do with an extra $774 in your pocket?

To see if your state offers a Circuit Breaker property tax refund, contact your local Department of Revenue or visit https://itep.org/category/property-taxes and select "State Policy" for more information.

INCOME SECRET NO. 28:

Let Your Pet Earn You Some Tax Deductions

When we welcome a pet into our homes, they are looked at as a source of companionship and entertainment. They bring warmth, love and laughter.

But did you know that they can also potentially bring some valuable tax deductions into your life, lowering your obligation to the IRS?

While it is not easy to claim your pet as a business expense, there are six avenues pet owners can potentially use to lower their taxes thanks to their beloved pet.

1. Eliminate Pests With Your Cat

If you use your cat to keep your business free of rats, mice and other vermin, you could potentially deduct costs associated with your cat. In one example, a court upheld a business expense deduction of $300 for cat food when a cat was used to deter snakes and rats from a family-owned junkyard.

In order to get the deduction, it's important that you convince the IRS that the cat is "ordinary and necessary." That means that using a cat must be "common and accepted in your trade or business." Furthermore, the cat must be "helpful and appropriate."

2. Guard Dog to Keep You Safe

The IRS might struggle to accept your cat is a necessary pest deterrent, but it has been more accepting in the past of guard dogs, particularly if a business is in a troubled neighborhood.

Keep in mind that size is key when convincing the IRS your pet is a guard dog. It's unlikely that your Yorkie is going to be believed as an effective guard dog.

If you are going to deduct expenses related to your guard dog, keep records of the dog's hours and work-related purpose.

You could potentially deduct expenses such as dog food, training and veterinary bills on Schedule C.

3. Service Animals

Do you have a service animal to help with your medical needs? You might be able to use it as a deduction since medical expenses are tax deductible if you itemize.

The first step is to get a doctor's prescription for your service animal or at least some documentation proving that you require a service animal as a medical necessity.

In addition, keep any documentation that shows your pet was trained to meet your medical needs. The IRS doesn't consider an animal a "service animal" unless it's been trained and certified.

You can also include the costs of purchasing and training guide dogs for the blind or hearing impaired. This includes veterinary, food and grooming expenses.

4. Foster Pet Deductions

Fostering animals can earn you tax benefits for charitable contributions. You can claim any unreimbursed expenses related to fostering animals from qualified nonprofit organizations. These deductions can be listed on a Schedule A as charitable donations. These expenses could include pet food, supplies and veterinary bills.

5. Offset Hobby Income

Has your show dog won prize money? While the IRS is happy to take a chunk of your winnings, you could potentially get some of that back by claiming related expenses such as training, showing, etc.

If you receive a 1099 each year for your hobby income, you can additionally deduct expenses related to that the hobby up to the amount earned.

Unfortunately, taking this deduction can be complicated. This deduction is subject to a threshold of 2% of your adjusted gross income (AGI).

For example, let's say that your AGI is $100,000 and you made $1,000 from pet shows. However, you accumulated $3,000 in expenses.

You would be allowed to deduct only $1,000 of expenses since you're allowed to deduct only up to the amount of income earned.

In this case, the $1,000 is less than 2% of your AGI, so you actually lose $2,000 from the pet shows — and you still have to pay taxes on the $1,000 in income you earned.

6. Moving Expenses

Have you moved for a job? Since you're already deducting your moving expenses, you can also deduct the cost of shipping your household pets to your new home.

To get this deduction, the IRS requires that you must prove:

- Your move must be closely related to the start of your work.

- You have to pass the distance test.

- You have to pass the time test.

For example, your new workplace must be at least 50 miles farther from your old home than your old workplace was. Furthermore, you must work full-time for 39 weeks or more during the first year after you relocate.

INCOME SECRET NO. 29:

Never Pay U.S. Taxes Again

It was good to be some place other than the land where I was born and raised. Maryland's Eastern Shore has its charms. But it just couldn't compete with what I was experiencing.

I was in a city built on the slopes of a stunningly beautiful mountain, surrounded by the sea on three sides. In 20 minutes, I could escape to fragrant forests cut by cool streams flowing from the mountain above. The air was always crystal clear, thanks to the steady ocean breeze. A few hours' drive to the north, and I'd be in a gorgeous desert. Head east and I'd find farmland and wineries that remind everyone who visits them of southern France.

The locals were friendly — not unlike the rough-edged but good-natured kids I'd known back in Maryland. They liked to drink a bit of beer, enjoy sunshine and waves, and check out live music in the city's numerous pubs. I made friends quickly and easily. I met a gorgeous girlfriend.

After a few months, I landed a nice job teaching at the city's world-class university, also built on the slopes of the mountain. I was a student as well, but the local tertiary education system was built around a "tutorial" system that generated a constant demand for tutors. It paid my tuition and then some.

After my first year, I was promoted to lecturer. By year three, I had been recruited by a top-notch economic research team to develop proposals for the country's manufacturing sector.

One thing led to another, and by year five, I was a senior executive at a nonprofit financial institution with a great salary, a permanent resident and had settled in for good. I had acquired a home in a quaint seaside village. I fell asleep to the sound of the Indian Ocean surf.

And the whole time, I didn't pay a dime in U.S. income tax.

Many of you have probably heard that there's a way you can pay no U.S. tax on a certain amount of your household income.

In fact, it's probably the single most popular topic with new subscribers to *The Bauman Letter*. People want to know how this works ... and for good reason! Who likes paying taxes?

It's not a hoax. Under certain circumstances, you can pay no U.S. tax on a portion of your income. After all, I did this for more than 20 years. It's something called the foreign earned income exclusion (FEIE). It allows you to exempt — completely — a certain portion of your annual earnings from U.S. tax. You report the income, but you just don't owe any tax on it.

The FEIE is the reason I didn't pay any U.S. income taxes from 1985 to 2007. I paid South African income tax, of course, but it was much lower than U.S. rates.

That meant I could save more and acquire a car, a house and other essential capital goods much more quickly than if I'd stayed in the U.S. Which I duly did.

You don't have to go as far as Cape Town to benefit from the FEIE. It's not for everyone, but it does provide a major incentive to move offshore. And when combined with the right business strategy, it can save you huge amounts in tax over your lifetime.

Let me tell you how.

The Strange Logic of U.S. Taxation

To understand the foreign earned income exclusion, you need to understand the way the U.S. government thinks about us, as citizens and taxpayers. It's not how most governments think.

That's for sure.

Most sensible countries only tax income earned within their own borders. There are exceptions, of course, but as a rule, most countries use a "territorial" tax system. This is based on the sensible logic that your earnings from the national economy are a proxy for your consumption of that economy's "public goods," such as roads, policing, courts, defense and so on. If you're not earning money inside the country, you're assumed to not be consuming those goods — at least, not as much of them. Hence, no taxes on foreign income.

The U.S. government — by pretty much full bipartisan agreement — takes the opposite course. Unlike most other countries, our tax system doesn't end at our borders. Instead, we Americans are taxed on our global income, no matter where we earn it or where we live. This is known as a worldwide tax system.

I never could figure out why the U.S. does this. My best guess is that two American peculiarities are at work.

First, Americans — government and citizens alike — tend to see the country as exceptional, a unique case in the world. We're so powerful, and there are so many benefits to being a U.S. citizen, that it's a bargain, not a burden, to be taxed on our global income.

We should gladly contribute to our glorious tax authorities, so the U.S. can continue the important work of being great and powerful. After all, so many foreigners want to live here!

Second, Americans living or working abroad come from many different states and congressional districts. There's no U.S. jurisdiction where there are so many U.S. voters living abroad that it would be worth a congressman's time to introduce and push a bill to change the worldwide tax system for Americans living abroad.

If they did, moreover, political opponents would scream bloody murder, claiming that "foreign Americans" were getting special treatment.

Whatever the reasons, when it comes to U.S. taxes, there's no essential difference between living in the U.S. and living abroad. American "persons" (i.e., a U.S. taxpayer, whether citizen or green card holder) living abroad must still report all their income, file their returns and pay their income taxes to the IRS.

As you may imagine, that poses a problem ... and creates an opportunity for you. There are a lot of Americans working abroad. They pay taxes to the countries where they work (unless they work for an American firm or the U.S. government, in which case they pay the IRS).

If the U.S. taxes them too, they're going to be major-league unhappy — as will foreign employers and governments that benefit from their work.

The solution, practiced by most countries in the world today, is what's known as a double-taxation agreement, or DTA.

DTAs aim to eliminate the taxation of income by more than one country. The U.S. has dozens of such agreements covering all major economies. They allow the country where the income arises to deduct income tax through their own withholding systems. They also require the IRS to grant the U.S. person taxed by them to receive a compensating foreign tax credit on their U.S. tax return.

The same applies in reverse for foreign taxpayers in the U.S. That way, everyone ends up paying what they would pay if they were working in their own country — unless, of course, the income tax rates between the two are very different.

To make DTAs work, however, the two taxation authorities must exchange information. That requires time and effort. In a rare instance of common sense, Congress decided that income earned by certain U.S. persons abroad below a cutoff would be exempted from U.S. income tax entirely ... because anything less than that just isn't worth pursuing.

Tax-Free Income ... Literally

Double-taxation agreements are the reason we have the foreign earned income exclusion.

The FEIE is essentially an admission that it's not worth the U.S. government's time and effort to reconcile tax records for individual filers earning under a certain amount. As odd as it may seem to us, the cost of pursuing tax on roughly $100,000 in annual foreign income cancels out the benefit.

Exempting such income saves the IRS lots of hassle over nothing ... and presents an opportunity for us.

The desire for tax efficiency also explains why the FEIE isn't a tax credit. It's a tax exemption.

Under the FEIE in 2019, the IRS literally exempted the first $105,900 of your foreign income from U.S. federal tax.

For a two-person household of U.S. persons where both were working, the amount is double — $211,800. The FEIE indexed annually for inflation and so increases every year.

In other words, if you qualified for FEIE in 2019 and you earned $105,900 or less in wages, you would have paid zero federal income taxes — zip, nada. You still would have had to file your 1040 and some other forms, but you wouldn't have owed any taxes.

Examples

1. Fred and Joyce, in their mid-60s, retired to a Central American country that has a tax treaty with the U.S. They sold their U.S. home and closed their U.S. business, investing the proceeds in a mix of U.S. and offshore financial vehicles.

   They planned to live on the proceeds of these investments and annuities, which would be transferred to their accounts in their new home country as needed. Before long, Fred began to get requests from local businesses for help in his areas of expertise.

   Unable to resist the lure of a little extra income, he began to oblige. Joyce also began to make and sell craft goods in local markets.

   Fred and Joyce pay U.S. tax on their U.S.-based investment income, receive U.S. tax credits for investment taxes paid in foreign countries, and pay no U.S. tax on their limited local earnings, since they qualify for the FEIE.

2. Rob decided to give life in the Mediterranean a try. The island nation where he hoped to settle didn't tax his investment income from the U.S., so he left it in U.S. investments for the first year.

Once he decided to buy a home and stay, he transferred most of his U.S. capital to investments in his new home country, since the tax rate on his earnings was much lower than in the U.S., as were the brokerage fees.

He no longer pays U.S. taxes on these offshore investments and receives a credit on his U.S. taxes for the taxes he does pay on these now foreign investment earnings.

If you earned more than $105,900 however, you'd have been liable for U.S. income tax on the excess. For example, if you earned $205,900 in salary, you would have paid U.S. federal income tax on $100,000 at 28% to 33%.

Note that even with the FEIE, your tax bracket is determined by your full earnings of $205,900. You are paying a rate on your last $100,000 as if you had earned $205,900 in wages, not just $100,000.

The FEIE exempts the first $105,900 from tax, but it doesn't change your overall tax bracket. If you pay tax in the country where you work, however, your U.S. tax on this $100,000 over and above the FEIE will be reduced. Every dollar you pay in foreign income tax should reduce your U.S. tax by $1.

Catch No. 1: You Must Leave

The FEIE is there for the taking. But it does come with a cost … at least, depending on your definition of cost.

You see, to qualify for the FEIE, you must be:

a. Physically out of the U.S. for 330 days during any 12-month period, or…

b. A legal resident of a foreign country for a full calendar year, and...

c. Earning foreign source income from employment or a business.

The 330-day test is simple math. It doesn't matter where you are in the world, so long as you're not in the U.S. You don't have to be a resident of any other country. You just can't be in the U.S.

That's what some folks call being a "perpetual traveler." If you are traveling physically outside the U.S. for 330 days out of 12 months, you qualify for the FEIE on your foreign income, even if you are using temporary visitor visas abroad and don't acquire residence anywhere other than the U.S.

I know a few folks who do this. For example, one guy I know spends three to four months each year in a variety of different countries. He owns homes in some of them and uses hotels or stays with friends in others. His income comes from a publishing business registered in a tax-free jurisdiction.

All the income earned by that foreign business is considered foreign sourced, even if it results from sales in the U.S. itself, because it is first booked to the foreign business, which then pays him a salary that is covered by the FEIE.

The residence test is more complex. It's based on your "intentions." This test involves moving to a foreign country for the "foreseeable future" and making it both your home and your home base — i.e., it's where you return when you travel. For that reason, it also must be a place where you're a legal permanent resident, with a residence permit or passport.

Finally, you must follow the country's tax laws as a legal resident, paying taxes if they are levied on income.

The residence test has one major advantage over the 330-day rule: It allows you to spend more time in the U.S. Under the 330-day test, you can spend a maximum of 36 days a year here. If you qualify for the residency test, you can spend four or five months a year in the U.S.

But remember that any income earned directly in the U.S. by you personally is taxable — the FEIE doesn't apply to U.S.-sourced income. If you work for 10 days in the U.S., the income from those days counts as a U.S. source of income and will be taxed.

As I've already noted, I'm a perfect example of residence-test FEIE. From 1985 to 2007, all my income from employment and self-employment was foreign sourced. Most of it was in South Africa, but I also received contract income from international agencies based in Europe.

From 1985 to 1990, I was a legal resident of South Africa on a student visa. After that, I became a permanent resident. In 2002, I became a South African citizen. The whole time, I paid South African income tax. My income never exceeded the FEIE limits, so I paid no U.S. income tax at all.

Catch No. 2: Unearned Income

The FEIE doesn't apply to income that's not "earned."

"Earned" income is money made in the current period from employment or a business.

"Unearned" income is passive income such as dividends, interest, capital gains, alimony, pensions, annuities and Social Security benefits. It's called that because you really earned this income years ago, but deferred using it until now.

In many cases, you may receive unearned income from a variety of sources around the world. The typical U.S. retiree abroad, for example, will receive a variety of unearned income, including Social Security, corporate pensions, private pensions, annuities and dividends on investments.

In most cases, this unearned income will be taxed exactly as if you lived in the U.S. Any U.S.-sourced investment income you receive, even if it is paid out abroad, will be taxed by the IRS just as if you were living here, at U.S. rates.

For example, if you live in Mexico on the proceeds of U.S. investments and Social Security, you'll report, file and pay tax on that income just as if you were living in the U.S. itself.

On the other hand, any foreign sourced unearned income you receive — such as dividends or interest — will be taxed per the laws of the country where the investment resides, at their tax rates. As I explained above, in most cases that foreign tax can be taken as a credit on your U.S. taxes.

For example, if you live in Mexico on the proceeds of investments located in Switzerland, you will pay tax to the Swiss government as per their laws. Any Swiss tax you pay can be deducted from your U.S. tax obligations, so you pay the same tax you would as if you received all your income in the U.S. itself.

Catch No. 3: Tax Rates Matter

One critical thing to understand about the FEIE is that only people living in low-tax countries will get much benefit.

If you are based in a place with a tax rate that is the same or higher than the U.S., then the foreign tax credit will prevent double taxation, without the need for the FEIE.

For example, if your U.S. federal tax rate is 35%, and your rate in France is 40%, you don't need the FEIE because you are already paying more in French tax than you would in the U.S. You can deduct your French tax on your U.S. tax return without concerning yourself with qualifying for the FEIE. Of course, you will end up paying more tax overall because the French rate is higher.

Conversely, if you are living tax-free in a place like Panama, drawing a salary of $100,000 and fail to qualify for the FEIE, 100% of your income is taxable in the U.S. Without the FEIE, there is no benefit to working in a low-tax country.

The Big Opportunity: The Offshore Business Loophole

The FEIE creates one of the greatest tax plays I know. Here's how it works.

Let's say you operate a small business through an offshore corporation. You pay yourself a salary up to $105,900. That makes it eligible for the FEIE. If spouses are both operating the business, they can draw a combined $211,800 and leave the rest of the money in the corporation.

But what if your net profits exceed the FEIE amount? What if you earn $1 million? Must you pay U.S. tax on $894,100? Yes … unless you structure your business to provide for retained earnings in your offshore corporation.

If you do that, you can shield those retained profits from U.S. tax until you decide to draw them down … including in the form of an FEIE-compliant future salary, making them tax-free.

In other words, if you take more than the FEIE out of the corporation as salary, you will pay tax on the excess as earned income. But if you leave the excess in the corporation's accounts, it will be classified as retained earnings and won't be taxable by the U.S. until it's distributed as a dividend.

It may even be possible to pay out retained earnings as FEIE-qualifying salary in future years, as long as the business is still in operation, and you can demonstrate a legitimate business need to pay salaries from retained earnings rather than current revenue. If you can't, it's considered a dividend and is taxable unearned income.

Bear in mind, as I noted above, that all this assumes you are living and working in a jurisdiction that levies no or low income taxes on the $105,900 that you draw as salary. If you're trying to do this in France, where the tax rate is 40%, you're not going to save anything … in fact, you'll pay more.

There are two important caveats to this trick. First, interest or capital gains on the retained earnings may be taxable, depending on the jurisdiction. Second, you may not borrow retained earnings or use them for your personal benefit. They must remain in the corporation.

So, what counts as a "properly structured offshore corporation"?

1. It must be a corporation — not a limited liability company (LLC), foundation, partnership or other pass-through entity. In other words, it must have a separate tax and legal identity from you.

2. It must be incorporated in a country that will not tax your profits. Otherwise, there is no point.

3. Retained earnings must arise from ordinary business income — income received from the sale of a product attributable to the normal and recurring operations of the company. You can't just book profits from other activities through a corporate shell.

   The product doesn't have to be physical; it is possible, for example, to sell your writings via a foreign corporation as a product. There are limits to this, as I'll show below.

4. You must report your activities and retained earnings of the offshore corporation on IRS Form 5471, report the corporation's foreign bank account under FATCA and keep up on all other U.S. reporting requirements.

One tricky aspect of this corporate loophole is the notion of an "ordinary business." Yours must be an ordinary business to qualify for the tax deferral on retained earnings. The definition of an ordinary business has two parts:

- First, you must sell something on a regular and continuous basis; you should make a profit in at least three of the last five years; you should work at the enterprise full-time; and it must be a business, not a hobby.

- Second, you should be selling a product, not providing a professional service such as consulting.

Now, it can be hard to determine where consulting ends and selling a "product" begins; this is where getting good legal advice is essential.

But if you are deemed by the IRS to be operating a consulting or professional service business, you may utilize the FEIE, but you are not allowed to hold retained earnings in your offshore corporation.

Other Useful Facts

1. The FEIE doesn't apply to self-employment tax (FICA), only income tax. A self-employed person living abroad and qualifying for the FEIE will still pay 15% in self-employment tax, i.e. $15,885 on a FEIE-qualifying income of $105,900.

2. Unearned passive income from interest, dividends and investments isn't active income and thus doesn't qualify for the FEIE. Unearned passive income flows through to you as shareholder of the foreign corporation and is taxable on your personal 1040 return.

   However, you can elect to pay U.S. tax on the appreciation in your corporate account each year, or you can pay U.S. tax on the gain when you sell funds or shares from your account. If you elect to pay tax when you sell, however, a punitive interest rate is added to the tax due to eliminate any benefit from deferral.

3. An offshore corporation may have shareholders who live in the United States. These shareholders must be passive investors who have no control over the company's day-to-day operations. The offshore corporation should not have a U.S. office or employees, or any U.S. agents working exclusively to market or distribute its goods in the U.S.

Reporting

Remember that you must file U.S. tax returns regardless of your FEIE status. I filed every year for two decades in South Africa without paying any U.S. taxes.

If you go the offshore business route, you must maintain records of income and expenses in accordance with U.S. accounting principles. Offshore corporations must file many U.S. tax forms, under threat of major penalties:

- Form 5471 — Information Return of U.S. Persons With Respect to Certain Foreign Corporations (https://www.irs. gov/pub/irs-pdf/f5471.pdf).

- Form 926 — Report of Transfer to Foreign Company, filed when you fund the offshore corporation (https://www.irs. gov/pub/irs-pdf/f926.pdf).

- FBAR — Financial Crimes Enforcement Network (FinCEN) 114, Report of Foreign Bank and Financial Accounts (https://www.irs.gov/businesses/small-businesses-self-employed/report-of-foreign-bank-and-financial-accounts-fbar).

- A foreign corporation or limited liability company must make an election to be treated as a corporation, partnership or disregarded entity using default classifications in Form 8832, Entity Classification Election (https://www. irs.gov/pub/irs-pdf/f8832.pdf).

- Form 8858 — Information Return of U.S. Persons With Respect to Foreign Disregarded Entities (https://www.irs. gov/pub/irs-pdf/f8858.pdf).

- Form 5472 — Information Return of a 25% Foreign-Owned U.S. Corporation (https://www.irs.gov/pub/irs-pdf/f5472.pdf).

- Form 8938 — FATCA (https://www.irs.gov/pub/irs-pdf/f8938.pdf). This applies to your personal accounts as well as the accounts of any corporate entity you control.

Conclusion: Not a DIY Matter

One thing that should be clear by now is that although FEIE can be simple — as it was for me in South Africa — it can quickly become very complicated indeed, especially if you opt to form an offshore corporation.

That's why I strongly recommend that you engage qualified, experienced tax counsel if and when you decide to eliminate taxes by moving abroad. Here are some of the key things to consider:

- An expatriate's tax return is more complicated than a normal U.S. tax return. That should be clear from what I've said here.

- You may have to reconcile your host-country tax year to the U.S. tax year. The U.S. tax year begins on January 1 and ends on December 31. Not all countries operate on this calendar. For example, Australia, Hong Kong, New Zealand and the U.K. all have different tax-year schedules that don't coincide with the calendar year.

- The IRS requires that you (or your tax preparer) prepare your return per the U.S. tax year, which means taking your tax statements from your host country for two years, extracting the appropriate information and then plugging it into your U.S. tax return.

- You must keep up with all changes in U.S. tax rules and legislation from afar. The U.S. tax code changes every year, especially when there are major changes in the political landscape. If you're not a tax professional, you probably don't have the time or inclination to keep up with these changes.

- You may be required to file a state return, even if you have not lived in the U.S. for a few years. Every U.S. state has its own rules, and certain states make it more difficult to avoid filing their tax return. You may have a state tax domicile if you maintain a state driver's license, state voter registration or bank accounts or property in that state.

- Commercial tax software isn't designed with expats in mind and may miss deductions or exclusions that could cost you money. You may save a few dollars up front by using them, but you could end up losing a significant amount in overpaid taxes or missed credits in the long run.

My go-to guy on these matters is my good friend Josh Bennett. He specializes in the intersection between U.S. and foreign tax and corporate rules. He can be reached as follows:

Josh N. Bennett, Esq.

440 North Andrews Avenue

Fort Lauderdale, FL 33301

Tel.: 1-954-779-1661

Mobile: 1-786-202-5674

Email: josh@joshbennett.com

Website: www.joshbennett.com

INCOME SECRET NO. 30:

Puerto Rico: The American Tax Haven

Did you know that the United States is the only country in the world that effectively taxes its citizens and former residents no matter where they live and make their money?

If you're a U.S. citizen or green card holder, you must file your taxes and pay up, even if all your income is from offshore sources and you live overseas yourself. Moving to a low-tax country like Singapore, the Cayman Islands or Dubai won't help. You'll still be on the hook. The only way to escape the IRS entirely is to give up your citizenship and pay a big U.S. exit tax.

But not if you live in Puerto Rico.

How is this possible? Because Puerto Rico is an "organized unincorporated territory" of the United States, not a state. It's basically a U.S. colony.

Puerto Ricans are U.S. citizens, with most of the rights and obligations that entails. However, residents of Puerto Rico are exempt from federal income tax. The trade-off is they cannot vote in any U.S. federal election.

Of course, residents of Puerto Rio are subject to U.S. tax on income from sources outside Puerto Rico. But they are exempt from federal tax on income generated in the territory.

It's relatively easy for a U.S. citizen or permanent resident to become a bona fide resident of Puerto Rico. You just have to move there. You don't need a passport, and there is no immigration control for arrivals from the U.S. mainland.

And once you're there, you pay no tax to the IRS on local income. Period.

Additional Tax-Friendly Incentives

Even with zero federal income tax, it only recently made sense for mainlanders to move to Puerto Rico. Income taxes there used to be just as high, if not higher than U.S. taxes. In

2012, however, the government of Puerto Rio passed Act 20 and Act 22, which provide a corporate tax rate of just 4% for companies exporting services outside Puerto Rico (Act 20), as well as a full exemption for individuals from taxes on most types of investment income (Act 22).

Since any Puerto Rico-based business or Puerto Rico resident individual pays no U.S. federal income taxes on local income, moving to the island and obtaining an Act 20 or Act 22 decree means you pay the IRS nothing on local income and minimal taxes to Puerto Rico itself.

Let's take a look at the finer details...

Act 20

Under Act 20, any service business operating in Puerto Rico for clients outside of Puerto Rico pays a tax rate of 4% — or even less under some circumstances. Service businesses include everything from hedge fund managers to marketers, public relations professionals, computer programmers, graphic designers ... even writers and researchers.

All it takes is the creation of a Puerto Rico-based company that sells its services to non-Puerto Ricans, such as an online business. That company must genuinely be physically present in Puerto Rico. It must create jobs for five employees — three after six months of commencing operations and the other two after two years. Here are the specifics:

- Puerto Rican corporate tax rate of 4%.

- Corporate tax rate of 3% in the case of "strategic services."

- Puerto Rican tax exemption of 100% on distributions from earnings and profits.

- Exemption of 90% of personal property taxes for certain business types up to the first five years of operation. (The taxable portion is subject to a regular property tax rate of up to 8.83%).

• Exemption of 90% from real property taxes for certain business types up to the first five years of operation. (The taxable portion is subject to a regular property tax rate of up to 11.83%).

• Exemption of 60% on municipal taxes. (The taxable portion is subject to a regular property tax rate of up to 0.6%.)

It should be noted that, as the owner of the company, you don't have to move to Puerto Rico to take advantage of this. You can still live in the U.S. or anywhere else and set up a separate U.S. company that receives fees for services performed on behalf of the Puerto Rican company.

Also, if you already have a U.S. corporation, any Puerto Rican subsidiary created under Puerto Rican laws will not be considered part of the consolidated company for U.S. tax purposes. A Puerto Rican corporation is considered a foreign corporation for U.S. tax purposes.

The U.S.-based company would pay U.S. taxes on those fee earnings. But most of the profits booked to the Puerto Rican entity — basically everything above the fees you pay yourself — would accumulate in the Puerto Rican company at just a 4% corporate tax rate. And those would not be taxable by the IRS, as long as you don't pay yourself a dividend from your Puerto Rican company.

Over time, your Puerto Rican retained profits would build up into a tidy sum. That's why the Puerto Ricans also enacted a second incentive to encourage investors to come down and enjoy that money, practically tax-free.

If you take advantage of it, you'll be able to pay out all the profits to yourself without paying a dime of tax — either to the IRS or to the Puerto Rican government. That's because Act 20 grants 0% taxes on dividend distributions.

Act 22

Unlike Act 20, which is for corporations, Act 22 is for individuals.

Here's how it works:

You acquire residential property in Puerto Rico, either by purchase or rental. You relocate and become a bona fide resident of Puerto Rico. You then get a 0% Puerto Rican tax rate on passive income sources such as investments, dividends or pension payouts — even if those investments are on the U.S. mainland.

Of course, the 0% tax on dividends applies to accumulated earnings in your Puerto Rican Act 20 business, if you have one.

Here's the breakdown:

- 100% tax exemption from Puerto Rican income taxes on all dividends and interest.

- 100% tax exemption from Puerto Rican taxes on all short-term and long-term capital gains accrued after you become a bona-fide resident of Puerto Rico.

- 0% capital gains tax on the sale of any Puerto Rican real estate acquired after you move there (if it is sold before 2036).

So, how does one become a bona fide resident of Puerto Rico?

First, you need to spend six months of the tax year in Puerto Rico.

Second, you need to ensure that your official "tax home" is in Puerto Rico, which entails filling out Form 8898 for the IRS, notifying it of your move.

Third, while you're living in Puerto Rico, you must have a "closer connection" to Puerto Rico than to the U.S. That means having a Puerto Rican driver's license, a bank account, a local doctor or a mixture of many other subtle conditions that say, "I really live in Puerto Rico."

Now, there are four critical things to bear in mind.

- First, no matter what, you are liable for U.S. capital gains tax for U.S. source dividends and capital gains.

- Second, under the American Taxpayer Relief Act of 2012, if your ordinary income in the year you realize capital gains puts you in the 10% or 15% tax brackets, you won't pay U.S. capital gains tax. This is in addition to 0% Puerto Rican capital gains tax on gains made while you live there.

- Third, if you sell stock after 10 years of living in Puerto Rico, you don't need to report any capital gains to the IRS — neither the unrealized gain at the time of the move nor the realized gain at the time of sales. That's because such gains are excluded under Section 865(g) of the Internal Revenue Code, for bona fide residents of Puerto Rico.

- Fourth, if you live in a high-tax state, such as New York or California, or a state that imposes additional capital gains taxes, this adds significantly to your overall potential tax benefit.

Sounds Great, But Can It Last?

Despite all that Puerto Rico has to offer as a viable tax haven for Americans, there are concerns that might give way to some skepticism.

For instance, can the government of Puerto Rico maintain its tax breaks for rich mainlanders, given that Puerto Rico is bankrupt and its economy is in a tailspin?

In 1917, the U.S. Congress exempted interest payments from bonds issued by the Puerto Rican government and its subdivisions from federal, state, and local income taxes. This triple-tax exemption made Puerto Rican bonds attractive to municipal bond investors, which led to the island issuing debt — regardless of its account balances to fund its expenses. Puerto Rico also began issuing debt to repay its older debt, as well as refinancing older debt that had low-interest rates with debt at higher interest rates.

Decades later, Puerto Rico is now $123 billion in debt to U.S. financial institutions, despite the fact that native-born Puerto Ricans are paying full tax rates. However, Puerto Rico cannot declare bankruptcy, which is explicitly forbidden by under Chapter 9, Title 11, United States Code by a 1984 Act of Congress.

However, it is in no one's interest to have the territory bled dry as Greece has been by its European lenders. Puerto Ricans are free to move to the mainland, and if Wall Street was to insist on full repayment without restructuring, the island would rapidly depopulate, leaving no economy to tax to raise funds for repayment.

That's the strongest case in favor of keeping Acts 20 and 22. With so many Puerto Ricans moving to the mainland in recent years, every person who takes advantage of Act 20 and/or Act 22 is providing tax income — 4% or thereabouts — that would not otherwise exist.

Another concern is whether the U.S. Congress would ultimately eliminate Puerto Rico's federal tax-exempt status. There are four reasons this is highly unlikely:

1. There are no mainland American jobs at stake as a result of Acts 20 and 22.

2. The tax boost provided by these acts is better than nothing.

3. The Contract Clause of the U.S. Constitution prohibits unilateral repeal on the part of the United States of any tax decrees issued under Acts 20 and 22, so those issued so far would have to be grandfathered in.

4. Most importantly, for Congress to take the drastic and rare step of overruling Puerto Rico's own laws, it would have to be willing to change Puerto Rico's status as an unincorporated territory. Otherwise, Puerto Rico would have no incentive to comply, and Congress would have to take over direct administration of the territory.

And then there is the concern about Puerto Rico's political "temperature," the fear that ordinary Puerto Ricans will not accept preferential treatment for rich mainlanders, thereby creating social and political instability.

However, very few Puerto Ricans pay much in tax at all, since they don't have much income. Those who do have good incomes tend to be invested in the Puerto Rican bonds that the government can't repay, so tax authorities are being lenient on them. Besides, most native Puerto Ricans are just glad to have somebody spending money on the island, even if it means a preferential tax rate.

How to Take Advantage of Acts 20 and 22

Acts 20 and 22 are considered "tax decrees," a unique feature of civil law. The decrees are valid for 20 years, but in some circumstances, they can be extended to 30 years.

The decree is a binding contract between you and the government of Puerto Rico and cannot be overturned by Puerto Rican legislation. Applying for such a decree involves a filing fee of $750, and if approved, a $5000 fee. To summarize the conditions:

- For Act 22, you must be physically present on the island 183 days of the tax year.

- You must have a Puerto Rican bank account.

- For Act 22, you must buy or rent property.

- For Act 20, you must form a Puerto Rican corporation and employ at least five locals.

- You cannot have a tax home outside of Puerto Rico.

- You cannot have been a resident of Puerto Rico within six years prior to the date on which the acts became effective in 2012. Puerto Rican expatriates who have been away longer than that are welcome to apply.

- Beneficiaries must file an annual report with the Office of Industrial Tax Exemption by April 15, showing compliance with conditions and requirements of the grant for the preceding tax year.

- To qualify for the Act 22 capital gains exemption, they must be recognized prior to January 1, 2036.

All of this can be done via an online application through the Department of Economic Development and Commerce, via the Office of Industrial Tax Exemption of Puerto Rico.

However, given what's at stake, I strongly advise that you work with a lawyer. I recommend contacting Ivonne Rodriguez-Wiewall, a highly regarded Puerto Rican attorney who offers a concierge service not only to obtain a decree, but also to handle issues associated with settling on the island. She can also put you in touch with developers who are building homes for Act 22 beneficiaries in high-quality beachfront developments.

Before you do anything, I advise you to take a short trip down to San Juan and have a look around. Meet with Ivonne and her colleagues to see what is offered. Explore the island yourself and see if it is a place where you could do business and/or comfortably retire.

All you have to lose is your obligation to pay the IRS every year.

RETIREMENT

A recent Gallup poll revealed that roughly 49% of people don't expect to have enough money saved for a comfortable retirement. Americans already have a poor track record when it comes to saving and when you throw in the multiple options available for retirement planning, many are simply too overwhelmed. In this section, there are tricks for boosting your Social Security payments, how to choose between a traditional IRA and a Roth IRA, and even how you can boost your retirement investment options by opening a self-directed IRA. Learn the steps you need to take to maximize your retirement savings.

INCOME SECRET NO. 31:

Boost Your Social Security Benefit
by Retiring Earlier

Social Security is a huge entitlement program that shells out more than $950 billion in benefits annually to about 67 million Americans. Most beneficiaries derive 50% or more of their retirement income from the program, while 21% of married recipients and 43% of unmarried individuals depend on it for 90% or more of their income.

You spend your working years contributing to the program, so why not try to get as much income out of the program in retirement as you can? After all, isn't that what Social Security is for?

Well, if you think the Social Security Administration is looking out for your best interests by encouraging you to delay drawing your benefits until age 70, you may want to reconsider that assumption.

At first glance, this might seem like a good idea since your benefits at 70 will be 32% higher than those you would receive at age 62. However, contrary to popular belief, you stand to make more money by taking your benefits as early as possible.

How can that be?

As you probably know, 62 is the earliest age you can start collecting your Social Security retirement benefits. However, you earn delayed retirement credits equal to 8% per year, plus inflation, for every year you delay claiming benefits past full retirement age — which is 66 for people born between 1943 and 1954, and 67 for those born after 1960.

On the next page is a table showing how much smaller your benefits will be if you elect to collect them before you reach your full retirement age:

Start Collecting At:	Full Retirement Age of 65	Full Retirement Age of 66	Full Retirement Age of 67
62	80%	75%	70%
63	86.7%	80%	75%
64	93.3%	86.7%	80%
65	100%	93.3%	86.7%
66		100%	93.3%
67			100%
Data source: Social Security Administration			

It would appear from that table that you'd be better off waiting until your full retirement age to collect Social Security. But there's a factor you must consider — namely, how long do you intend to live?

You see, the Social Security system is designed in such a way that if you live an average length of time, your total benefits received will be more or less the same regardless of when you start collecting them. Payments that begin at age 62 will be substantially smaller, but you'll receive many more of them. So, whether you live a little longer or shorter than average, there isn't that much difference.

Nevertheless, many Americans refrain from claiming Social Security benefits as soon as they reach 62 because they've been told that the longer they wait, the more they will be paid — which is true on a short-term basis. But since the average U.S. lifespan is 78, you're more likely to lose money in the long run by waiting.

True, if you live a little longer or shorter than average, your total benefits received will not be vastly different whether you start collecting at age 62 or age 70. And if longevity runs in your family and you can keep working longer, waiting might make more sense.

But why gamble on living a very long life if you can start enjoying that retirement income now?

Besides, the sooner you start collecting Social Security benefits, the more money you'll receive in the long run.

Consider this: A 50-year-old who earns $60,000 annually stands to make $199,212 by age 75 if he or she retires at 62, versus $145,140 from retiring at 70. That's $54,072 more in Social Security benefits!

Of course, not everyone can afford to retire at age 62. It depends on how much money you'll need to live comfortably for the rest of your life. Social Security is just one source of income — and not a lucrative one at that.

The average monthly retirement benefit was recently $1,461, amounting to $17,532 per year, while the overall maximum monthly Social Security benefit for those retiring at their full retirement age was $2,861 — or roughly $34,332 for the whole year. Compare that to those who retired at age 70 in 2017, who could collect monthly checks as large as $3,770, or $45,240 per year — though most people likely received less.

To find out what you can expect to receive from Social Security, go to www.ssa.gov, and set up a "my Social Security" account. It will provide you with information on your estimated benefits.

Even if the numbers don't seem all that impressive, you may still be able to retire early depending on how far from retirement you are. Why? Because your money is growing at an annual average rate of 8%, as illustrated in the following table:

Growing at 8% For:	$10,000 Invested Annually	$15,000 Invested Annually	$20,000 Invested Annually
3 years	$35,061	$52,592	$70,122
5 years	$63,359	$95,039	$126,719
10 years	$156,455	$234,682	$312,910
15 years	$293,243	$439,864	$586,486
20 years	$494,229	$741,344	$988,458
25 years	$789,544	$1.2 million	$1.6 million

But even if you take longevity out of the equation, there may be other good reasons to start collecting Social Security early:

- So you can retire earlier. Early retirement means you can enjoy your money while you're still relatively young, healthy, active and able to travel — provided, of course, you have other savings or sources of income. Note, however, if you take your benefits before your full retirement age, you'll be taxed for your benefits if you are still employed, depending on how much you earn.

- You're married and want to take advantage of an overall spousal strategy. If you and your spouse have very different earnings records, the spouse with the lower lifetime earnings record might start collecting benefits early, while the higher-earning spouse delays collecting their benefits. That way, you both get to enjoy some income earlier, and when the higher earner hits 70, you can collect their extra-large checks. Also, should the higher-earning spouse die first, the spouse with the smaller earnings history can collect those bigger benefit checks.

- You have no choice but to retire early. Sometimes, you aren't the one who gets to decide when to retire — your circumstances choose it for you. Some retirees are forced to leave the workforce sooner than they planned due to health problems or a disability. For others, it might be because of corporate downsizing or because their company went out of business. In those situations, having Social Security benefits available sooner rather than later provides a relatively modest, but nevertheless welcome safety net.

This is just one of several hidden strategies to boost your Social Security income. In the next Income Secret, we'll show you how you can significantly increase your income by NOT filing for two types of Social Security benefits simultaneously.

INCOME SECRET NO. 32:

How to Collect an Extra $5,600 per Year in Social Security Benefits

Marriage certainly has its perks — love, companionship, emotional support ... and potentially extra Social Security benefits.

There are numerous strategies that enable married couples to maximize their benefits by coordinating the timing of their claims.

For example, they have the option to claim benefits based on their own earnings or choose to receive up to 50% of the amount for which their spouse is eligible at full retirement age. This game plan can provide an important safety net for parents who stayed out of the workforce for an extended period of time in order to care for their children.

There is also the strategy of claiming twice. Dual-earner couples who have reached their full retirement age may be able to claim spousal benefits, and then later, switch to payments based on their own work record — which will then be higher due to delayed claiming. That way, if you're planning to delay drawing benefits until age 70, you can receive some benefits between ages 66 and 70.

However, there is another marriage-related income booster that stands out among the rest. It comes right out of the Social Security Administration's public documents, but is buried amid so much other confusing information that many retirees completely miss out on it.

It enables you to collect an extra $5,600 in Social Security benefits each year by filling out two forms instead of one. The trick, however, is to NOT file for two types of Social Security benefits simultaneously, but rather to file for one (typically the smaller one) at 62, then wait until age 66 to file for the other.

If you're eligible for a retirement benefit and a survivor benefit, for example, you'll lose out on one if you file for both simultaneously. That's because, under Social Security rules, you can only collect the larger of the two. The better strategy is to take the smaller benefit first, then claim the larger one later.

Here's an example: Edith is a 62-year-old widow. She lost her husband before he could claim any Social Security benefits. At her age, Edith is eligible for her own monthly retirement benefit ($1,800) and a survivor benefit ($2,000). But if she claims both at once, she'd only receive a check for $2,000 a month for the rest of her life.

Edith would do better to claim her retirement benefit at 62 and wait until age 66 — her full retirement age — to claim her survivor benefit, which will now equal what would have been her husband's benefit at his full retirement age — $2,469. That way, she'd get $1,800 a month for four years (from 62 to 66), then $2,469 a month for the rest of her life.

That's a 23% higher real benefit from age 66 to her death, versus if she had settled for the $2,000 a month survivor benefit. It means that Edith would pocket an extra $5,628 per year.

With that higher payment, it would take Edith less than two years to make back the $200 a month she forfeited from ages 62 to 66.

Not only that, but let's say Edith lives at least another 20 years (to age 86). That's approximately $5,600 per year times 20 equals $112,000 in extra benefits … not including Social Security cost-of-living adjustments.

You've already discovered two ways to significantly boost your Social Security income. Next, however, you'll learn how to potentially score the biggest payoff of all…

INCOME SECRET NO. 33:

Add $1,140 per Month (or More) to Your Social Security Benefits

Rules are funny things — especially when they pertain to government entitlement programs.

For example, just because you've elected to take your Social Security benefits at an earlier age — say, 62 — doesn't mean you're locked into collecting only the minimum monthly allowance due to you. Not when there's an often-overlooked Social Security "reset" rule that can boost your benefits by a whopping $1,140 per month.

Let's say you jumped at the opportunity to claim Social Security benefits when you reached 62, but now realize that you don't need this source of income just yet.

Or perhaps you changed your mind about retiring and decided instead to continue working.

Or maybe you just have "beneficiary's remorse" and wish you would have waited until you reached your full retirement age — or even 70 — to take advantage of your Social Security benefits.

Well, you can. You're entitled to a "do-over" and can actually postpone collecting benefits until you're older. In fact, making such a move could be the difference between collecting only $1,277 per month at age 62 and getting $2,419 per month at age 70.

Perhaps financial need was behind your initial decision to take those early benefits. Or maybe you were worried about the long-term viability of the Social Security program, which many have warned will go bankrupt within the next two decades. Regardless of the reason, the consequences of taking early Social Security benefits can be significant.

If your full retirement age is 66 and you start taking payments at 62, it would result in a permanent 25% reduction in benefits. Put another way, if your full retirement age (FRA) benefit was expected to be $2,000 per month, electing to collect benefits at age 62 would reduce that amount to $1,500 per month. It would produce a shortfall that — when you take into consideration that Social Security benefits are indexed for inflation — would add up to thousands of dollars in lost income.

But there is a way to mitigate such a decision after the fact, and it's perfectly in compliance with Social Security rules.

Upon reaching full retirement age, you can stop receiving benefits until later in the future. In the meantime, under the program rules, delayed benefits after full retirement age are entitled to earn credits of 8% per year up to age 70. This means that if your full retirement age (FRA) is 66 and you delay your benefits until you reach age 70, you will receive delayed credits totaling up to 32% — or 132% of your primary insurance amount (PIA), as shown in the chart below.

Age when you claim retirement benefits	Amount of retirement benefit
5 years before FRA	70% of PIA
4 years before FRA	75% of PIA
3 years before FRA	80% of PIA
2 years before FRA	86.67% of PIA
1 year before FRA	93.33% of PIA
at FRA	100% of PIA
1 year after FRA	108% of PIA
2 years after FRA	116% of PIA
3 years after FRA	124% of PIA
4 years after FRA	132% of PIA

Here's an example of this strategy...

John was gainfully employed up until he lost his job at age 62. Unable to find other work, he decides it best to just retire and live off his savings, a modest pension and his Social Security benefits. Had he waited until his full retirement age of 66, John's monthly Social Security benefits would have been about

$2,000. Instead, it was reduced to $1,500 (or 75% of what he would have collected at age 66) due to his decision to take an early benefit.

However, John belatedly learns about this "reset" rule. So, when he reaches his full retirement age of 66, he decides to suspend his benefit until age 70. This benefit now starts earning delayed credits at a rate of 8% per year. This means that at age 70 (four years after his full retirement age), he will be entitled to 132% of his PIA.

So, when John resumes taking his benefit at age 70, he recovers 99% of the original primary insurance amount (0.75 times 1.32 equals 0.99) and receives $1,980 per month for the rest of his life, along with any inflation adjustments.

Of course, had John originally delayed taking his benefit until age 70 (four years beyond his FRA), it would have increased to $2,640 per month with delayed credits ($2,000 times 1.32 equals $2,640). Nevertheless, by suspending his benefit for a time, he has considerably improved his financial circumstances despite his prior decision to take early benefits.

Thanks to the "reset" option, allowing suspension of Social Security benefits at full retirement age, many beneficiaries can not only undo the impact of having taken early benefits, but also significantly boost their monthly and yearly income to meet their spending needs throughout retirement.

In fact, doing so could be one of the best "secret" income moves you'll ever make.

To apply, simply fill out the SSA-521 form within 12 months of becoming entitled to your retirement benefits. You are limited to one withdrawal. For more details on applying for a "do-over," visit https://www.ssa.gov/planners/retire/withdrawal.html.

INCOME SECRET NO. 34:

Roth or Traditional IRA: Don't Let Taxes Eat Into Your Retirement

Quick: How do you set your annual retirement savings goal?

Very wealthy households usually seek professional assistance. Once you get to the point where planning for estate taxes is an issue — when you and your spouse expect to leave more than $11 million in gross estate value — it's indispensable, since you must juggle multiple types of taxes.

But if you're like most people, you base your savings on a combination of IRS contribution limits (for IRAs), 401(k) employer matches (if you're employed) and rules of thumb, such as saving 10% of your pretax income.

A recent study found that most American retirement savers do exactly that. They let the system decide for them how much to save based on the tax rules and their employers' whims.

That's understandable. But the interesting fact is that they do so regardless of the type of savings vehicle they use, with remarkable results … results that provide a fascinating free lesson in retirement planning.

To Roth or Not to Roth: That Is the Question

Individual retirement accounts (IRAs) and 401(k) plans come in two flavors: traditional and Roth. Contributions to the former are tax-exempt — i.e., you don't pay taxes on the income you set aside for them. Your accumulated contributions plus investment growth are taxed when you withdraw them in retirement.

Since the IRS gave you a tax break when you saved into a traditional vehicle, it insists on its pound of flesh when you retire in the form of annual required minimum distributions (RMDs). Those can create massive headaches and tax complications for retirees.

Contributions to a Roth vehicle, on the other hand, are subject to tax ... but the proceeds are tax-free when you retire, and there are no RMDs.

At the level of logic and math, the decision to go the traditional or Roth route should depend on a combination of your cash flow needs during your working life and your expectation of future tax rates.

All else being equal, if you need more money now and/or expect taxes to remain the same or fall in the future, you'd go the traditional route. If you can spare the extra tax now and/or expect tax rates to rise in the future, you'd choose Roth. That's because, if you expect future taxes to be higher, it makes sense to pay them now, when they're low.

Dumb Luck

In 2019, a married couple filing jointly could contribute a maximum of $6,000 (if under 50 years old) or $7,000 (if 50 years old and older), whether Roth or traditional. Contributing to a traditional IRA lowers their current tax bill (they'll pay later). Contributing to a Roth leaves it unchanged, but future withdrawals are tax-free.

In theory, that sets up a complex net present value calculation of current versus future income, tax rate expectations and other factors.

But most Americans don't think about that. They contribute the same amount, whether it's to a traditional or Roth vehicle. As Harvard Business School researchers found, that's because they simply save according to the IRS maximum, whether it's a traditional or Roth IRA.

If they have a Roth IRA, this accidental choice creates a huge, unintended retirement windfall.

Let's say the couple saved $5,000 a year in an IRA for 40 years, earning a 5% annual return. Their balance at retirement will be more than $600,000.

If the IRA is a Roth, the full balance is available for their retirement spending. If it's traditional, taxes are due on the balance.

Let's say their tax rate is 20% in retirement. That's what they'll pay on withdrawals from their traditional IRA — which they must take whether they need them or not, due to the RMD rules.

If they opt for a Roth, on the other hand, their taxes will already have been paid, and they'll enjoy $120,000 worth of extra spending power in retirement — about $700 a month more.

A No-Brainer

I've said it before, and I'll say it again: U.S. income tax rates will be higher in the future. That makes a Roth IRA a more sensible choice.

Our current income tax rates are the lowest in over a century. Our national debt is enormous and growing. Those in charge of the federal government show no signs of reining it in — quite the opposite. The population is aging, but retirement benefits are politically sacrosanct. Our national infrastructure requires urgent and expensive repairs. And so on.

When taxes do go up, having a Roth IRA and/or a 401(k) means you'll be able to ignore them. Some people will be in that situation accidentally.

You, on the other hand, can choose it consciously. My advice is to do so ... it's a no-brainer.

INCOME SECRET NO. 35:

Why the Self-Directed IRA Is Your Key to Long-Term Prosperity

I'm a do-it-yourself (DIY) sort of guy. It's taught me something I want to share with you.

In my personal life, I'm biased toward solutions that give me maximum choice and control. I like to service my own motorbike. I do my own basic electrical repairs and plumbing. I file my own taxes … unless they get really complicated, in which case I know where to draw the line and bring in an expert.

I've learned — often the hard way — that trusting big, remote institutions to make decisions or do things for me is asking for trouble. Retirement planning is an excellent case in point.

For a few years, I had a 403(b) plan from a previous employer. It offered a fixed range of investment options. Some of them were superficially attractive, but once I took into account plan fees and the costs associated with specific funds, it became clear that I'd do better by ending my participation in the plan, paying taxes on the compensation that would have gone to contributions and investing it myself.

That's why I now manage my own retirement funds … with the help of the right experts.

The fact is that most garden-variety institutional retirement plans — including individual retirement accounts (IRAs) — are designed to gather people's retirement savings and direct them to U.S. stock markets. An entire "food chain" has grown up around the U.S. retirement system that more or less guarantees that you won't do any better than inflation, even if the underlying investments occasionally do.

But the biggest problem with conventional retirement plans is a lack of investment options. Why should you have to limit yourself to someone else's choices, made for their own convenience and profit? You don't. You don't have to limit yourself to dollar-based U.S. equities and bonds. You can pursue almost any investment option imaginable … real estate, business startups, intellectual property, precious metals … you name it.

You want more for your IRA. And you can have it … a lot more.

Take Control of Your Future … and Your Present

There's about $17.5 trillion in all U.S. private pensions. More than 25% of it is in personal IRAs. For a clever few, some of that money is in "self-directed" IRAs … about 2% of the total. Those are the folks who have found that a more flexible approach to retirement planning provides the best returns and asset protection.

A self-directed IRA is a critical tool, regardless of how DIY you are. It's legal, profitable and can be as simple or as complex as you'd like it to be. And it can open up offshore opportunities for your retirement investment that are unavailable any other way. A self-directed IRA is just like a conventional IRA in all the important ways:

- You can have multiple IRAs, so a self-directed IRA can coexist with others.

- Capital gains, dividends and interest earnings within the account incur no tax liability.

- Contributions are tax deductible (subject to conditions).

- Distributions are taxed as ordinary income and can begin when you turn 59 ½ or if you become disabled.

- You can withdraw funds for qualified unreimbursed medical expenses that are more than 7.5% of your adjusted gross income (AGI), or for qualified higher education expenses for yourself, your children and grandchildren.

- When you die, your spouse can roll both of your IRA accounts into one IRA account.

The big difference is that with a self-directed IRA, a specialist IRA "custodian" permits you to actively choose and design investments far beyond everyday stocks, bonds and mutual funds. You can invest in real estate, private mortgages, private equity, precious metals, intellectual property ... and much more.

You can reap incredible gains, tax-free, on both the income from your investments and their underlying appreciation ... gains that go way beyond what a conventional IRA custodian can provide.

And if you like, you can do it outside the U.S.

Who's Who in the IRA Zoo

In strict legal terms, a self-directed IRA is a bit of a misnomer. In most cases — with one important exception that I'll show you — your IRA assets will actually be held by a custodian, like the trustee of a trust. The Internal Revenue Code requires a custodian for all IRAs — and they must be based in the U.S.

The custodian is responsible for records management and safekeeping of your IRA, processing transactions, filing required IRS reports, issuing statements and performing other administrative duties on your behalf. Custodial firms generate revenue from fees, not from trading your money for themselves. In fact, your IRA funds must be "segregated" from the firm's own funds, so they're safe if the company goes bust. That's their core business, and they do it for millions of Americans.

But some provide a lot more value for that service than others. There are two types of IRA custodians.

One offers garden-variety securities, such as stocks, bonds and funds. This is what you'll get if you have an IRA with most big U.S. commercial custodians, such as Fidelity, American Express, Entrust or T. Rowe Price. Although you can choose from a variety of investment profiles, most of these plans are focused on the plain-vanilla U.S. market. You can forget about most "alternative" investments ... especially if they are located outside the U.S.

The other type of IRA custodian, often called a "self-directed custodian," is willing to entertain alternative investments that you choose yourself. They add value by helping you decide what your IRA is going to invest in, and if you wish, put them in safe offshore jurisdictions. There aren't many of them, but I watch them carefully to make sure you can access the best of them.

Self-directed IRA custodians allow you, the IRA owner, to choose and design specific investments, or have it done by an independent asset manager (IAM) of your choice, either in the U.S. or abroad. That's the key to supercharging your IRA — DIY style.

We're at a time when the U.S. economy is looking shaky. Unemployment is down, but there has been a dramatic decrease in labor force participation as well as quality of jobs created. U.S. equities are peaking ... at any moment, a U.S. interest-rate hike could bring them crashing down. And the ever-present threat of wealth confiscation looms. That's why these alternative investments are where you want to be.

The World's Your Oyster ... Even Oysters Can Be Your Oyster

I've heard of a case of a self-directed IRA investing in an oyster-farming venture ... hence the cheeky section title.

But the U.S. Internal Revenue Code places some restrictions on IRA investments, as I will show.

Most mainstream IRA custodians impose additional restrictions of their own, limiting you to garden-variety U.S. investment funds. That's because their job is to generate mass investment in U.S. equity markets, not to allow for customization.

But customization is exactly what you need. That's why self-directed IRA custodians, on the other hand, allow alternative investments and embrace the increased complexity involved.

What sort of alternative investments are we talking about? The range is enormous ... and most of these investments can be in the U.S. or abroad.

In fact, the Internal Revenue Code doesn't describe what a self-directed IRA can invest in, only what it cannot invest in.

Let's start with some of the things people have invested in successfully:

Real estate: A self-directed IRA can purchase any type of real estate, including residential and commercial properties, farmland and raw land — both U.S. and foreign. It can be new construction or renovation of an existing property. Your self-directed IRA funds can be used for purchase, maintenance and expenses such as taxes and utilities. When the property generates income, either from rental or sale, those funds go back to your IRA, tax-free. They can then be used to invest in other assets.

For example, your IRA could buy a home now that you'd plan to use in retirement. Your rental income goes back to your IRA and is used to maintain it, and to fund other investments.

Unlike an annuity or private insurance policy, where you can't self-direct your investments, with a self-directed IRA, you can select the property and negotiate the terms of the deal yourself. You just direct your self-directed IRA custodian to pay for the purchase. The custodian must be the legal owner, so all documents associated with the offer and purchase, as well as anything associated with the ownership of the property, must be in the name of the custodian. Although, they can specifically reference you as the IRA owner, such as "XXX Company Custodian for Benefit of (Your Name) IRA."

If you wish, real estate purchased in a self-directed IRA can even have a "non-recourse" mortgage against the property (i.e., one where neither you nor the custodian have personal liability for the mortgage — only the property as collateral). That can help leverage your self-directed IRA funds. However, according to Section 514 of the tax code, if you do this on a real estate investment, some of the income from the property will be subject to "unrelated business income tax" (UBTI).

Bear in mind that an IRA-owned property won't qualify for tax deductions for property taxes, mortgage interest or depreciation. Also, neither you nor any "disqualified person" may live in or vacation on the property. You can make decisions about how the property is maintained, but you can't do the work yourself.

(A "disqualified person" is basically you and your descendants, as well as any entity that you control. Investments involving your self-directed IRA must always be handled in a way that benefits your retirement account, not you or others close to you right now. Your self-directed IRA has to avoid any investment that would appear to involve immediate benefit for you, any descendants or any entity in which you hold a controlling equity or management interest.)

One of the interesting aspects of real estate in a self-directed IRA is that you could purchase a retirement home for yourself with it. You'd have to avoid any involvement in the property while it is in your IRA, but you could rent it out and use the income to fund renovations and improvements in anticipation of moving in one day. When you do, taking the title of the house will count as a distribution from your IRA. You will then pay an ordinary income tax on the appreciation of the house's value since the IRA purchased it, at the current rate.

For example, let's say you establish a self-directed IRA LLC with $100,000 to purchase a house. Assume you operate the LLC for 10 years and that it appreciates at an average annual rate of 8%. Your rental income is all tax-free, since it all returns to the IRA. After 20 years your $100,000 investment would be worth $215,890, and you'd pay income taxes on the $115,890.

Business investments and private equity: Self-directed IRA funds can be invested in private companies. Ownership is usually expressed as a percentage or number of shares of stock. A self-directed IRA can even fund a start-up business or other venture, as long as it's managed by someone other than you or a disqualified person. This is especially attractive if the startup does well: Your IRA's value will increase along with the fair market value of the company. And of course, it's all tax-deferred.

The IRS does put a few restrictions on private equity investments by a self-directed IRA. It can't purchase stocks that you already own. In most cases, neither you nor any disqualified persons can be employed by a company while the IRA has an equity position in that company. Also, the IRA cannot be a general partner in a limited partnership, nor can it invest in an S-corporation.

Private loans: The IRS also allows self-directed IRAs to make private loans. You can choose the borrower, the principal amount, the interest rate, the length of the term, the payment frequency, the amount of the loan and whether or not the loan will be secured. The IRA custodian makes the actual loan in its name, for the benefit of your self-directed IRA. (Such loans cannot be made to yourself or to prohibited persons.)

Other investments: You can choose self-directed IRA investments based on your own expertise. Depending on your area of specialty, you could direct your self-directed IRA to invest in currencies, commodities, hedge funds, commercial paper, royalty rights, intellectual property or equipment and leases. Self-directed IRAs have invested in golf courses, racehorses and mineral rights.

Precious metals: I know that metals are of big interest to people like us. You want them, and you'd prefer them to be offshore. That's smart thinking these days. Fortunately, self-directed IRAs are an ideal way to hold part of your retirement kitty in precious metals.

A self-directed IRA can hold gold, silver, platinum and palladium. The Taxpayer Relief Act of 1997 created this option for you.

The rules for taking distributions from a "gold IRA" are the same as those for a regular IRA. You can liquidate your IRA metals for cash or take physical possession of them. Both actions are equivalent to taking a taxable IRA distribution.

Your self-directed IRA can hold coins — as long as they aren't considered collectibles — and bullion.

- **Coins:** In order for coins to be held inside a self-directed IRA, they must be 99% pure (or better). They must be "bullion coins," not "collector's coins." That rules out Krugerrands, older Double Eagle gold coins and numismatic coins. Allowed bullion coins include:

    o One, one-half, one-quarter or one-tenth ounce U.S. gold coins.

o Other gold coins, such as the Australian Kangaroo/ Nugget, Austrian Philharmonic, Canadian Maple Leaf, Australian Kookaburra, Mexican Libertad, Isle of Man Noble and Australian Koala.

o 1-ounce silver coins minted by the Treasury Department.

o Any coin issued under the laws of any U.S. state.

- **Bullion:** Your IRA can hold bullion, such as gold, silver, platinum or palladium in bars, as long as it's of the requisite fineness.

What about storage? Unless you opt to use an LLC as the vehicle for your IRA assets (see below), your bullion coins or bars must be in the physical possession of an IRS-approved trustee, which must be a U.S. bank or approved depository, not a foreign bank. The one exception is the American Gold Eagle coin. Because these are legal tender — like the paper U.S. dollar — they can be held in an offshore account.

Of course, there are other options for including metals in your self-directed IRA:

- The Hard Assets Alliance (HAA) offers you the ability to own gold, stored internationally, inside a pre-existing IRA without having to go through a complex process. That's because it uses the American Gold Eagle, which is considered a form of U.S. currency.

- Another IRS-approved option is to buy shares of an exchange-traded fund (ETF) that tracks the value of particular precious metals.

- You can have your self-directed IRA buy stock in a mining company.

LLCs and IRAs: I'm sure you're wondering about the safety of keeping your IRA metals inside the U.S. After all, the federal deficit is about the same amount as the total U.S. retirement savings. That's an ominous thought.

The answer to this threat is an offshore IRA LLC.

In this structure, your self-directed IRA exclusively owns an offshore LLC, and you as the IRA owner become the manager of the LLC. This gives you the ability to manage your retirement funds directly, as long as you play by the "rules."

By forming the LLC offshore, you can hold metals offshore, open brokerage accounts in foreign countries, hold or trade foreign currencies and make more aggressive investments. Plus, you get the added benefit of having your assets securely offshore as an extra layer of protection from the greedy U.S. government.

When you form an offshore IRA LLC, no one has access to or control over your investments but you. Your custodian is merely responsible for moving your IRA assets into your new LLC and for reporting your offshore LLC to the IRS, since it's your only self-directed IRA asset. All the other assets are under the LLC itself.

From there, it's up to you — as a member of the LLC — to determine how and where to invest, including offshore gold or other precious metals.

As an added benefit, the custodian will no longer charge a transaction fee on your investments in the LLC, saving you a lot of money.

When it comes to holding precious metals offshore, LLCs are critical. Several European banks and other financial institutions are willing to hold American IRAs, offering a variety of precious metal storage programs. But to access them, you must have an offshore LLC — IRS rules prohibit your U.S. custodian from doing this on your behalf.

Sounds too good to be true? Don't worry — it's perfectly legal.

Getting Expert Help

I mentioned that although I'm a DIY guy, I know when to trust the experts. For example, before I start soldering the circuit board on my precious Fender Deluxe Reverb guitar amplifier, I run my plans by a trusted specialist in Seattle who knows a lot more than I do about such matters.

The same applies to your self-directed IRA. Whether your IRA is managed by your custodian or by you via an LLC, you are welcome to use the services of an independent asset manager (IAM) to help you plan and execute your investments. For a fee, the IAM can help you decide what to instruct your custodian to do with your self-directed IRA assets.

This is especially useful — even essential — when it comes to offshore investments, especially via an offshore LLC. IAMs in Europe, for example, have well-developed relationships with European banks and other institutions that can host LLC accounts and arrange precious metal transactions and storage.

And of course they know European markets much better that most U.S. advisers. With the European economy looking up these days, an offshore IAM can help you take advantage of the rising tide.

Play by the Rules

The IRS has rules about IRA investments, and you don't want to break them. They're not too complicated, but it's critical to be aware of them ... especially if you take the offshore LLC route with your self-directed IRA.

Here's why: If the IRS decides that there's been a "prohibited transaction" under Internal Revenue Code Section 4975, your IRA loses its tax-exempt status. The entire fair market value of your IRA is treated as a taxable distribution, subject to ordinary income tax. You'd also pay a 15% penalty, as well as a 10% early distribution penalty if you're under the age of 59 ½.

You don't want that to happen. But it won't, if you know the rules, and obtain and follow good advice from a qualified tax attorney like the ones I recommend.

There are three types of prohibited transactions: those involving specific investments, those involving disqualified persons and self-dealing.

Prohibited investments: Your self-directed IRA can't invest in life insurance. It can't invest in collectibles such as artwork, rugs, antiques, gems, stamps, alcoholic beverages or collectible coins (there are exceptions, as I explained before).

Disqualified persons: This is based on the premise that investments involving your self-directed IRA must always be handled in a way that benefits your retirement account, not you or others close to you right now. Basically, your self-directed IRA has to avoid any investment that would appear to involve immediate benefit for you, any descendants or any entity in which you hold a controlling equity or management interest. That means things such as:

- Borrowing money from your IRA.
- Selling property to your IRA.
- Receiving compensation for managing your IRA.
- Receiving compensation from a disqualified entity, such as a company your IRA owns.
- Personally guaranteeing an IRA loan.
- Using your IRA as security for a personal loan.
- Using it to pay for a personal expense.
- Living in a property owned by your IRA.

Self-dealing and conflict of interest: This is when the IRS can show that you or a disqualified person received some indirect personal benefit from your IRA. Examples include issuing a mortgage on a residence purchased by a disqualified person, or buying stock from yourself, from any entity in which you have a controlling equity position or from a disqualified person.

Fortunately, there are excellent tax attorneys who specialize in staying on top of the rules and case laws involving prohibited transactions … and they are an essential part of your self-directed IRA strategy.

How to Convert Your IRA to a Self-Directed IRA

Moving money from your existing IRA (or even from a 401(k) or 403(b)) to a self-directed IRA can be done in two ways. They're both legal and tax-free as long as they're done the right way.

- A transfer is the method used to move your retirement funds from your existing IRA to a new IRA. In a direct transfer, the distribution check is not sent to you. Instead, your IRA's assets are transferred from your old custodian directly to the custodian of your new self-directed IRA. You can choose to transfer your existing plan at any time, tax-free.

- A rollover is used to move your retirement funds between two qualified retirement plans, such as from your current 401(k) to a self-directed IRA.

With a rollover, the distribution from your existing retirement plan is paid directly to you. This distribution is tax-free as long as you redeposit your funds into your new IRA within 60 days. It is important to note that if the 60-day period is exceeded, you will be liable for taxes and penalties on the funds withdrawn. You may rollover funds from an existing IRA tax-free once per year.

Choosing a Custodian

Self-directed IRA custodians aren't responsible for your investment choices ... you are. If you tell them to invest in something that doesn't work out, it's not their problem. Indeed, most IRA agreements clearly state that investors are solely responsible for making investment decisions in connection with their funds.

Some investment promoters seeking self-directed IRA business require exclusive use of certain custodians. With a few exceptions, I'm wary of such arrangements. The exception is when an offshore IAM has an existing relationship with a trusted U.S. custodian and prefers to work with it.

On the other hand, an investment scheme that says "You can buy in as long as you use custodian 'X'" should be treated with caution.

Needless to say, it's critical to choose the right self-directed IRA custodian. Here are some of the things to consider:

Specialization: Make sure you work with an IRA custodian that genuinely specializes in alternative investments. A few IRA custodians will work with both types of investments. An IRA custodian that specializes in traditional investments typically won't be the best choice to also manage your alternative investments.

The reverse holds true as well. When you work with a self-directed IRA custodian, you want one whose specialty matches up with your needs. Remember, you can have more than one IRA.

Fees: Every IRA custodian charges fees for their services. They are often surprisingly low — several hundred dollars to set up and between $100 and $150 a year thereafter. Nevertheless, there are two fee models — either a per-transaction fee model or an asset-based percentage fee model. Make sure the custodian's fee schedule aligns with your investment strategy. Your choice will affect the total returns of your self-directed IRA. The bigger your account, the more negotiating room you'll have when it comes to fees.

Number of transactions: Your investment strategy might involve frequent transactions. Some custodians also offer automated investment services. Make sure your IRA custodian understands and is prepared to handle your investment habits.

Miscellaneous costs: Many alternative investments provide a variety of services as part of the investment strategy, and almost all IRA custodians charge fees for them. They include federal funds wires, notarizing documents, document storage, account setup fees, statement fees, transfer fees, account termination fees, and servicing fees such as check writing, processing documents and so on. Some custodians include these services in their custody fees, while others itemize the fees and charge them separately. My preference would be for most fees to be included in your custody fees, unless they are unavoidable pass-through fees such as federal funds wires or postage. Make sure your expected return on investment takes all these miscellaneous fees into account.

Service: This is really the key, and why due diligence is so important. You want to consider your custodian's depth of knowledge, timeliness of response, precision, consistency of a process, speed of resolution of any issues and willingness to adapt to a changing environment. Remember, investing in a piece of real estate inside a self-directed IRA requires the custodian to process all documentation associated with the property (e.g. paying taxes, expenses, insurance, maintenance personnel or other expenses). If the service team at the custodian isn't experienced at this, is slow in its response time or are sloppy with their documentation processing, your investments could be negatively affected.

A Final Example

Let's wrap up our tour of self-directed IRAs with an example.

Rob is in his late 50s, self-employed and in the real estate business. He knows U.S. markets reasonably well, but he's not convinced that they are the key to his retirement future. He knows property, however, and how to make money out of it.

Rob has three current IRAs: two self-employment IRAs with about $500,000 in each and a Roth IRA with $250,000. He also has an old 401(k) from earlier in his career, worth about another $250,000. He wants to keep the Roth as a place to put occasional windfalls. But the two SEP-IRAs are weak performers.

So, he decides to look for an appropriate custodian that has a lot of experience in handling U.S. real estate transactions. He also wants to form an offshore LLC on the island of Nevis to hold any self-directed IRA property acquisitions, and also so he can open gold accounts in Europe via an independent investment manager.

Rob identifies a suitable custodian and has an attorney execute due diligence on it. His attorney also advises him on the mechanics of the process of setting up and running his self-directed IRA before he takes the plunge.

When he's ready, he decides to request that his current IRA custodian transfer his two SEP-IRAs to the new self-directed IRA custodian, which invests them in an offshore LLC set up by his attorney. But he decides to take a rollover of his old 401(k), because he wasn't sure whether he wanted to put it into his existing Roth or his new self-directed IRA. New IRS rules that his attorney told him about stipulate that he can only do this once a year — the reason he decided to move his SEP-IRAs by direct custodian-to-custodian transfer.

Within a few months, money that had accumulated in his SEP-IRAs purchased a range of investment properties in the U.S. and abroad that he knew well, thanks to his real estate expertise. He chose high-growth markets in the U.S. and Panama, where returns were in the double-digits. He used about 50% of his IRA value to do that. He put another 30% of his self-directed IRA value into offshore gold storage in Liechtenstein. The remaining 20% he invested in a variety of foreign stocks, bonds and currencies.

With three years, the value of Rob's retirement portfolio had doubled. That's because he had the flexibility to invest in areas he knew intimately.

Before that, he'd just been a spectator as someone else managed his money ... and not very well.

If that sounds like a story you'd like to be part of ... start now. There's no reason to wait.

INCOME SECRET NO. 36:

Use Your "Secret IRA" to Save as Much as $591,000

Planning for retirement is no easy task. With the likelihood of Social Security and even pensions failing on the rise with each passing year, the burden of supporting yourself through your golden years is falling more and more on you.

In fact, a GOBankingRates poll revealed that 64% of Americans expect to retire with less than $10,000 in savings. And according to a Northwestern Mutual 2019 Planning & Progress study, 15% of Americans have no retirement savings.

But many people are looking for ways to maximize their retirement savings while still getting the best tax benefits. There are, of course, the standard 401(k) and IRA savings plans ... assuming that you are even eligible to enjoy the tax benefits of an IRA.

However, what if you could grow your money for retirement in a "Super IRA" that allows you to invest tax-free and withdraw the money without incurring taxes?

I know, it sounds too good to be true.

The truly remarkable thing is that this incredible retirement savings plan isn't technically meant for retirement. It's part of your health insurance.

The health savings account (HSA), sometimes referred to as an (H)IRA, was created as a way to put more control over health expenses into the hands of individuals in hopes of bringing down costs. When it was pushed through Congress in 2003 as part of the Medicare Prescription Drug, Improvement, and Modernization Act, few realized that it provided Americans with an interest loophole when it came to their retirement savings. A loophole that could save you as much as $591,000.

What Is an HSA?

A health savings account (HSA) is similar to a regular personal savings account that you use to stash away money for a rainy day. The only difference is that this money is being stored for qualified health care expenses. An HSA can be established with you as the sole beneficiary, or for you plus your spouse and/or dependents.

However, to establish an HSA, you must be enrolled in a high-deductible health plan (HDHP). These HDHPs have much smaller monthly premiums than most health insurance plans, which makes them enticing to individuals who are attempting to cut down on up front health care costs. The goal of HDHPs is to cover serious injury or illness.

But HDHPs require that you first meet your annual deductible in medical costs each year before your plan starts to pay any benefits. This is where your HSA comes in handy. Out-of-pocket medical expenses that aren't covered by your HDHP can be funded by the savings you've stored away in your HSA.

But what if you don't use all the savings you've stored over the year for medical expenses?

The great thing about the HSA is that it's not a "use it or lose it" scenario. If you don't use all the funds that you've stored in your HSA during the year for medical expenses, then that money rolls over and continues to accumulate.

Year after year. On and on and on ... you can see where I'm going with this. It's just like a savings account, but better, because the money that you've invested in the HSA is pretax dollars. The savings are growing tax-free. And if you withdraw the money for qualified medical expenses, you won't be taxed on those withdrawn funds either.

That's something an IRA or a 401(k) can't even claim.

The HSA Tax Advantage

The HSA is a great way to save for, as well as pay for, health care expenses, but one of the great added bonuses is that it offers some great tax advantages.

An HSA is largely funded through pretax contributions. For the most part, contributions to your HSA are made through payroll deposits (through your employer) using pretax dollars. Your employer can also make contributions on your behalf, and the contribution is not included in your gross income. As a result, you will owe fewer taxes because your gross annual income is lowered by the amount that you paid into your HSA.

Your Estimated Tax Savings			
Without HSA		With HSA	
Gross annual pay (estimate)	$60,000	Gross annual pay (estimate)	$60,000
Estimated tax rate (22%)	-$13,200	Maximum annual family coverage HSA contribution	-$7,100
Net annual pay	=$46,800	Adjusted gross pay	=$52,900
Estimated current + future healthcare expenses	-$7,100	Estimated tax rate (22%)	-$11,638
Final take-home pay	=$39,700	Final take-home pay	=$41,262
		Take home this much more $1,562	

All figures in this table are estimates based on an annual salary of $60,000 and maximum contribution limits to the benefit account. Your salary, tax base, healthcare expenses and tax savings may be different.

All figures in this table are estimates based on an annual salary of $60,000 and maximum contribution limits to the benefit account.

Your salary, tax base, health care expenses and tax savings may be different.

What's more, contributions are not subject to state income taxes either (unless you are a resident of Alabama, California or New Jersey — these are the only states that require you to pay state income taxes on your HSA contributions).

But what if you pay into your HSA with after-tax dollars? Don't worry. You're covered. You can deduct any after-tax dollar contributions from your gross income on your tax return.

Now, remember that those contributions to the HSA aren't just sitting in cash. That money can be invested in a variety of vehicles such as stocks, bonds, mutual funds and exchange-traded funds. What's more, any growth enjoyed during the year — whether through price appreciation, dividends or interest payments — is also growing free of federal taxes, as well as most state taxes. Right now, the only states to tax HSA earnings are New Hampshire and Tennessee.

And finally, with an HSA, withdrawals can be tax-free. Withdrawals from your HSA are not subject to federal (or in most cases, state) income taxes if they are used for qualified medical expenses. As you can see from the table below, other retirement savings plans such as the 401(k), IRA and Roth IRA can't even claim all of those tax benefits.

	401(k)	IRA	Roth IRA	H(IRA)
Tax-free before investing	✓	✓	X	✓
Tax-free while growing	✓	✓	✓	✓
Tax-free withdrawals	X	X	✓	✓

The Other Benefits of an HSA

The tax benefits of an HSA are tempting enough to entice most investors into this kind of savings plan, but those aren't the only advantages offered.

Did you know that other people can actually contribute to your HSA?

Contributions to your health savings account aren't limited to the funds pulled from your paycheck. In fact, anyone from your employer to your spouse or a relative can add to your HSA. The Kaiser Family Foundation reports that 72% of employers contribute to HSAs — an average $1,655 for singles and $1,600 for families.

In addition, the funds in your HSA don't disappear at the end of the year if you don't use them. Many people have been burned over the years using flexible spending accounts to help pay for medical expenses.

They would dutifully contribute to the account all year, but if they overestimated what their medical expenses would be and didn't spend all the money ... poof! Gone when the year ended.

That's not the case at all with an HSA. If you have money left in your HSA at the end of the year, it rolls over to the next year. That allows you to keep the money invested and growing for the future and your retirement.

What if you change health insurance plans?

Don't worry. The money is still yours and is available for future qualified medical expenses.

Life comes with many shifts and changes, and you need your HSA to follow you. Should you change your health insurance plan, employer or even retire, your funds will remain in your HSA to grow tax-free.

What if you don't want to bother with mailing in copies of receipts and waiting for reimbursement?

HSAs are far more convenient than other savings accounts, as most HSAs issue a debit card. This will allow you to pay for your prescription medication and other expenses right away. If you wait for a bill to come in the mail, you can call the billing center and make a payment over the phone using your debit card. You can even use the card at an ATM to withdraw cash.

The Drawbacks of an HSA

No plan is perfect, and it is critical that you understand the few disadvantages that come with an HSA.

The first and most important is that an HSA requires you to have a high-deductible health plan (HDHP).

And while you may be enjoying smaller insurance premiums each month, it can be difficult — even with help from money in an HSA — to come up with the cash to meet a high deductible.

Furthermore, if you have health care expenses that surpass what you had planned for, you may find that you have not saved enough money in your HSA to cover your costs.

While you can add pretax money, allowing the fund to grow tax-free, and even withdraw funds tax-free for qualified purchases, there is a chance that you could pay taxes and penalties. If you withdraw funds for nonqualified expenses prior to turning 65, you'll owe taxes on the money withdrawn from the HSA, plus a 20% penalty.

After the age of 65, you'll owe only taxes on the money withdrawn, but not the penalty. (Keep in mind that this is a bit different from an IRA, where there's no 10% penalty tax for withdrawals from an IRA if you're over the age of 59 ½.)

It is important you are organized, because you will need to keep your receipts to prove that withdrawals from the HSA were used for qualified health expenses.

And finally, some HSAs charge a monthly maintenance fee or a per-transaction fee, which can vary from one institution to another. While these are usually low, they can easily eat away at the savings and growth that you've achieved.

These disadvantages are not insurmountable in the least. They simply require some careful planning, a little bookkeeping and some research on the best place to set up your HSA to keep fees to a minimum.

Taking Advantage of Qualified Expenses

Health care costs might have slowed compared to years past, but PwC's Health Research Institute predicts a medical cost increase as high as 10% for 2021. What's more, a study showed that the net cost of prescription drugs in the U.S. has risen more than three times faster than the rate of inflation.

And even without an HDHP, we find ourselves paying more and more of those medical expenses out of our own pockets — and those expenses tend to skyrocket as we get older.

In fact, Fidelity reports that a 65-year-old couple leaving the workforce today can expect to spend $285,000 on health care and medical expenses.

So why not use tax-free funds to pay for those medical expenses?

The fact is that there are hundreds of health expenses that qualify for tax-free payments from an HSA. Some of those expenses include:

- Acupuncture.
- Alcoholism treatment.
- Ambulance services.
- Chiropractors.
- Contact lens supplies.
- Dental treatments.
- Diagnostic services.
- Doctor's fees.
- Eye exams, glasses and surgery.
- Fertility services.
- Guide dogs.
- Hearing aids and batteries.
- Hospital services.
- Insulin.
- Lab fees.
- Prescription medications.
- Nursing services.
- Surgery.
- Psychiatric care.
- Telephone equipment for the visually or hearing impaired.
- Therapy or counseling.
- Wheelchairs.
- X-rays.

What's more, health insurance premiums are not eligible as qualified medical expenses if you are under the age of 65. However, after the age of 65, you can use the fund from your HSA to pay for health insurance premiums including Medicare Part B premiums and long-term-care insurance premiums.

To see a full list of medical and dental expenses that you can use tax-free with your HSA funds, please read the IRS Publication 502, Medical and Dental Expenses (https://www.irs.gov/forms-pubs/about-publication-502).

Can You Open an HSA?

So, you now understand what an HSA is, the advantages and the few disadvantages.

You've gone over your past medical expenses and made estimates on what you think your future medical needs are likely to be.

You believe that an HSA will not only fit your current medical expenses, but that it will allow you to save on taxes that you're paying right now on your income, and grow a nice tax-free nest egg to help fund your retirement.

Yes, it looks like a great plan for you.

But are you eligible?

Just as there are limitations on whether you can deduct your IRA contribution due to your income levels, there are federal guidelines on whether you can open and contribute to an HSA.

To open an HSA, you must be:

• Covered under a HDHP on the first day of the month.

• Not covered by any other non-HDHP plan (with some exceptions for certain plans with limited coverage, such as dental, vision and disability).

• Not enrolled in Medicare.

• Not claimed as a dependent on someone else's tax return.

Each year, the IRS sets up guidelines for HSAs and HDHPs, based on individual and family coverage.

For 2020, all HDHPs must have a minimum deductible of $1,400 for individuals and $2,800 for families. The out-of-pocket maximum (including deductibles, copayments and coinsurance, but not premiums) cannot exceed $6,900 for individuals and $13,800 for families. As long as you can check all these boxes, you can open an HSA.

Establishing Your HSA

First step, of course, is to join a high-deductible health plan.

Then you can sign up for a health savings account. Your health insurance provider can provide you with more information on setting up an HSA through its recommended bank.

But you don't have to use the bank your health insurance provider recommends ... and that might prove to be in your best interest.

Not all HSA providers are equal. Some will require that you hold a minimum amount in cash (which obviously limits the amount that you have invested and are growing toward your retirement), and others will have a variety of fees that can cut into your savings.

When you're shopping for the provider of your HSA, here are some things to look for:

- No minimum balance. Most HSAs don't require you to maintain a minimum balance, but some can require that you keep a certain amount in cash to cover potential medical expenses. However, some providers may waive certain fees if you do.

- Beware of fees. Some accounts charge for monthly account maintenance, debit cards and various transactions. Carefully read all information regarding fees and ask questions about any charges that you don't understand.

- Shoot for the highest interest rate. In this environment of low interest rates, finding a good return for your investment isn't an easy task.

That doesn't mean you can't find some good deals. Some accounts are similar to a regular bank savings account that pays a modest interest rate. Others have an investment option where you can choose securities, such as mutual funds or individual stocks.

- The best payment options. Look for accounts that offer both paper checks and a debit card. This will allow you to pay for medical expenses in just about any situation, either in person or online.

- Get online convenience. Use an account that you can access online for transactions, statements and records. This allows you to save time and makes electronic payments for your medical expenses.

The thing to remember is that unlike medical savings accounts or health reimbursement arrangements that are controlled by employers, an HSA belongs exclusively to you, the account holder. You can spend the funds at your discretion (though nonqualified medical expenses will result in taxes and penalties) and are free to take along with you if you change jobs.

Maximizing Your HSA

Just like with IRAs, there are limits on how much you, your employer or anyone else can contribute to your HSA each year. The IRS adjusts these limits each year based on inflation calculations.

	2019	2020
Individual	$3,500	$3,550
Family	$7,000	$7,100

However, if you are 55 or older, you are permitted to contribute an additional $1,000 as a "catch-up" contribution similar to 401(k) or IRA contributions.

If you are married, and both of you are at the age of 55, each of you can contribute an additional $1,000.

Unfortunately, it gets a little more complicated if you and your spouse aren't both 55 or older. That's because an HSA is in an individual's name — there is no joint HSA even when you have family coverage. Only the person age 55 or older can contribute the additional $1,000 in his or her own name.

If only the husband is 55 or older and the wife contributes $6,900 to her HSA for their family coverage, the husband must open a separate account for the additional $1,000.

If both husband and wife are age 55 or older, they must have two HSA accounts if they want to contribute the maximum. There's no way to hit the maximum with only one account.

You can make contributions to your HSA at any time during the calendar year and up to April 15 of the following tax year. Funds can be added to your HSA in regular amounts or in one lump sum.

One great way to fund your HSA is with a one-time tax-free transfer of funds from your IRA to an HSA. This is not like a rollover, as it counts toward your annual HSA contribution limit.

It does allow you to move a small amount of money from an IRA. It's a smart move, particularly if you would have been using those IRA funds to pay medical expenses. In that case, you would have had to pay taxes on that IRA disbursement. If you take the money out of your HSA for medical expenses, you don't have to pay taxes on those funds.

Investing for Tomorrow With Your HSA

One of the key things to remember if you plan to use your HSA to fund your retirement is that you must have funds left-over at the end of the year to rollover into the next year.

While it might seem a little counterintuitive since the HSA was designed to help cover your annual medical costs, the benefits of having a vehicle that allows you to triple the tax benefits can't be overlooked when saving for your retirement.

The more you can have left over at the end of the year from your annual contributions, the better. In fact, many financial planners will argue that to really grow the HSA, you could dedicate it to retirement by paying health costs with other savings. If possible, use other savings to pay for smaller expenses so that you can allow the funds in your HSA to grow.

When you are planning the investments for your HSA, be sure to carefully look over your options and make sure that your HSA custodian will meet your investing needs.

Some custodians offer fewer than 20 mutual funds. While HSA Bank, for example, offers a full brokerage via TD Ameritrade. And HealthSavings Administrators (https://healthsavings.com) lets you pick from 22 low-cost Vanguard funds.

One way to compare your options is through HSASearch. com.

Keep in mind that your HSA withdrawal strategy can influence your investment strategy. If you are planning to use your HSA to pay for current medical expenses, you may want to avoid substantial stock market investments that can decline at any time and look for liquid investments that conserve principal.

If you are planning to use your HSA more for future medical expenses during your retirement, you may have a longer time frame that will allow you to take on more risk through significant stock investments to grow your nest egg.

In fact, if you can postpone accessing your HSA account until your 80s, when you might have high medical or long-term-care expenses, you would benefit from a very long investing horizon.

When it comes to funding and ranking your retirement accounts, it's important to not only take into account the tax benefits, but the potential penalties on withdrawals as well. It may be best to set your hierarchy of contribution at:

1. 401(k) or IRA up to any match.

2. HSA to contribution limit.

3. 401(k) nonmatched limit.

4. IRA nonmatched limit.

Building Your Retirement With Triple-Tax Benefits

How does the math actually shake out for an HSA over other retirement accounts?

As an example, let's say you start out with $100,000 to invest in your retirement account.

In a Roth IRA, you will have to pay taxes on it at both the state and Federal level. For the sake of simplicity. Let's assume that you pay the U.S. average of 32%, which reduces your initial investment to $68,000.

	401(k)	IRA	Roth IRA	H(IRA)
Tax-free before investing	$100,000	$100,000	$68,000	$100,000
Tax-free while growing	$1,000,000	$1,000,000	$680,000	$1,000,000
Tax-free withdrawals	$680,000	$680,000	$680,000	$1,000,000

As you can see, the HSA is the only account that can truly grow 100% tax-free ... leaving you with a $1 million retirement. That's an additional $320,000 — money you don't get to keep with an IRA, Roth IRA or 401(k).

Of course, this is a pretty simple example. It assumes you make only one initial deposit and nothing more.

Most people contribute money to their retirement account on a regular basis.

Let's look at another example, where you just put an extra $5,000 into the account each year...

The total amount for each retirement plan would look like this:

	401(k)	IRA	Roth IRA	H(IRA)
Tax-free before investing	$100,000	$100,000	$68,000	$100,000
Tax-free while growing	$1,848,810	$1,848,810	$1,257,191	$1,848,810
Tax-free withdrawals	$1,257,191	$1,257,191	$1,257,191	$1,848,810

As you can see, the 401(k), IRA and Roth IRA end up at nearly the exact same amount ... $1,257,191.

But the HSA soars to $1,848,810, thanks to its triple-tax benefit — giving you an extra $591,000 for your retirement.

None of those traditional retirement plans can give you this level of freedom.

All you have to do is put your money into an HSA ... and watch it grow.

And, unlike a traditional retirement plan ... you can withdraw money tax-free before you are 59 ½ for some of retirement's most worrisome and unexpected expenses ... like health care costs.

Plus, if you don't need the extra money during retirement, you're not required to take it out. Unlike IRAs, Roth IRAs and 401(k)s, you can leave it in, and let it grow ... even after you are 70 ½.

The HSA may have been born out of a health care plan, but it has become the "Super IRA" you need to grow your nest egg and see yourself through a worry-free retirement.

INCOME SECRET NO. 37:

13 States That Won't Loot Your Retirement

Often, a secure retirement isn't just about when you decide to retire or how much money you have to retire; it's also about where you choose to retire.

That's because some U.S. states offer certain financial benefits to retirees that other states do not.

In considering places to retire, the first that often comes to mind is Florida. After all, it's where millions of Americans from all over the country choose to live out their golden years for a variety of reasons — the weather, no state tax, and plenty of communities specifically catering to the needs of older Americans.

But there are at least a dozen other states that are just as retiree-friendly, if not more so. Choosing the right one depends on your personal priorities. But one thing's for sure, there are many variables to consider. And maintaining the same standard of living in various parts of the country can require radically different incomes.

That means, besides things like crime, culture, weather, amenities, attractions and senior citizen wellbeing, you need to consider the basic essentials as well:

- What is the overall **cost of living**?
- What is the **state tax burden**?
- How much does the **state tax structure** matter, given your specific retirement strategy?
- What's the **cost of housing**?
- How much will **health care cost** you?

As you can see, this all involves trade-offs. Having a firm grasp of your personal likes and dislikes is the first step to creating a framework to identify the perfect place to retire inside the U.S. Knowing beforehand the things you'll get — and the things you'll lose — when you move to a new state is critical.

But let's focus on the financial variables since ultimately it all depends on whether you can *afford* to live your dream retirement, starting with the most important variable of all.

Cost of Living

Surveys of retirees routinely show that cost of living is the most important issue determining retirement strategies.

There are many different tabulations of state-by-state cost of living, but ranking states this way is harder than it looks. One reason is that nonfinancial factors can affect the cost of living.

For example, the high cost of living in states like Vermont and Maryland can be offset by the many free or low-cost things to do, such as skiing in Vermont or boating on the Chesapeake Bay. The reverse is also true. You could move to a low-cost state like Arkansas or Alabama and forced to spend lots of money traveling elsewhere.

Another complication is that cost of living is tangled up with taxation and the cost of health care, two of our other critical variables. The best rankings of cost of living take this into account.

Based on an index that includes costs associated with housing, utilities, groceries, health care, transportation and miscellaneous expense — but excludes taxation — here are the 10 cheapest and 10 most expensive cost of living states:

10 Cheapest Cost of Living States			
1	Mississippi	6	Tennessee
2	Arkansas	7	Michigan
3	Oklahoma	8	Kansas
4	Missouri	9	Georgia
5	New Mexico	10	Alabama

10 Most Expensive Cost of Living States			
1	Hawaii	6	Massachusetts
2	Washington, DC	7	Alaska
3	California	8	Maryland
4	New York	9	Connecticut
5	Oregon	10	New Jersey

As you can see, the cheaper states are clustered in the Deep South and the lower Midwest, whereas the most expensive states are in the Northeast or on the Pacific.

Taxation

Determining a state's tax burden is also complicated. In addition to income tax, you must also consider property and sales tax. Other important considerations are whether the state taxes Social Security benefits, and how it treats retirement investment income.

	Top 10 States With the Highest Taxes		Top 10 States With the Lowest Taxes
1	New York	1	Alaska
2	Hawaii	2	Delaware
3	Maine	3	Tennessee
4	Vermont	4	Florida*
5	Minnesota	5	New Hampshire
6	Connecticut	6	Oklahoma
7	Rhode Island	7	South Dakota*
8	Illinois	8	Alabama
9	New Jersey	9	Montana
10	California	10	Virginia
			* No income tax

The highest tax states have several features in common. They tend to be in the Northeast, which is highly urbanized, densely populated and has a lot of transportation infrastructure to maintain. They tend to be "blue" states politically and make significant investments in social services for their residents.

Hawaii's high-tax burden is a result of its unique location, it's strong social services system and, above all, high property values and, thus, property taxes.

On the other hand, three of the 10 lowest tax states have no income tax. Two others on the list, New Hampshire and Tennessee, don't tax wages. The other states have an income tax, but it's either so low or so favorable to retirees that they are still considered comparatively low-tax.

By 2025, there will be nine U.S. states that levy no income tax: Alaska, Florida, Nevada, South Dakota, Texas, Washington, Wyoming, and joining the list by 2021, Tennessee and New Hampshire. (And those living in Alaska, once you've established residency there, the state actually pays you every year from its "Permanent Fund" oil industry trust fund. Requirements are listed here: https://pfd.alaska.gov/Eligibility/Requirements.)

Much depends on how you plan to finance your retirement. If you are going to continue receiving business income in retirement — for example, if you continue to retain ownership interest in a medical practice, a car dealership, or some other family business — you'd want to live in a state with low or no income tax, especially on out-of-state income.

On the other hand, if you are going to rely largely on Social Security benefits, the income tax system wouldn't matter as much as whether those benefits were subject to taxation. In fact, 37 U.S. states don't tax Social Security benefits. Seven of them currently have no income tax at all, and one — Alaska — has no sales tax.

States with no Social Security Tax include: Alabama, Alaska, Arizona, Arkansas, California, Delaware, Florida, Georgia, Hawaii, Idaho, Illinois, Indiana, Iowa, Kentucky, Louisiana, Maine, Maryland, Massachusetts, Michigan, Mississippi,

Nevada, New Hampshire, New Jersey, New York, North Carolina, Ohio, Oklahoma, Oregon, Pennsylvania, South Carolina, South Dakota, Tennessee, Texas, Virginia, Washington, West Virginia and Wyoming.

If you look for overlaps, you'll find 10 states that are at the bottom of the tax burden list that also don't tax Social Security benefits. They are Wyoming, South Carolina, Idaho, Virginia, Alabama, South Dakota, Oklahoma, New Hampshire, Florida, Tennessee, Delaware and Alaska.

Of those 10, Idaho, Alabama, Oklahoma, and Tennessee are all amongst the 10 lowest cost of living states in the country. Rounding out the top 20 are Georgia, Texas, Wyoming and Ohio.

Housing

One of the major components of America's cost of living is housing. For a variety of reasons, the cost of a place to "be" in the U.S. has skyrocketed over the last two generations.

The fastest rise in housing costs has been in the older cities of the Northeast, coastal Florida, the urban areas of Texas and practically everywhere west of the Great Plains.

By contrast, housing prices have not risen much on the last 20 years in the Midwestern states around the Great Lakes, or in the small towns and rural areas of the South and the Plains states.

Overall, the states with the most affordable housing costs are geographically within the same range as lowest cost of living states. They are located between the Appalachians in the east and the Great plains in the west, and between the inland regions of the Deep South and the Great Lakes and Canadian border.

That doesn't tell the whole story, however. As the list below shows, after housing, the second biggest expenditure for retirees is transportation. For most people that means a car or two, fuel, maintenance and insurance.

Housing Affordability Rank			
1	Iowa	11	North Dakota
2	Ohio	12	Arkansas
3	Indiana	13	Kentucky
4	Oklahoma	14	South Dakota
5	Michigan	15	Mississippi
6	Nebraska	16	Wisconsin
7	Missouri	17	Illinois
8	West Virginia	18	Georgia
9	Kansas	19	Alabama
10	Pennsylvania	20	Louisiana

One of the defining features of the low-cost housing environment in the region above is lack of good public transportation systems. Few of the cities in the big swath of Middle America where housing is cheap have well-developed train systems. That means a car is a necessity.

On the other hand, popular retirement states like Florida also have poor public transport, but their low-tax burdens offset this to a degree.

Once again, this highlights the importance of trade-offs in determining the best environment for retirement — and therefore of doing your homework to see the best fit for you.

Analyzing the Big Picture

A widely accepted rule of thumb is that you'll need to replace from 70% to 90% of your pre-retirement income to maintain your standard of living in retirement.

That suggests that the first step to discovering the best value in retirement locales is to compare where you are now with where you might go. There are two calculators at the following links that show you how far your expected retirement income will go in different locales:

- https://smartasset.com/mortgage/cost-of-living-calculator

- http://money.cnn.com/calculator/pf/cost-of-living/index.html

For example, the first calculator shows that you'd need to have an income of $50,279 in El Paso, Texas, to have the same standard of living that $65,000 provides in Boston — a drop of 23%!

The second calculator shows that you'd save 62% on housing, 38% on utilities, and 28% on health care by moving to the city on the banks of the Rio Grande.

Finally, here is a list of the **30 cheapest cities to retire in the U.S.** The cheapest is indeed El Paso. In fact, seven of the 10 cheapest places to retire in the U.S. are in Texas:

30 Cheapest Cities for Retirement			
1	El Paso, TX	16	Greensboro, NC
2	Brownsville, TX	17	Mobile, AL
3	Fort Wayne, IN	18	Louisville, KY
4	Pasadena, TX	19	Beaumont, TX
5	Amarillo, TX	20	Fayetteville, NC
6	Corpus Christi, TX	21	Tulsa, OK
7	Laredo, TX	22	Columbus, OH
8	Montgomery, AL	23	Akron, OH
9	Lexington, KY	24	Birmingham, AL
10	Lubbock, TX	25	Augusta, GA
11	Oklahoma City, OK	26	Des Moines, IA
12	Columbus, GA	27	Macon, GA
13	Omaha, NE	28	Wichita, KS
14	Winston-Salem, NC	29	Huntsville, AL
15	Pittsburgh, PA	30	Shreveport, LA

Making a move in retirement all comes down to the numbers. Hopefully this information gives you a good head start.

INCOME SECRET NO. 38:

In the Red Zone? Don't Fumble Your Retirement

The one thing guaranteed to ensure that you don't run out of money in retirement is an annuity. It's a contract between you and an insurance company in which you make a lump sum payment — or series of payments and, in return, you receive regular disbursements which can begin immediately or at a later date.

However, if you haven't retired yet, you shouldn't consider investing in one unless you are already contributing the maximum to other retirement plans, such as an individual retirement account (IRA) or 401(k).

That's because traditional retirement plans provide the same tax deferral as annuities — but without the fees. Of course, you can invest in an annuity inside a tax-advantaged account, but you get no extra tax benefit.

Also, be aware that early-withdrawal penalties and surrender (early termination) fees mean an annuity is useless for short-term saving. You'd need to hold a variable annuity at least 15 years for the benefits of tax deferral to outweigh the extra costs.

That means the ideal pre-retirement annuity buyer is someone who:

- Is making the maximum contributions to other retirement plans.
- Can live without the money until after age 59 1/2.
- Who is in at least the 25% tax bracket to take advantage of the tax deferral.

But that's only relevant to folks still working.

So what about those in the "red zone" — five years before and five years after retirement (or longer)? If that's your position, you also might be a viable candidate if you're concerned about outliving your savings.

That's because annuities can provide a guaranteed stream of income in retirement.

How Annuities Work

Oddly, annuities are insurance products, even though we tend to think of them in terms of investment.

To start one, you make a payment to an insurer — either an upfront lump sum or a series of payments over time. The money grows tax-deferred, like a traditional IRA or 401(k), at a fixed or variable rate — the "accumulation phase."

You pay taxes at regular income rates when you take annuity payments, which the insurer undertakes to make to you for the rest of your life — the "payout phase."

The thing that makes annuities an insurance product is the guaranteed payouts. Even if the insurer loses money on its investments, it is still obligated to pay you. Moreover, annuities can also include a death benefit. This entitles the beneficiary of the annuity — a spouse or children — to the value of your annuity or a guaranteed minimum, whichever is greater.

There are two types of annuities: deferred and immediate. The distinction overlaps with the "accumulation" and "payout" phase of annuities. Here's why:

Accumulation Phase Annuities: Deferred

There are three subtypes of accumulation annuities, the key variable being how much exposure to the equity market they involve:

- **Fixed deferred annuity** — You lock in a guaranteed rate of return for periods ranging from one year to 10 years. The rate is set by the insurer, based on market rates. It can fluctuate, but it will never drop below your guaranteed rate.

  As a result, you won't lose money, but you won't have the potential for growth you'd get by investing in stocks or stock funds. A fixed-rate annuity is worth considering if you have low-risk tolerance and a shorter time horizon to retirement.

Fixed deferred annuities are like certificates of deposit (CD) in that if you hold the money in the annuity to maturity, you will receive a scheduled amount of interest. Unlike a CD, the annuity interest isn't taxed along the way. Tax is deferred until the earnings are withdrawn.

If you pull your money out before the term ends, however, you could incur a surrender charge. At the end of the annuity's term, the insurer will offer a renewal rate with no new surrender charges.

- **Indexed annuity** — This is a type of fixed deferred annuity with a growth rate pegged to the performance of an equity index over a certain term, such as the S&P 500. But the money isn't invested directly into the market. Instead, the market becomes the benchmark for your interest payout.

The key to an indexed annuity is understanding the formula behind your return. You might have a "participation rate" of 50% of S&P 500 index gains during the contract term. If the market rises 10%, you're only going to get 5%. If the market falls, it has a floor, which is generally zero.

While some indexed annuities are tied to the performance of a well-known index, others are tied to one developed by the insurance company. Make sure you ask what investments comprise the index.

The surrender period is usually seven to 10 years for indexed annuities.

- **Variable annuity** — This is the riskiest type of annuity. Your money is invested in accounts that are like mutual funds. You can see substantial gains — or the opposite. That means you have considerable risk because the underlying investments may lose value. It is possible, however, to buy some downside protection by paying extra for a rider that offers a guaranteed minimum withdrawal benefit.

You defer paying tax on earnings while your money is invested by the annuity. You can take a cash distribution after the annuity reaches maturity, and without IRS penalties, after age 59 ½. Those withdrawals are taxable at your ordinary income rate. Because you contributed post-tax money to the annuity, however, part of the payout will be considered a return of capital and not taxable.

When a variable annuity matures, you can choose to "annuitize" it: You turn the accumulated money into an immediate annuity.

Payout Phase Annuities: Immediate

There is nothing preventing you from buying deferred annuities in retirement. But because the surrender period is typically seven to 10 years — and life is uncertain — many people avoid deferred annuities, which are inaccessible until maturity, in favor of immediate annuities.

With immediate annuities, you turn over a lump sum to the insurer, who agrees to give you guaranteed payouts over a certain term — 10 to 20 years, perhaps — or for as long as you live. The guarantees never change. Payouts begin anytime within 13 months of starting the annuity.

The most important variables with an immediate annuity are the size of the contract and the interest rate. But age is important too. The older you are when you buy, the bigger your regular payouts.

The insurance company looks at your age and possibly your health, lifestyle and estimates how long you are expected to live. It then designs the payout of the annuity based on that lifespan.

That means men and women receive different payouts for the same size of annuity and interest rate. Women have longer average lifespans, so their payouts are smaller than men's.

Immediate annuities also offer the flexibility of inflation adjustments and death benefits. For example, you could buy a rider that provides five years of income to you or your beneficiaries or lets you or your heirs receive your full investment. But there's a cost: Reducing risk this way reduces the payout.

A 72-year-old man who invests $100,000 will receive about $675 in immediate lifetime monthly income. But that payout would be cut to $579 a month if he opted for an heir to receive a lump sum of any premium balance at his death.

The Advantages of Annuities

Annuities offer retirees a number of benefits. Here are some pros:

1. **To provide a hedge against longer life spans.**

   According to the Centers for Disease Control (CDC), anyone who reaches 65 years old will likely live into their 80s. Men can expect to live another 18 years and women an additional 20.5 years.

   The longer you expect to live, the more annuities make sense. A longer life span means your money needs to last longer, too.

   Because annuities provide a guaranteed lifetime income, you can avoid depleting all your assets. And since an annuity is a form of insurance, some of the "longevity risk" — the risk of running out of money — moves to the company offering the annuity product.

2. **To impose budget discipline.**

   Annuities force you to manage your money more efficiently. Because the payouts are predetermined, and the form of annuity I'm going to recommend can't be cashed in, you must live within your means.

   As many retirees know, it's easy to tap your retirement portfolio more often than you intend. The biggest threat is "lifestyle creep." You start retirement with 75% of your expenses covered by a pension or other stable monthly income source, but five years later, it's down to 50%. It's all those extra trips to see the grandkids or vacations in the Caribbean.

   The bottom line is that with the right annuity, you can spend only what it's going to pay out every month. Of course, you can generate additional income beyond your annuity payments, but the annuity becomes your baseline.

3. **To ensure peace of mind.**

   You may be a risk-taker, but retirement has a funny way of curing you of that — and fast. Many people are essentially forced to gamble in high-risk investments because they don't have enough money to last. They take huge risks ... and, as is often the case, they lose.

On the other hand, many people are forced to sell stocks during a big market pullback — or worse, they panic. Selling a large chunk of your portfolio in a down market means you'll have less equity to generate income over the rest of your retirement.

Consider two 30-year periods. The first (Scenario A) has three down years, minus 20%, minus 12% and minus 10%, followed by an average annualized return of 6% over 30 years. The second (Scenario B) 30-year period has exactly the reverse sequence of returns — average annualized returns of 6% over 30 years with three down years at the very end.

With a $500,000 portfolio that you want to withdraw $25,000 from every year, the first model runs out of money in 20 years. The second never does.

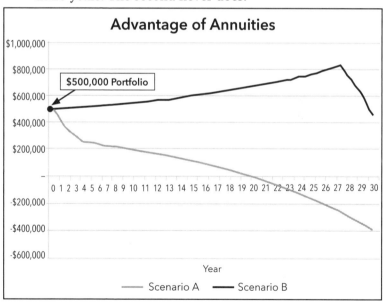

By forcibly preserving capital in the present and generating guaranteed income in the future, the right annuity can ensure that you don't end up like the first model.

Interest Rates and "Laddering"

In recent years, low interest rates have depressed monthly annuity payments. However, there is a risk in waiting for interest rates to rise to buy an immediate annuity.

The Federal Reserve has temporarily kept interest rates steady but has signaled that more hikes may be in the offing. That may prompt you to postpone an annuity purchase until those hikes take effect. But if the market nose-dives, the Fed could put off those increases or reverse them. Buying an annuity then would mean you take a chance to lock in current rates.

One way around this problem is to build an annuity ladder.

Say you have $300,000 to invest in an immediate annuity. You would invest $100,000 this year, another $100,000 in two years and the remaining $100,000 the year after that. By spreading out your purchases, you'd potentially benefit from higher interest rates in later years.

Laddering also allows you to vary the type of annuity. Immediate annuities can be tailored to all sorts of variables. You can specify the number of years you get guaranteed income. You can include life insurance. You can opt for an immediate payout rider.

How Much Is Enough?

Even if you're convinced that an annuity is right for you, DO NOT put your entire portfolio into one. Instead, add up your guaranteed income sources, including Social Security. Then add up your basic expenses, such as housing costs and food. Don't cheat. Factor in nonessential things you know you'll be doing, like travelling and buying gifts for the grandkids.

If there's a gap between your steady income and these essential expenses, buy an immediate annuity to fill it and no more.

That allows you to use the rest of your retirement funds to play the market — to the extent of your risk preferences, of course.

Five Tips When Shopping for an Annuity

Unbeknownst to annuity purchasers, most major annuity providers reward agents for selling their products. These perks include cruises, luxury car leases, theater tickets and golf outings.

Sales rewards like these drive an adviser to recommend an annuity based on his reward, not your needs. Here's how to combat that.

First, ask yourself two questions, and don't let the salesperson distract you from them:

1. What do you want the annuity to guarantee?

2. When do you want that guarantee to start?

Second, avoid being distracted by "hypothetical return" illustrations or costly bells and whistles, such as stepped-up death benefits, that you may not really need. Focus on the bottom line.

Third, ask the agent to show you annuities from multiple companies. If he's only offering products from a single company, or if you're having trouble comparing different products, seek out an opinion from another agent, and pit them against each other.

Fourth, as you narrow your options, ask for a "specimen policy." This is a copy of the actual contract you'd receive after purchasing the annuity. It will help ensure that you see everything before buying.

Finally, after purchasing an annuity, you typically have a "free look" period of about 10 to 30 days, depending on your state. You can review all the details of the contract … and if you decide you've made a mistake, you can terminate it and get a full refund.

Choose Wisely

A sense of caution should be applied when choosing an annuity. That's because in addition to interest rates and actuarial values, immediate annuities can vary based on the financial strength of the insurer.

There are two issues involved — your return and the safety of your money.

First, all else being equal, an insurer with a high credit rating will be able to finance their operations at lower rates. That means they will be able to pay higher average payouts than other insurers.

Second, the insurer's rating also offers the expectation of financial stability. If you're using annuities to generate income over two or three decades, you want to make sure the insurer will be around for the whole time.

What happens if an insurer goes bankrupt? Unlike bank accounts and other types of financial accounts, annuities are governed by state law, not federal law. Each state has its own rules and regulations, and the degree to which they ensure annuities depends on the size of the state's insurance guaranty association pool. That's one reason why many annuity insurers are clustered in states like New York, which have large insurance pools.

Protect your investment by narrowing your search to insurers rated A-minus or better. Above all, find out how much of your investment is covered by the state's insurance guaranty association. Most state guaranty associations cover $250,000 or more in annuity benefits per insurer. (You can check state guaranty limits at the National Organization of Life & Health Insurance Guaranty Associations at www.nolhga.com) If you plan to invest more than your state's limit, divide your money among several companies.

In conclusion, annuities are a great option if you are uncertain about how long your retirement money can last. As long as you discipline yourself and are realistic about your expenses over the years to come, you can decide how much to put into this type of product — which is essentially "income insurance."

Just be careful. Shop for an annuity the way you'd shop for something in which you take a special interest. Don't buy the first thing that comes along. Look for the absolute best you can get for your money.

INCOME SECRET NO. 39:

Get Paid $565 a Month, for LIFE, Simply for "Insuring" Your Nest Egg

"Son, you scared the heck out of us."

The two ladies' gentle Southern drawls strained at the burden of speaking of such distasteful matters. Where I live in the Deep South, dignified ladies don't talk to strangers about their financial affairs.

And they hadn't actually said "heck," either. But I wasn't exactly a stranger.

The ladies had been reading *The Bauman Letter* for some time now. They got it as a trial with one of my colleagues' products. If they weren't sure about renewing before, they certainly were now, they told me.

We had just emerged from one of my presentations at the recent Total Wealth Symposium in Hollywood, Florida. I'd spoken about something I call the "red zone" — the five years before and after retirement.

It's the decade of your life that matters most ... at least when it comes to the way you'll be able to live the rest of it.

I had just presented a chart showing what happens when you retire in a down market and have to liquidate stocks at discount prices to satisfy the IRS' required minimum distribution (RMD) requirements — or simply to survive.

Not to mention supporting an Oscar de la Renta shopping habit.

Taking distributions from a stock portfolio during a historically average 34%, 18-month long bear market drop would mean running out of money in 20 years instead of 30, I'd warned.

I showed scarier charts illustrating why I feel the current bull market is at its top. Lots of red.

"Low interest rates have lashed investors into a stampede to equities that has little to do with the underlying economy or future earnings," I'd said. Everyone is chasing yield ... often using dangerous margin debt to leverage their investments. It's like a loaded mousetrap.

Testing the convention against mixed metaphors, I'd gone on to compare markets to a ballistic missile. A rocket keeps going upward for a while even after the motor cuts out. But gravity ensures that it starts to curve downward at an ever-accelerating pace.

Thus terrified, the ladies had asked to know more about my *Alpha Stock Alert* service, designed to hedge such calamities before they happen.

"But there is another way to avoid running out of money, as well," I told them. Their blue eyes stared at me as if I were the Delphic oracle itself. At least I knew I was making more sense that a half-drugged chief priestess of Apollo.

"But it requires adopting an attitude like Zen Buddhism. You have to take a leap of faith. You need equanimity." I wasn't sure how well references to the Buddha played in Baptist country, but it seemed OK. And I was deep in mixed-metaphor territory now.

"I don't mean pure faith without evidence. In fact, as the Dalai Lama himself would tell you, true faith is always backed by empirical science. I simply mean having faith that what you are doing is the wisest course based on all the factors at play and all the information available ... even if others are telling you differently based on less rational forms of faith."

This Income Secret is about the money-preserving strategy I offered the ladies: The humble annuity.

It's the only thing guaranteed to ensure that you don't run out of money in retirement.

After all, that's the single most common concern I hear from my faithful readers of *The Bauman Letter*.

Why an Annuity?

Let's get one thing straight: If you haven't retired yet, you shouldn't consider investing in an annuity unless you are already contributing the maximum to other retirement plans, such as an individual retirement account (IRA) or 401(k).

That's because traditional retirement plans provide the same tax deferral as annuities — but without the fees (more on that in a moment). Of course, you can invest in an annuity inside a tax-advantaged account, but you get no extra tax benefit.

Also, be aware that early-withdrawal penalties and sur-render (early termination) fees mean an annuity is useless for short-term saving. You'd need to hold a variable annuity at least 15 years for the benefits of tax deferral to outweigh the extra costs.

That means the ideal pre-retirement annuity buyer is someone:

- Who is making the maximum contributions to other retirement plans.
- Who can live without the money until after age 59 1/2.
- Who is in at least the 25% tax bracket to take advantage of the tax deferral.

But that's only relevant to folks still working. The focus here is on those in the "red zone" — five years before and five years after retirement (or longer). If that's you, you also might be a viable candidate if you're concerned about outliving your savings ... as so many of my readers are.

That's because annuities can provide a guaranteed stream of income in retirement. Here are some pros:

1. To provide a hedge against longer life spans.

According to the Centers for Disease Control (CDC), people who were 65 years old in 2017 will likely live into their 80s. After reaching 65, men can expect to live another 18 years and women an additional 20.5 years.

The longer you expect to live, the more annuities make sense. A longer life span means your money needs to last longer, too.

Because annuities provide a guaranteed lifetime income, you can avoid depleting all your assets. And since an annuity is a form of insurance, some of the "longevity risk" — the risk of running out of money — moves to the company offering the annuity product.

2. To impose budget discipline.

Annuities help — no, force — you to manage your money better. Because the payouts are predetermined and the form of annuity I'm going to recommend can't be cashed in, you must live within your means.

As many retirees know, it's easy to tap your retirement portfolio more often than you intend. The biggest threat is "lifestyle creep." You start retirement with 75% of your expenses covered by a pension or other stable monthly income source, but five years later, it's down to 50%. It's all those extra trips to see the grandkids or vacations in Saint Maarten.

The bottom line is that with the right annuity, you can spend only what it's going to pay out every month.

Of course, you can generate additional income beyond your annuity payments, but the annuity becomes your baseline.

3. To ensure peace of mind.

You may be a risk-taker. I know I am. But retirement has a funny way of curing you of that ... and fast.

I hear from many folks who are essentially forced to gamble on high-risk investments because they don't have enough money to last. They take huge risks ... and, as is often the case, they lose.

On the other hand, many people are forced to sell stocks during a big market pullback — or worse, they panic. Selling a large chunk of your portfolio in a down market means you'll have less equity to generate income over the rest of your retirement.

Consider two 30-year periods. The first has three down years, minus 20%, minus 15% and minus 10%, followed by an average annualized return of 6% over 30 years. The second 30year period has exactly the reverse sequence of returns — average annualized returns of 6% over 30 years with three down years at the very end.

With a $500,000 portfolio with an initial 5% annual withdrawal, the first model runs out of money in 20 years. The second never does.

By forcibly preserving capital in the present and generating guaranteed income in the future, the right annuity can ensure that you don't end up like the first model.

How Do Annuities Work?

Oddly, annuities are insurance products, even though we tend to think of them in terms of investment.

To start one, you make a payment to an insurer — either an upfront lump sum or a series of payments over time. The money grows tax-deferred, like a traditional IRA or 401(k), at a fixed or variable rate — the "accumulation phase."

You pay taxes at regular income rates when you take annuity payments, which the insurer undertakes to make to you for the rest of your life — the "payout phase."

The thing that makes an annuity an insurance product is the guaranteed payouts. Even if the insurer loses money on its investments, it is still obligated to pay you. Moreover, annuities can also include a death benefit. This entitles the beneficiary of the annuity — a spouse or children — to the value of your annuity or a guaranteed minimum, whichever is greater.

There are two types of annuities: deferred and immediate. The distinction overlaps with the "accumulation" and "payout" phases of annuities. Here's why...

Accumulation Phase Annuities: Deferred

There are three subtypes of accumulation annuities: fixed deferred, indexed and variable. The key variable is how much exposure to the equity market they involve.

With a fixed deferred annuity, you lock in a guaranteed rate of return for periods ranging from one year to 10 years. They offer a guaranteed interest rate for a certain term, such as five or 10 years. The rate is set by the insurer, based on market rates. It can fluctuate, but it will never drop below your guaranteed rate.

As a result, you won't lose money, but you won't have the potential for growth you'd get by investing in stocks or stock funds. A fixed-rate annuity is worth considering if you have low-risk tolerance and a shorter time horizon to retirement.

Fixed deferred annuities are like certificates of deposit (CD). As with a CD, if you hold the money in the annuity to maturity, you will receive a scheduled amount of interest. Unlike a CD, the annuity's interest isn't taxed along the way. Tax is deferred until the earnings are withdrawn.

If you pull your money out before the term ends, however, you could incur a surrender charge. At the end of the annuity's term, the insurer will offer a renewal rate with no new surrender charges.

Indexed annuities are a type of fixed deferred annuity with a growth rate pegged to the performance of an equity index over a certain term, such as the S&P 500. But the money isn't invested directly into the market. Instead, the market becomes the benchmark for your interest payout.

The key with these annuities is understanding the formula behind your return. You might have a "participation rate" of 50% of S&P 500 Index gains during the contract term. If the market rises 10%, you're only going to get 5%. If the market falls, it has a floor, which is generally zero.

While some indexed annuities are tied to the performance of a well-known index, others are tied to one developed by the insurance company. Make sure you ask what investments comprise the index.

The surrender period is usually seven or 10 years for indexed annuities.

A variable annuity is the riskiest type. Your money is invested in accounts that are like mutual funds.

You can see substantial gains — or the opposite. That means you have unlimited upside but also unlimited downside. It is possible, however, to buy some downside protection by paying extra for a rider that offers a guaranteed minimum withdrawal benefit.

You defer paying tax on earnings while your money is invested by the annuity. You can take a cash distribution after the annuity reaches maturity, and without IRS penalties, after age 59 ½. Those withdrawals are taxable at your ordinary income rate. Because you contributed post-tax money to the annuity, however, part of the payout will be considered a return of capital and not taxable.

When a variable annuity matures, you can choose to "annuitize" it: You turn the accumulated money into an immediate annuity, which I will discuss below.

Payout Phase Annuities: Immediate

There is nothing preventing you from buying deferred annuities in retirement. But because the surrender period is typically seven to 10 years — and life is uncertain — many people avoid deferred annuities, which are inaccessible until maturity, in favor of immediate annuities.

With immediate annuities, you turn over a lump sum to the insurer, who agrees to give you guaranteed payouts over a certain term — 10 to 20 years, perhaps — or for as long as you live. The guarantees never change. Payouts begin anytime within 13 months of starting the annuity.

The most important variables with an immediate annuity are the size of the contract and the interest rate. But age is important too. The older you are when you buy, the bigger your regular payouts.

That's because immediate annuities are based on actuarial values of life span. The insurance company looks at your age and possibly your health, lifestyle and estimates how long you are expected to live. It then designs the payout of the annuity based on that lifespan.

That means men and women receive different payouts for the same size of annuity and interest rate. Women have longer average lifespans, so their payouts are smaller than men's.

Immediate annuities also offer the flexibility of inflation adjustments and death benefits. For example, you could buy a rider that provides five years of income to you or your beneficiaries, or lets you or your heirs receive your full investment. But there's a cost: Reducing risk this way reduces the payout.

For example, a 72-year-old man in Washington, D.C., who invests $100,000 will receive about $675 in immediate lifetime monthly income. But that payout would be cut to $579 a month if he opted for an heir to receive a lump sum of any premium balance at his death.

Interest Rates and "Laddering"

In recent years, low interest rates have depressed monthly annuity payments. But rates have begun to move up and are expected to climb higher. As a result, annuity payouts are rising as well.

For example, right now, a 65-year-old Georgia man who invests $100,000 in a single-life immediate annuity would receive an average monthly payment of $543. The average monthly payment was $506 in late 2016. That's a 7.3% difference in less than a year.

But there's a risk in waiting for interest rates to rise to buy an immediate annuity.

The Federal Reserve has signaled that it plans for more hikes. That may prompt you to postpone an annuity purchase until those hikes take effect. But if the market nose-dives, the Fed could put off those increases or reverse them. Buying an annuity then would mean you take a chance to lock in current rates.

One way around this problem is to build an annuity ladder.

Say you have $300,000 to invest in an immediate annuity. You would invest $100,000 this year, another $100,000 in two years and the remaining $100,000 the year after that. By spreading out your purchases, you'd potentially benefit from higher interest rates in later years.

Laddering also allows you to vary the type of annuity. Immediate annuities can be tailored to all sorts of variables. You can specify the number of years you get guaranteed income. You can include life insurance. You can opt for an immediate payout rider.

Here's a table showing the options available to a 65-year-old man in Georgia, where I live:

Life	$543
Life insurance & 5 years guaranteed	$542
Life insurance & 10 years guaranteed	$532
Life insurance & 15 years guaranteed	$514
Life insurance & 20 years guaranteed	$489
Life insurance with cash refund	$492
5-year period guaranteed	$1,705
10-year period guaranteed	$914
15-year period guaranteed	$661
20-year period guaranteed	$546
25-year period guaranteed	$482

As you can see, you have many options — each of which can be implemented for each annuity in your ladder.

How Much?

Even if I've convinced you to consider an annuity, don't put your entire portfolio into one. That's certainly not what I'm suggesting!

Instead, add up your guaranteed income sources, including Social Security. Then add up your basic expenses, such as housing costs and food. Don't cheat. Factor in nonessential things you know you'll be doing, like traveling and buying gifts for the grandkids.

If there's a gap between your steady income and these essential expenses, buy an immediate annuity to fill it and no more.

That allows you to use the rest of your retirement funds to play the market — to the extent of your risk preferences, of course.

To take an admittedly self-interested example, if you set up your laddered annuity plan and then invested $100,000 in my Alpha Stock system, your pretax return at the end of August would look like this compared to the S&P 500:

Investment: $100,000	
Alpha Stock return	$10,569.45
S&P 500 return	$4,886.64
Excess: $5,682.80 • Excess %: 116%	

That extra return is a nice trip to the Bahamas, or a lot of presents at Christmas.

Of course, the Alpha Stock system is quite low-risk, so it might be possible to do even better if you have the appetite for it.

Beware of the Fees Monster

A recent study by Senator Elizabeth Warren (D-Mass.) examined 15 major annuity providers. It found that all but two offer perks to reward agents for selling their products. The perks include cruises, luxury car leases, theater tickets and golf outings. None of the companies clearly disclosed the sales incentives to annuity purchasers.

Sales rewards like these drive advisers to recommend an annuity based on their reward, not your needs. Here's how to combat that.

First, when you shop for an annuity, ask two questions, and don't let the salesperson distract you from them:

1. What do you want the annuity to guarantee?

2. When do you want that guarantee to start?

Second, avoid being distracted by "hypothetical return" illustrations or costly bells and whistles, such as stepped-up death benefits, that you may not really need. Focus on the bottom line.

Third, ask the agent to show you annuities from multiple companies. If he's only offering products from a single company, or if you're having trouble comparing different products, seek out another opinion from another agent, and pit them against each other.

Fourth, as you narrow your options, ask for a "specimen policy." This is a copy of the actual contract you'd receive after purchasing the annuity. It will help ensure that you see everything before buying.

Finally, after purchasing an annuity, you typically have a "free look" period of about 10 to 30 days, depending on your state. You can review all the details of the contract ... and if you decide you've made a mistake, you can terminate it and get a full refund.

Don't Choose Poorly

In the great flick "Indiana Jones and the Last Crusade," there's a memorable scene where a greedy Nazi drinks from the wrong cup and disintegrates into dust. The ancient knight who's been guarding the real grail comments drily: "He chose poorly."

That sense of caution applies to annuities, too, although the stakes aren't so high — and the odds are far, far better than picking one cup out of dozens. That's because in addition to interest rates and actuarial values, immediate annuities can vary based on the financial strength of the insurer.

There are two issues involved: your return and the safety of your money.

First, all else being equal, an insurer with a high credit rating will be able to finance their operations at lower rates. That means they will be able to pay higher average payouts than other insurers.

Second, the insurer's rating also offers the expectation of financial stability. If you're using annuities to generate income over two or three decades, you want to make sure the insurer will be around for the whole time.

That raises an issue that many people ask me: What happens if an insurer goes bankrupt, like a bad holy grail copy?

Unlike bank accounts and other types of financial accounts, annuities are governed by state law, not federal law. Each state has its own rules and regulations, and the degree to which they ensure annuities depends a lot on the size of the state's insurance guaranty association pool. That's one reason why many annuity insurers are clustered in states like New York, which have large insurance pools.

The good news is that only six insurers licensed to sell annuities and life insurance have entered receivership since 2008, and most were small, regional companies. Even so, protect your investment by narrowing your search to insurers rated A-minus or better.

Above all, find out how much of your investment is covered by the state's insurance guaranty association. Most state guaranty associations cover $250,000 or more in annuity benefits per insurer. (You can check state guaranty limits at the National Organization of Life & Health Insurance Guaranty Associations, at www.nolhga.com.) If you plan to invest more than your state's limit, divide your money among several companies.

Conclusion

Annuities are a great option if you are uncertain about how long your money can last. As long as you discipline yourself and are realistic about your expenses over the years to come, you can decide how much to put into this type of product — which is essentially "income insurance."

But be careful. As one commenter has said, annuities are the "Wild West" of U.S. financial markets. Salesmen have powerful incentives to sell you products that may not be your best choice.

So, shop for an annuity the way you'd shop for something in which you take a special interest. For me, it's guitars. For you, perhaps it's cars or jewelry.

In other words, don't buy the first thing that comes along. Look for the absolute best you can get for your money.

After all, it's a big chunk of all the money you're ever going to have.

PASSION TO PROFITS

Adding to your income doesn't mean that you need to take on a typical nine-to-five job. Resourceful people have come up with creative sources of income in the new "gig economy." This is an opportunity to dedicate a little of your free time and possibly some skills that you've learned over years to rake in some extra cash. Learn how you can earn extra money with the photos you took on your last vacation. Turn your favorite hobby into an easy source of cash. You can even get paid doing routine activities such as watching TV. Turn your passion into profit.

INCOME SECRET NO. 40:

Turn Your Hobby Into a Secret Income Gold Mine

Using the collectibles market to increase your fortune means honing in on some of your hobbies or special interests, and putting your unique knowledge to work. If you love baseball, you'll have fun gathering old trading cards. If you're a comic collector, then I'll bet the idea of hunting down a rare variant cover of your favorite issue appeals to you.

The same goes for coin collectors, watch enthusiasts, art lovers, wine connoisseurs, fans of rare manuscripts and so on. And no matter what, you have the thrill of the hunt — all while using an investment strategy that's proven to be exceedingly profitable for those who know how to search for the right collectibles.

Historical price charts for collectibles tend to show a very similar pattern. Be it coins, comic books or rare wines, collectibles have a history of outperforming traditional assets over time. And they tend to do so with far less volatility or correlation to traditional investment assets.

It's only logical when you consider that collectibles tend to be held in "strong hands," meaning they're largely owned by aficionados who rarely part with their collections just because of economic tribulations. That gives them stability and provides a certain counterbalance to an investment portfolio.

Of course, that doesn't mean collectibles won't fall in value; they can and do at times. But if you're investing in the long haul with the idea that you will sell a collection at auction one day — to supplement retirement or maybe pay for a kid's college education — then the growing demand for certain areas of the collectibles world means that key items will likely retain their value or grow in value over time.

These assets are called "quiet wealth" for a reason: They can help you keep some of your wealth out of the government's hands. Various organizations and Western governments around the world these days are talking about a "wealth tax" — let's call it what it truly is: wealth confiscation — as the last, best way to extinguish what is now an unmanageable debt load that our elected leaders have accumulated for us. If we ever reach the point where America imposes such a tax, the hit men in the IRS aren't likely to include hard-to-value, nonfinancial assets in their calculations. Collectibles, then, would be a perfectly legitimate and legal means of shielding your assets from a government that is increasingly desperate for money. It's a store of wealth that potentially has a government buffer built around it.

And collectibles — true collectibles that can't be mass-produced — hold value over time because of the nostalgia factor. Sometimes they even become a part of pop culture. Collectors want to hold on to their conquests and are willing to pay big money for them.

And that means huge profit potential.

For example, the Codex Leicester, a compilation of scientific writings by Leonardo da Vinci, was purchased in 1980 for $5.148 million and it sold for about $30 million just 14 years later. The profit-gain increased by 443.9%, or 31.7% per annum.

Another example is the Fender Stratocaster guitar. One went on sale for a whopping quarter of a million dollars. It originally listed for about $250, so that's a 10,000% appreciation.

Not bad!

Nice profits aren't that rare, either. In fact, collectibles have been known to outperform other, more common investing avenues. In December 2014, CNBC reported that overall, investing in high-end collectibles was more lucrative than investing in stocks. Even during the incredible bull market from 2010 to 2020, the Knight Frank Luxury Index (which tracks collectibles from cars and art to stamps, wine, coins and furniture) was up about 150% while the Dow Jones Industrial Average was up 132%. (By itself, rare whisky was up 540%.)

This is one investment avenue that is too often overlooked by investors, and I want to give you some key tips to get started.

8 Beginner Tips for Making Money in Collectibles

Each collectible category demands a unique approach for making the most of your investment. But no matter if you're investing in wine, coins or comics, there are commonalities to keep in mind. Because the basic strategy is always the same: You need to buy the right item at the right time, preserve it well and sell it at the right moment to the right buyer.

It's deceptively simple. See, although the strategy seems like common sense, it takes an intimate knowledge of the market to execute correctly. If you don't have a healthy knowledge, it becomes extremely difficult to successfully invest money in collectibles.

Just consider the wide range of questions you have to answer: How do you begin your search? What trends are peaking? Which dealer is the perfect candidate to rate your item? What's the best way to keep your collectible in tip-top shape? What auction house should you use — if you use any?

To get you started, I've put together a list of eight tips a novice collector should keep in mind.

Let's jump right in and start with the most important piece of advice...

1. Stay on top of the market you're invested in. All collectibles depend on three main factors: interest, scarcity and condition. Those are the biggies that span every area of the market, and each category demands that a collector be aware of the area they're invested in. So do your homework! That means keeping up on the latest trends, from current interests to the speculative market.

For example, many comic books shoot up in value once they've made it to the big screen. So there's an entire speculative market built around any superhero movies slotted for an upcoming release. I suggest joining a blog or an online community that will keep you updated on your area. For instance, in our sports memorabilia report, we suggest joining Sports Collectors Daily, a blog devoted to delivering sports collecting news stories. You can also set up Google alerts to let you know whenever a key word/phrase is mentioned in a news story. Basically, make sure that you have a way to hear about a new development as soon as it occurs.

And for those of you who might like to step away from your computer, it's never a bad idea to familiarize yourself with a local collectibles store. The owners are on the ground floor, dealing with comics on a daily basis. It's the ideal environment for getting a better handle on which characters or issues are rising in demand. The same goes for trading card stores, etc.

You should also visit a local auction if you get the chance. It will give you a behind-the-scenes look at the auction process — and that will help you out immeasurably once you decide to sell your collectible. Plus, there are social networking sites which not only connect you with fellow collectors, but also can be a source for finding items for sale.

That just covers interest — the first factor. As for **scarcity**, a little research will get you a long way. After you narrow down the items you're interested in, you should dig around to find out how many baseball cards come in a certain set, how many variant covers of a particular comic book issue were released, how many coins are in circulation, and so on. Basically, learn everything you can about the history and current status of your item. It'll give an idea of why people would want a certain collectible … and then you must ask yourself if this reason will always exist. That knowledge is a major factor when considering a buy.

Of course, there are also plenty of dealers and experts out there who are intimately acquainted with this knowledge, but it's never a bad idea to do your own research. As for finding your ideal dealer, I'll get to that in a moment. For now, just keep in mind that you will want to consult an expert, either when you're looking for an item or when you've already scored one and need to know the value.

Finally, you have to consider the **condition**. One tear, smudge or crease can mean thousands of dollars gone. On the other hand, a rare misprint could mean thousands more. So again, research is your friend! By learning everything you can about a collectible, you'll be able to get an idea of the value of various conditions.

For example, by looking up PSA Sports' trading card price guides, you can find the value PSA Sports assigns to a mint card, as opposed to a poor card. It's not much different than when researching the value of a car. Better condition vehicles can be worth more than poorly maintained vehicles. There are also price guides for just about any collectible you can imagine: comic books, coins, guitars, wines, movie posters, etc.

Ultimately, just remember this: Don't invest in collectibles when you aren't familiar with the market. If you're not interested enough in the hobby to spend some time each week — or, at the very least, each month — to keep up with the fluctuations in the market, you probably shouldn't invest in that hobby. It's no different than investing in stocks: In order to make the best of a trade, you have to keep up with the company.

2. Don't let emotions get in the way. Since this is an investing practice tied to hobbies and special areas of interest, emotions have a habit of getting in the way. For example, if your dad took you to every Mets game growing up, you'll probably have great memories of going to the ballpark. Like getting a hot dog, while watching a player such as, say, future Hall of Fame pitcher Nolan Ryan walk across the field. Then you might be willing to spend an exorbitant amount just to own his glove — and end up paying much more than the value.

So you should always ask yourself this: What is the value of my collectible, and will it appreciate?

The bottom line is that by admiring a collectible too much, you risk losing money. And if your goal is to make money, then too much admiration will get in the way of good decisions. If you really are investing, not collecting, don't let your emotions get in the way of your business sense.

While I recommend loving the item you get, you should also be logical. Refer to your research and/or a professional, and always remember that an item is an investment. Buy when it's cheap and sell when it's expensive. That's the long and short of it.

3. Find the best dealer. There are plenty of disreputable dealers out there, and fraud has been a problem in more than one area of the collectibles market. Know who you're buying from. Don't buy from eBay or an unknown auction house when you're first getting started. In fact, buy directly from the best dealer if possible — one you know you can trust. That means researching your candidate thoroughly.

In early 2000, forged signatures and fraudulent memorabilia of famous athletes were a rampant issue. In 2000, the FBI's Operation Bullpen revealed that $500 million to $900 million of autographed sports memorabilia were attributed to forgeries. In 2016, a man was charged in connection to a $2.5 million wire fraud scheme that involved an alleged five-year span of selling counterfeit sports memorabilia. This is why it is important to do your research and confirm authenticity.

So, many athletes now enter contract agreements with memorabilia retailers, where they promise to autograph items that will be sold only through that company. By doing your research, you can easily tell if a dealer has the right to sell a signed piece.

Of course, that's only for certain pieces of sports memorabilia. If you're in the market for another collectible area, though, doing your due diligence and researching the dealer will place you with a reputable company more often than not.

In the end, the old saying rings true here: If you come across a deal that seems too good to be true, it probably is.

4. Have your most valuable items professionally graded. As much research as you accomplish, you still want to have the experts take a look at your item. Professional grading means having an independent company assess the authenticity and condition of your item.

Grading can only increase the value, so the cost is normally worth it — specifically for any item with a value of $500 or more. For items of lesser value, the cost can become a significant part of an item's value, so it should be considered on a case-by-case basis.

And if you choose to do so, you can always discard the professional grading. It's not written in stone.

A professional service will also often seal it so that the condition can't be altered. For example, the Certified Guaranty Company (CGC) provides encapsulation storage that gives the optimum long-term protection for a comic book copy.

So this is something I stress: Professional grading is only helpful with your most valuable items.

5. Keep your collectible secure. As I mentioned, condition is key. The value of many collectibles is directly tied to the state of the item, and the reason makes sense. Since much of a collectible's value is tied to nostalgia — and is therefore based on emotional value — buyers are picky about the condition. That means if you improperly store an item, you can run the risk of losing your investment.

Again, I suggest getting a professional service to seal your item. And when considering storage, keep in mind the environment. A damp, humid environment is a comic book killer. Direct sunlight can fade your rare manuscripts or baseball cards, and so on. Remember that most categories of collectibles have price guides classifying how much an item is worth in pristine condition and what sort of damage degrades it, by what percentage of value. For instance, a well-read copy of The Amazing Spider-Man No. 1 may be worth only 30% to 60% of the $6,000 list price, depending what degree of wear it displays.

You can prevent that type of scenario by learning how to properly store and treat your collectibles.

6. Plan your exit strategy. It's easy to fall in love with a purchase, hide it away and forget that you need to have an exit plan. Years can pass as your rare movie poster signed by Marilyn Monroe gathers dust. Trends can come and go, and you may have missed your sterling opportunity to get the best price.

This ties directly back to my advice about staying on top of your market and about finding a reputable dealer. First off, being in the know means being knowledgeable enough to recognize the best opportunities for banking on your investment. So you always want to be up to date.

Second, you should have an idea of the dealer you want to use when you decide to sell. Dealers exist primarily to serve the needs of collectors — so investors should proceed with caution. Many investors do their research on which collectible to buy, and haggle with dealers to get the best possible price, but they forget to consider their exit options. When it's time to sell, they find that a large chunk of their profits are wiped out by an auctioneer's commission (which can go up to 25% oftentimes) or by dealer margins (often more than 50%).

So, even when you first buy your collectible, plan an exit strategy. That way, you're not hit with unexpected fees upon selling your collectible.

7. Diversify your investments. One of the reasons many investors get into collectibles is to diversify their portfolio. It's the basic rule of thumb: Never have all of your eggs in one basket. So, just as it doesn't make sense to have all of your money in stocks, it doesn't make sense to have all of your money in collectibles.

Figure out how much of your wealth you're willing to devote to collectibles, and stick to it.

8. Be patient. It's always nice when you can make an event-based stock trade and collect gains within a couple of weeks or months. Well, the collectibles market oftentimes doesn't work that way. Collectibles are simply not an avenue for immediate profits. They can take years to surge in value, even decades. Of course, there are those happy moments when you buy the first issue of an obscure comic series right before the movie gets announced, and the comic's value soars. But that's not something to bank on because it's a fairly rare event.

When collecting, you generally have to think in terms of a five- to 15-year plan in order to realize profits. Just be patient, and remember that you should love what you're buying in the event that you're stuck with your item. I always like to think that if I'm buying what appeals to me, there's probably someone else to whom it will appeal, as well. It's a win-win.

A Final Note

If there's one message when starting your collection, it's this: Do your homework, buy what you love, deal with reputable people and have fun with it. That's the collectibles market boiled down.

Although this can be an area that requires some time and effort, it's clearly a great hobby that can reward you with fantastic profits. And it's an ideal way to diversify your portfolio with inflation-proof wealth while doing something you genuinely enjoy. I can't think of many investment areas with that definition.

INCOME SECRET NO. 41:

Get Paid to Do Routine Activities

In a perfect world, they'd pay you to watch TV. You'd get a bonus for paying your bills each month, and you'd collect $100 or more for stopping by your hair salon or barber shop.

Well, welcome to that perfect world.

You can do all of those things. And here's how...

First of all, there are numerous companies that will pay you to watch videos and TV shows. For example, Netflix, the most popular subscription video streaming service on the planet, periodically hires "taggers" — or editorial analysts, if you want to get technical about it. These are folks who watch Netflix's programming and enter relevant metadata (words or phrases that describe the content) into the company's database to make it easier to search and categorize and also to provide accurate recommendations to fellow subscribers.

According to MoneyPantry.com, Netflix taggers watch approximately 10 to 20 hours of programming per week. These positions are posted on the Netflix job board (https://jobs. netflix.com) and are perfect if you like to binge-watch movies, TV series and special programming.

Of course, there are only a limited number of positions available at Netflix, and the competition for them is fierce. But they're not the only game in town. There are many other pay-to-watch TV services.

One of them is Marketforce Information, which has a "Certified Field Associate" program (https://www. certifiedfieldassociate.com) that pays you $10 to $20 per hour to watch Netflix or to be a Theater Checker, visiting movie theaters on the weekends and — among other things — collecting box office information or recording all trailers on all screens prior to the assigned feature.

And then there's Swagbucks (https://www.swagbucks.com), where you can earn money for watching a variety of themed videos ranging from world news to sports and entertainment. When you're ready to be paid, you can redeem your bucks for gift cards or PayPal cash.

Inbox Dollars (https://www.inboxdollars.com) also allows you to make money watching short videos on a daily basis. You get paid with cash and earn your first $5 just for signing up.

Not interested in spending a lot of time at the movies or in front of the tube? Here's another option: Download the MoneyLion app (https://app.moneylion.com). It offers rewards — including gift cards to restaurants, such as Chili's, Romano's Macaroni Grill, Maggiano's Little Italy and On the Border, plus to AMC Theaters — just for staying on top of your finances.

That's right — you earn rewards by:

- Signing up for a free MoneyLion account.
- Downloading the mobile app.
- Connecting a bank account to track spending.
- Sign up for free credit monitoring.
- Make bill payments on time.
- Get a loan.
- More rewards with MoneyLion Plus Cashback bonuses — $1 every day just for logging into the MoneyLion app (exclusive to MoneyLion Plus members).

For more information or to join, visit https://www. moneylion.com.

Now, while discussing ways to earn rewards for doing what otherwise are daily routines, here is a way to get cash back.

Rakuten Rewards (formerly Ebates) is a cash back and discount website that helps its members earn when spending. What does that mean for you? All you have to do it become a member — free of charge — and begin your online shopping at www.rakuten.com. From there, you'll find over 2,500 of the biggest stores and boutiques, including Amazon, Macy's, Kohl's,

Zulily, Nike, even Travelocity. From that, you can earn as much as 10% cash back.

Simply search for the store you want, sign in and shop. From that, you get a check in the mail or can be paid through a PayPal payment. It's that simple! Seemingly almost too good to be true. Plus, you can get a $10 bonus just for signing up. This is the ultimate easy way to make money for doing what you would be doing anyway.

And finally, this hair-raising opportunity...

Every time you go for a haircut, your locks end up on the salon or barbershop floor, where they usually get swept up and disposed of. Instead, you can sell your hair for anywhere from $100 to $4,000!

As long as you have hair that is at least six inches long, there are buyers from around the world — often wig manufacturers — who'll pay good money for those precious strands. All you need to do is go to Hairsellon.com, register for a free account, post an ad and wait for the offers to come pouring in.

And the great thing about hair is that it'll grow back, so you can make this an ongoing, profitable side hustle. For more information, visit www.hairsellon.com.

INCOME SECRET NO. 42:

Earn Thousands Per Year Writing About Your Favorite Hobby Online

Do you have a favorite hobby? Perhaps it's collecting memorabilia, restoring vintage cars, photography, crafting ... the list goes on and on.

Chances are, many other people share your interest and would like to learn more about it and/or profit from this knowledge. So, why not start a blog and write about it on a regular basis?

How exactly do you make money from blogging? By being more than just a writer, but also an entrepreneur running a small business and using your blog as a lead generator for products and services.

Blogging can earn you money in several ways ... from simple Google AdSense revenue to affiliate sales.

With AdSense (https://www.google.com/adsense), you place Google ads on your website. When a visitor clicks on it, Google pays you 68% of what the advertiser pays them.

Affiliate sales are a business model in which you endorse someone else's products or services in exchange for a commission — typically 50% or more.

How much you make by blogging depends on the quality of your blog, how long it's been online and how much traffic is directed to your site.

A survey of 1,500 ProBlogger readers found the majority made only about $1,278, but 9% made between $1,000 and $10,000 per month and 4% made over $10,000 per month.

So, how do you become a part of the 13%? The process, according to ProBlogger, involves:

- **Setting up your blog.** First, you choose a topic for your blog (for example, health, marketing or gardening) and focus on that one topic. Next, you pick a relevant domain name and purchase it. Then, find an affordable web host, install WordPress and upload a good-looking template so your blog looks professional.

• **Creating useful content.** To make your blog worth reading, you'll need to research keywords your audience is typing into search engines. You'll find these using keyword tools such as SEMrush, Ahrefs and the Google Keyword Planner. Also, research the kind of content shared on social media. This can be done by running blogs on the same topic as yours through BuzzSumo, which analyzes what content performs best.

• **Converting visitors to email subscribers.** How much money you make as a blogger will depend on how many recurring visitors you have. Ways to lure subscribers include an email marketing platform (to send mass emails), sign-up forms on the blog and a bribe to subscribe in the form of a free giveaway.

• **Building engagement with readers.** Before sending readers links to your sales pages, build their trust by delivering content that provides them with great value for free. When they realize your advice actually works, they'll not only trust you but also be more likely to purchasing the products or services you have to offer.

• Making money from a variety of income streams by selling products or services your audience wants. These can include:

   o Education such as coaching, courses, books, e-books and seminars.

   o Services such as financial, programming, design, copywriting and marketing.

   o Digital goods such as templates, music, software, photography and games.

   o Physical goods such as art, electronics, clothing, supplements and food.

There are many sites devoted to showing you how to build a successful blog. These include: Backlinko, DigitalMarketer and Smart Passive Income. And for more tips on starting and maintaining a moneymaking blog, visit: https://smartblogger.com/make-money-blogging.

INCOME SECRET NO. 43:

Turn a Lifetime of Knowledge Into Cash

When your children were growing up, there were probably a lot of nights that you sat at the kitchen table, helping them with their math or science homework. Or maybe you were an ace at flashcards. Or maybe you helped them achieve that next reading level through nightly lessons.

While your kids might be grown and raising their own kids, that doesn't mean your nights of tutoring are over.

Only this time, you could get paid for your time in actual cash.

At Tutors.com, it costs anywhere from $25 to $100 per hour for tutoring help in the subject areas of math, economics, languages, sciences and programming. Most tutors start at around $11 per hour, but your pay rate varies based on the difficulty of the subject and can increase as you gain experience.

Some high demand areas of knowledge include:

- Calculus.
- Discrete Math.
- Physics.
- Chemistry/Organic Chemistry.
- Statistics/College Statistics.
- Finance.
- Economics.
- Accounting.
- German.
- French.
- Italian.
- Nursing.

Another option is Chegg Tutors (https://www.chegg.com). The company has higher requirements for its tutors, but those tutors will be paid $20 per hour at the start.

Use your free time to help someone expand their knowledge and earn money.

INCOME SECRET NO. 44:

Spending Time With Man's Best Friend Can Increase Your Income

We love our four-legged friends. They are companions and a frequent source of amusement and love in our lives.

But vacations and emergencies that draw us away from home mean we need someone reliable to care for our dog or cat.

That's where the reliable pet sitter comes in.

According to Statista.com, pet industry expenditures in the United States were estimated to reach $99 billion in 2020, while pet care services such as sitting, board, grooming and walking are estimated to reach $8.1 billion in 2023. And it's still growing.

Pet sitting offers the pet a calm, private home rather than the noise and anxiety of a kennel environment.

And if you're an animal lover, this is an easy way to make some extra money out of your own home without a lot of effort. For pet sitting, there's no extensive training or certifications required.

On sites such as Rover (https://www.rover.com) or Care. com (https://www.care.com/pet-care), you can post a profile, which will include your rates (e.g., $25 per night or $15 to $20 per hour), your availability and photos of yourself, your family, any pets you may have and the space your animal guest will be staying in.

The director of operations for Rover.com estimates that a person who treats pet sitting as a part-time job, taking two or three dogs for two weeks out of a month will earn $1,000 per month on average.

Someone treating pet sitting as a full-time job can earn roughly $3,300 a month on average.

If you're an animal lover, that's an easy way to rake in a little extra income doing something you already enjoy.

AROUND THE HOUSE

G reat sources of potential income and cost-cutting ideas don't have to be limited to your investments and retirement planning strategies. There are plenty of opportunities to increase your savings around your own home. From making smarter decisions with your brand-name prescriptions to taking advantage of the cash-back rewards to attending a class that could potentially trim up to 15% off your auto insurance to making money off the clutter you're already planning to clear out, there are several overlooked options that could put money back into your pocket.

INCOME SECRET NO. 45:

Switch to a Cash-Back Rewards Gas Credit Card

Gas prices are once again on the rise. As each trip to the pump threatens to take a bigger bite out of your wallet, it's time to take back a little more of your money.

If you haven't done so already, consider applying for a gas-company credit card that offers cash-back rebates with your purchases. You can save up to $600 per year on this kind of program.

For example, BP has a loyalty rewards program called BPme Rewards. It allows customers to earn at a rate of $0.05 off per gallon for every $100 spent on BP or Amoco fuel.

For your added convenience, you can link your BPme Rewards account to your qualified debit or credit card and automatically earn and use fuel rewards every time you swipe your card at a BP or Amoco gas pump.

For more details about the BPme Rewards program or to join, visit www.bp.com/en_us/united-states/home/products-and-services/our-rewards/bpme-rewards.html.

Other gas companies such as Shell and Speedway offer similar rebate programs. For example, Shell Fuel Rewards members earn $0.05 per gallon at Shell stations. You can also save up to $0.10 per gallon for every $50 you spend at participating restaurants, car rentals, events and more when using a linked card. For more details or to participate, visit www.fuelrewards.com/fuelrewards.

Meanwhile, Speedway Speedy Rewards members earn 20 points per dollar on in-store purchases and 10 points per gallon on their fuel purchases. These points can be redeemed for free featured items such as food, beverages, fuel discounts and gift cards using Speedway's mobile app. For more information, visit www.speedway.com/SpeedyRewards.

If you depend on personal transportation, cash-back programs are a great way to fill up your tank and get rewarded for your customer loyalty.

INCOME SECRET NO. 46:

Save 15% on Auto Insurance by Taking This Course

Sick of paying high auto insurance premiums — especially when you've never had an accident?

Then enroll in a defensive driving safety course to save up to 15% on your auto insurance.

If 15% doesn't sound like a significant savings, do the math: For every $1,000 per year you spend on auto insurance, you could be saving $150. Depending on where you live and your previous driving record, that could mean savings of anywhere from $150 to $450 or more ... every year you drive.

Defensive driving classes are often sponsored by groups such as AARP, AAA and the Safety Council to promote better motoring skills — and therefore, less risk of accidents — among both older and younger drivers. These courses, which can be conducted in a classroom or online, usually range in cost from $15 to $100, but are worth the investment.

According to AARP: "By taking a driver refresher course you'll learn the current rules of the road, defensive driving techniques and how to operate your vehicle more safely in today's increasingly challenging driving environment. And you'll learn how you can manage and accommodate common age-related changes in vision, hearing and reaction time."

AARP notes that 34 states and Washington, D.C., mandate a discount for safe-driving classes. These states include Alabama, Alaska, Arkansas, California, Colorado, Connecticut, Delaware, Florida, Georgia, Idaho, Illinois, Kansas, Kentucky, Louisiana, Maine, Minnesota, Mississippi, Montana, Nevada, New Jersey, New Mexico, New York, North Dakota, Oklahoma, Oregon, Pennsylvania, Rhode Island, South Carolina, Tennessee, Utah, Virginia, Washington, West Virginia and Wyoming.

The mandated discounts cover all drivers who take the courses, regardless of their age, with the exception of New Mexico, which prohibits the discount for drivers under 50.

However, some but not all insurers in non-mandated states offer discounts for course participation, according to the Insurance Information Institute.

Also, some state-mandated insurers do not accept online classes, so you should speak with your insurance company or agent before signing up for a defensive driving course to verify whether you can get credit for taking an online class and find out how much of a discount you can expect.

Age requirements can vary from state to state and among insurers. Some offer discounts after the age of 50. Meanwhile, some insurers offer discounts for those 25 and younger, while others reserve the discount for those 21 and below.

Here's a rundown of what some of the major insurers have offered (depending on the state) for both older and younger drivers who take a defensive driving class, according to company representatives and the insurer's website:

- Farmers Insurance — About a 10% discount for older drivers and up to 10% for younger drivers.
- State Farm — Up to 10% for both older and younger drivers.
- Nationwide — About 5% for both older and younger drivers.
- Esurance — About 5% for older drivers and up to 15% for younger drivers.
- Geico — About 5% for both older and younger drivers.
- Allstate and The Hartford — Up to 10% for all drivers, any age.
- Liberty Mutual, Progressive and USAA — About 5% for both older and younger drivers.

Besides saving you money on your insurance premiums, a defensive driving course could also result in a reduction of points on your driver's license and waiver of a fine following a driving violation ticket.

But best of all, it'll help make you a better driver and safer on the road.

INCOME SECRET NO. 47:

Review Your Auto Insurance Bill to Save $531

We've all seen the commercials telling us to shop around for a better rate because we may be paying more than necessary with our current carrier. And in some cases, it can be true.

According to the federal Consumer Price Index (CPI), car insurance rates usually rise an average of 3% to 4% per year, but rates have been jumping faster in recent years.

In December 2016, car insurance rates shot up 7% from the same time a year earlier. In 2017, it was 5%. In 2018, it was up 6%.

And it was up another 2% in 2019 in the wake of revenue losses due to costly car accidents and natural disasters.

Advances in safety and technology within cars have resulted in a steeper price increase over the past several years. Even if you haven't gotten a new, more advanced car, you might have seen your insurance increase with everyone else's.

So, it's best to at least shop around to see if you're getting the best rate possible. A couple of phone calls or web searches can really pay off.

For example, if you or your spouse are 50 years of age or over, requesting a rate quote from the AARP Auto Insurance Program from The Hartford may prove very fruitful. This insurer offers competitive rates that are worth investigating and may reward you with significant savings.

Also, an auto insurance policy through AAA can save members an average of $531 per year. Please visit your local AAA website or office for further details.

Some other tips for lowering your auto insurance include:

1. **Bundle your policies** — If you get your car insurance from the same company that offers your homeowners or renters insurance, you can possibly save up to 25% on each policy from some companies.

2. **Purchase a cheaper car** — Consider a preowned car without the advanced gadgets such as backup cameras. Older cars are also less risky for insurers because they are less expensive to replace. If your car's value is less than 10 times the premium, you may want to reduce or drop your collision and/or comprehensive coverage, as well.

3. **Pay your bills on time** — A low credit score often results in higher car insurance. Paying your bills on time will improve your credit score and lower your car insurance payment. You may also be able to get a discount if you choose auto-billing and if you pay for a full year up front versus paying month by month.

INCOME SECRET NO. 48:

Chop Your Cable Cord ... and Save Big

"Not wasting money is just as important as making money in any prudent investment strategy," I said in my presentation at an Offshore Investment Summit.

Out of the corner of my eye I saw a little man's head snap up, his eyes fixed on me. He'd been taking notes up to then, head bowed to the table. But from that moment onward, he stared at me in rapt attention.

After I was done — my session was just before the afternoon coffee break — he cornered me on my way out of the hall.

Uh-oh, I thought. No coffee for me. I had to be back onstage to introduce the panel discussion in 15 minutes.

"Until you spoke, I was worried that nobody really understood the secret of wealth," he said in a thick Swiss-German accent. "But you clearly do." I nodded politely, the smell of fresh coffee and leche tugging at my nostrils. "What you just said is the wisdom of the ages, as far as I am concerned."

"You mean the part about not trusting any politician who isn't Uruguayan?" I ventured. Instantly I recognized my father's brand of irreverent humor, albeit unsure of its appropriateness in conversation.

The apple doesn't fall far from the tree, for better or worse.

The little man looked right past my quip in the way that only the Swiss can.

"No, I mean about not wasting money as the key to wealth."

Free Your Mind, Then Your Wallet

OK then ... I know a bit about that! After all, I spent the bulk of my career working in the nonprofit sector, where salaries are nothing to write home about.

But my interest in good value and savings goes beyond dollars and cents. I see it as a critical aspect of my more general passion ... to live as freely as possible, to escape traps laid for me by the powers that be and to help others do the same.

The problem is that in today's America, mainstream media and pundits — all working for big private corporations — strongly encourage us to focus our discontent on the government and politicians. And they certainly deserve a lot of that! But a mono-focus on Washington distracts us from problems that are at least as important as an out-of-control government.

Thanks, perhaps, to my many years spent outside the U.S., I see the country from a slightly different perspective — one that is also sensitive to the ways in which accumulation of power outside of government shapes our fortunes in negative ways.

For example, I know for a fact that on a like-for-like basis, I pay a great deal more for my broadband internet service in the U.S. than I would if I lived in any other developed country, as well as a number of less-developed countries. The same is true for health care, education and other crucial services. The reason for this? As *The Economist* puts it:

> *One problem with American capitalism has been overlooked: a corrosive lack of competition. The naughty secret of American firms is that life at home is much easier: their returns on equity are 40% higher in the United States than they are abroad. Aggregate domestic profits are at near record levels relative to GDP. America is meant to be a temple of free enterprise. It isn't.*

An average 40% return on equity is unheard of in economic history. An individual firm may be capable of sustained returns like that for a while, but would expect to see its profits "competed away" eventually. Today, however, a very profitable American firm has an 80% chance of being that way 10 years later. In the 1990s, the odds were only about 50%.

The problem is that steep corporate earnings aren't luring in new entrants because established firms are abusing monopoly positions or using lobbying to stifle competition. Indeed, two-thirds of the U.S. economy's 900-odd industries have become more concentrated since 1997. A tenth of the economy is at the mercy of a handful of firms. At the same time, the rate of small-company creation in America is close to its lowest mark ever.

What are we to do about this if our politicians won't do anything? Well, you can't "vote the b******s out" when they are private corporations, industry associations or lobbyists. The best way I can think of to fight back is to explore the ways they rip us off and how to stop that from happening by adopting smart, little-known techniques to avoid doing business with them altogether.

Cable: How (and Why) They're Ripping You Off

For most of us, television in the first half of our lives meant tuning into the broadcast networks CBS, ABC and NBC, and enduring commercials (and poor reception) as the price of free entertainment.

All that changed with the rapid spread of cable TV in the 1980s. By the end of the decade, there were about 30 channels available on most cable networks. By the mid-'90s, the numbers had exploded into the hundreds — cable's vastly greater bandwidth made that technically feasible.

This plethora of content led to the development of "tiered" cable offerings, in which a higher monthly subscription fee gave you more channels to watch. The trick was that the most desirable content — especially professional sports, which migrated early to cable-only formats — was limited to the most expensive subscription tiers. The cost of these top tiers has risen at two to three times the rate of inflation ever since, joining cable with education and health care as the key drivers of escalating household budgets.

Sports Über Alles

Of course, just because cable can carry a lot of channels doesn't mean it has to. The driving force behind this tiered-bundle model is the cable companies' need to cover the costs of broadcast rights for sports and other premium content. A cost breakdown of the typical top cable tier shows that the bulk of your monthly subscription fee goes to broadcast rights for a small number of channels — usually four to five.

The main culprit is sports. Every U.S. league makes millions or billions of dollars from the content networks that want to broadcast their sports. Those networks, in turn, reap money from cable networks, which recoup it from you via the bundle model whether you want sports or not. Anyone who wants just a few special channels has to pay for the whole bundle regardless, keeping the money flowing up to the leagues.

One reason for this is that the content cable companies buy is also sold in bundle form. ESPN, for example, is owned by Disney, which will only sell ESPN to a cable network if it buys a range of other Disney channels as well. Each of those channels attracts a per-subscriber fee paid by the cable network, which then passes it on to subscribers whether we watch them or not.

Merging Content and Distribution

Starting with Comcast's acquisition of NBC in 2009, cable companies have rapidly merged with content producers — the people who make movies and TV shows. Cable companies realized that they might as well be the ones receiving the money they were paying for content broadcast rights, so they started acquiring the companies that produced it. In that way, they could increase their own profits — notably, by refusing to allow their now-proprietary content to be shown on competing cable networks — creating a de facto monopoly pricing situation.

Cable networks now commonly require small content programmers to give up much of their companies' equity stock just to get carried at all. As one CEO explained: "Cable and satellite TV companies want to own you before they put you on television." Cable networks are known to blackball any programmer that resists this — something illegal under federal communications and antitrust laws, but largely unenforced.

Oligopoly

The third factor behind high and rising cable prices is regional monopolies and national industry consolidation. Many

Americans rely on a single provider in their neighborhood, which can dictate prices at will. That's because most cable operators received exclusive franchises from local authorities when the cable network infrastructure was first being built out in the 1980s, using public utility rights-of-way. Otherwise, they wouldn't have laid the cables.

For example, in my neighborhood, Comcast was the only option for years, until AT&T figured out how to deliver cable via the existing telephone infrastructure it already owned. They're my only two choices now.

Nationally, the U.S. cable television industry is an unmistakable oligopoly, with the top four companies serving over 60% of the market. Coupled with limited regional options, this allows cable companies to jack up prices and neglect service quality at will.

Getting You Coming and Going

Finally, cable TV distributors derive extra "rent" from leasing set-top boxes to consumers. These boxes are often needed for on-demand and high-definition (HD) offerings and frequently include recording capabilities. The cable networks dominate the market for these boxes and deliberately make it difficult for consumers to use independent boxes. As a result, the set-top box is not subject to competition or innovation (many rely on old technology). Nevertheless, cable companies can and do charge high monthly prices for them.

The Specter of the Internet

The bottom line is that the average American household pays about $100 a month for hundreds of cable channels ... but only watches 10 to 12 of them regularly. The price of these cable packages continues to rise at more than the inflation rate, contributing to monopoly profits at our expense.

Most people instinctively react to this situation with the reasonable proposal that we should be able to buy cable channels a la carte, picking only those we actually watch. Surely, if we can put a man on the moon, we can pick and choose what to watch and when, paying as we go.

Indeed, there is absolutely no technological obstacle to a la carte television. The problem is that the cable companies rely on the current distorted market structure to extract economic rent from the U.S. consumer.

Internet streaming is the key to fighting back against this rip-off. It is considered such a threat that contracts between content producers (such as ESPN) and cable networks — which are often as long as seven years — limit what the producer can make available on its own internet streaming service ... and particularly on third-party services such as Netflix or Apple TV. For example, ESPN still doesn't allow most live sports to be broadcast on its own streaming service, WatchESPN.

That's done specifically to ensure that streaming distributors can't compete with cable networks, so we have to keep paying excessive costs for inferior products. It's market manipulation plain and simple, really.

But the cable companies aren't stupid, and they know they need to cover their flanks. So they've used those massive excess profits (rents) to buy up the broadband internet networks so that we need to watch streaming TV and ditch cable.

Consequently, nowadays most folks get their internet and cable from the same company — AT&T, Verizon, Comcast, Charter or Time Warner. That gives the cable companies even more market-distorting leverage over content producers ... and viewers like you and me. Here's how they use it:

- **TV everywhere** — In the late 2000s, the cable networks and the big content providers secretly colluded to create an internet-based streaming ecosystem called "TV Everywhere." The idea was to allow people to receive some streaming content — like hit cable series — only if they already had a valid cable subscription.

   For example, there is a nice Cartoon Network app available for the iPhone, but you can use it only if you enter your subscription details to one of the major cable companies that carries Cartoon Network. In this way, the cable industry hoped to satisfy the demand for a la carte streaming without giving up any profits. They assumed what we want is the convenience to watch TV anywhere — but what we really want is the freedom to buy only what we want to watch.

- **Network neutrality violations** — In mafia-like fashion, cable/broadband companies like Comcast have tried to force internet-based distributors like Netflix to pay "protection money" to prevent their streams from being "throttled," or slowed down, on their internet networks, which would make it hard to watch them online. By contrast, Comcast goes out of its way to ensure that content that it owns, such as NBC shows, streams beautifully. Although the Federal Communications Commission outlawed this in 2015, it still persists in hard-to-detect forms.

- **Content lockout** — Cable networks that own content (such as Comcast's NBC titles) refuse to license that content to streaming TV services such as Netflix, Hulu or Apple TV, forcing consumers to subscribe to Comcast cable to get it.

- **Targeted cap-and-metered pricing** — A bit ago, I got a notice from AT&T, my current internet provider, saying that my internet data would be capped at 600 megabytes a month, after which I'd have to pay $25 for blocks of 50 MB. I ditched Comcast before this because it was doing the same thing (at a 300 MB cap). This led to internet bills of $200 or more a month because I use streaming services instead of cable. There is no technological reason for them to do this, as they typically claim. Instead, they do it purely to compensate for the loss of cable subscribers to streaming services and to make returning to cable look more attractive.

An Epidemic of "Cord Cutting"

In these ways — despite the absence of technological barriers and the rapid spread of high-speed broadband internet —

the cable cabal has basically blocked the natural progression to a la carte content in the U.S. That's why we have slower and costlier internet service and higher TV prices than any other developed country.

But 2013 turned out to be a historic inflection point: the first full year the cable industry lost subscribers. The losses widened in 2014 and rapidly grew even faster in 2015. Cable TV viewing has been dropping at around 10% a quarter, a plunge that has advertisers terrified. In 2016, for example, there were a reported 1.4 million fewer cable subscribers from the year prior.

Fast-forward to 2020, when a combination of record unemployment from the COVID-19 pandemic, high cable prices and the pause of live sports sparked an overall drop of 1.8 million pay-TV subscribers in the first quarter of 2020 — the fastest shrinkage of the sector on record.

Not only is the number of cable subscribers falling, but the customers who remain are buying much slimmer bundles. One result was that ESPN lost 14 million viewers in seven years. The trend became particularly noticeable in 2016, when ESPN had the worst reported month in its history, losing over 620,000 cable subscribers, which also meant a drop in revenue of over $52 million. Overall, the number of pay-TV households is projected to decline, slowly but consistently.

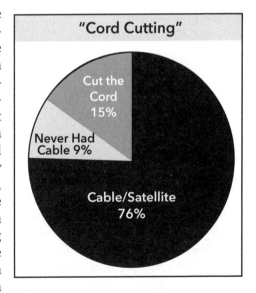

For example, *eMarketer* predicts that nearly 25% of households in the U.S. will drop traditional TV by 2022. The driving force behind this change is "cord cutting" — the rapid uptake of streaming devices and online content-delivery services. Pew

Research Center's "Home Broadband 2015" study found that 24% of all American adults do not subscribe to a cable TV service. Of those, 15% have become cord cutters in recent years, while 9% never had cable at all. The high cost of cable TV packages was cited by 74% of the cord cutters as the reason for dropping a service. Two-thirds of those who don't subscribe to cable cited alternate sources of streaming content as the reason for not having a traditional cable service. And 45% said they had reduced their cable or satellite TV service because they could get some desired content via streaming.

This was enough motivation for the content providers to finally take the plunge and start experimenting with streaming-only options, over the strenuous objections of the cable giants.

How I Fight Back

My household canceled its last cable subscription a few years ago. At the time, I was paying almost $200 a month for cable. Now I pay around $45 ... and could be paying even less. And if anything, our viewing options have expanded rather than contracted ... and we have vastly more control over what and when we watch.

My weapon of choice in the fight against the great cable rip-off is a little box that sits next to the TV called a Roku. (We actually have three — one in the living room, one for my daughter's room and one for the basement.)

The Roku box we use costs about $100, but the Roku Ultra can be had for less on special or used on eBay, while the Roku Streaming Stick, which does the same thing, is only about $50. There is no subscription charge — you just buy the Roku of your choice.

The Roku connects to our broadband internet by wireless or Ethernet cable. Once it's fired up, there's a menu of streaming "channels" to choose from. Most are free, and those that aren't are dramatically lower in price than a cable package, as you'll see shortly. We load and unload specific channels as needed — for example, during cricket season, we watch our South African national team via a special channel that we unload during the rest of the year. The same is true of many other specialized channels.

Here's the core of our Roku channel lineup:

- **Movies and TV shows** — The popular Netflix channel gives us unlimited access to tens of thousands of titles, with monthly plans that go from $8.99 for Basic to $15.99 for Premium. It also has a number of its own series, such as the popular hits *House of Cards*, *Orange Is the New Black* and *Stranger Things*.

  Then there's Amazon Instant Video, part of Amazon Prime. It costs as low as $8.99 a month for Prime Video only, or just $12.99 a month ($119 a year) for the additional Prime perks, including two-day shipping and unlimited music streaming, photo storage and reading. This gives us access to a large variety of video material that's "free" — i.e., covered by the Prime membership. Other titles are available to buy or rent on demand, costing anywhere from $0.99 to several dollars per title. We typically pay $4.99 for the standard-definition version of a movie that has just been in theaters. After a few months, the price of such films drops to $2.99 or $1.99. High definition is also available, usually for $1 more per title. Amazon Prime added the ability to stream versions of popular cable channels, such as Starz, Showtime and HBO, with free trials or monthly fees ranging from $8.99, $10.99 and $14.99, respectively.

  Finally, my wife subscribes to the CBS All Access channel ($5.99 a month), which carries her favorite soap opera.

- **News** — All the major American news networks, including CNN and PBS, have Roku channels that provide both a live feed and a menu of specific stories viewable on demand. The live feed isn't always the same as what you'd see on cable, but it's pretty close. Some of the networks display advertisements between news segments, just like a broadcast signal, but they are much shorter and less obtrusive. Local news channels are available on Roku for every major and medium-sized city in the U.S. I also subscribe to a range of alternative news networks — the list of available channels grows every day.

- **Sports** — Here's where my household is atypical. Since we're South African Americans, we follow cricket, rugby and soccer, mainly. We can get those sports either via a special channel (Willow TV) or as part of a free ESPN or Fox Sports Roku channel. We pay for the cricket channel, which has live broadcasts, but for rugby and soccer we often watch free replays the next day.

On the other hand, if we were into American sports, we could simply subscribe to Sling TV for $30 a month, which would give us ESPN, ESPN 2, NBA basketball and a number of entertainment channels. In addition, we might add MLB.TV for our favorite baseball team ($50 a year) and NFL Game Pass ($100 a year). Both are also available month by month. The NHL GameCenter platform and Major League Soccer's MLS Live provide similar access for those sports. College sports channels are also available at similar prices for games that aren't already on ESPN.

Note, however, that this may not be enough if you're a die-hard fan. The old-fashioned, network-oriented licensing and marketing rules usually entail a blackout of local team games, forcing you either to watch them on local network TV affiliates or to watch them later on replay.

History Repeating: Broadband Consolidation

The top high-speed internet access providers include cable companies AT&T, Comcast, Verizon, Time Warner, Cox and others. These companies charge you twice — once for internet access and once for a cable TV subscription.

Most analysts predict that as customers desert cable TV packages for internet-based streaming services, the telecom giants will try to charge more for internet, wiping out some or all of the cable savings. Indeed, the raw economics of internet delivery favor the cable companies. Internet service is much cheaper to offer than TV, so having customers shift the balance of their bills to data instead of TV is pure profit for the industry. It costs broadband providers virtually nothing if you use more data, so the overage charges they are starting to apply for the higher data usage arising from streaming cord cutters is essentially easy money for them.

That's why it's important to pay attention to the debates about competition in the broadband market and issues like net neutrality. The cable/internet giants are lobbying furiously for special favors from national and local politicians to protect their extraction of excess profits from the rest of us.

For example, some states have passed laws that make it difficult or impossible for municipalities to invest in low-cost broadband networks for their residents. They have also erected barriers that make it hard for newer businesses to string fiber-optic cable on utility poles or below ground in order to compete with established cable and phone companies.

The Digital Antenna Hack

But there's a way around that, which also gives you access to local broadcast stations in real time — the digital antenna or HD antenna. Local affiliates of commercial broadcast networks such as CBS, NBC, ABC and Fox still broadcast free-to-air the way they always have, except that now the signal is digital. With a digital antenna, you can ditch cable but still get real-time broadcast networks for free. Modern HD antennas don't have to go on the roof — they're simple affairs you set up next to the TV. (Outdoor antennas remain a viable option.) You'll have to play with the antenna position to maximize reception, just like fiddling with rabbit-ear antennas in the 1970s.

Before you do this, make sure you have over-the-air HD as an option where you live. Visit AntennaWeb.org or TVFool. com for a listing of the stations broadcasting near you and the sort of antenna you might need to pick them up. Top-rated HD indoor antennas include the Winegard FlatWave Amplified Indoor HDTV Antenna (model FL5500A) and the Mohu Leaf 50 Amplified Indoor HDTV Antenna, both in the $50 to $60 range.

Your Options for Low-Cost Streaming

There are a lot of ways to watch streaming TV across the internet like I do. For these services, a 5 MB per second broadband internet connection is generally fine, although high-definition streams may require a bit more.

Your viewing options include your smartphone, tablet, computer and, of course, your TV. On your computer, just visit a streaming service's website to view them — or connect your laptop to your TV using a monitor output, as I sometimes do for special events that are only on the internet.

An increasingly popular option is to use "smart" TVs, which have built-in streaming software like Roku and connect to the internet. I was in Best Buy recently and saw excellent 52-inch models on sale for under $450.

If you don't have a smart TV, there are many streaming hub options like the Roku I use with an 8-year-old flat screen. They include game consoles such as the Xbox 360, Xbox One, PlayStation 3 and PlayStation 4. Several Blu-ray players also have streaming hub apps.

Dedicated streaming devices like my Roku have two main forms: a thumb drive-sized unit that plugs into the HDMI port on the TV or a separate box the size of a portable CD player. Excellent small "stick" streaming devices include the Google Chromecast ($35), Roku Streaming Stick ($50) or the Amazon Fire TV Stick ($40). Larger units that give slightly better performance and onboard memory storage include the Amazon Fire TV Cube and the Apple TV.

Every single one of these products supports the "holy trinity" of cord cutter video-streaming apps: Netflix, Hulu and Amazon Prime Video. If you've got a specific service you want to watch, however, you need to do some research. Not every streaming device or game console gives access to every streaming service. For example, PlayStation 4 users who have Comcast cable have found that the company blocks them from using the HBO Go app.

What You'll Save

Below is the list of apps that would give you almost complete programming coverage — at least of prime-time TV across networks and cable channels. Many of them offer a free trial month too. From this, you can do a quick calculation against your current cable bill. Remember that you'll need to keep internet service, so be sure to deduct that from your current bill if you get bundled service to arrive at your cable-only cost. In any case, our household has saved a substantial amount of money each month. Now, we don't subscribe to all the streaming services — I don't have Hulu, HBO Now or Sling TV. But everyone in my household is perfectly happy with what we get. We do purchase on-demand movies and TV shows two to three times a week, which probably adds another $40 to our monthly outlay — but remember, these are things we choose to watch and when to watch them. We don't need to set up a recording — just click and view on demand.

Service	Monthly	Yearly
Netflix "Standard"	$12.99	$142.89 (w/ first month free)
Hulu	$5.99	$59.99
Amazon Prime	$12.00	$119.00
Sling TV ("Orange" or "Blue")	$30	$350
HBO Now	$14.99	$179.88
CBS All Access	$5.99	$59.99
TOTAL	$81.96	$911.75

Is Cord Cutting for You?

The decision to "cut the cord," as I've done, depends on how you balance the various factors. To help you do that, here's a summary of the pros and cons.

Pros:

- **Savings** — If you're like me, you'll definitely save money. Theoretically, you could pay almost as much as you do for cable if you subscribe to a lot of streaming services. I did initially try a number of the other streaming services that I don't use, but just found that I didn't watch enough on them to justify the cost. When the dust settled down, I was saving almost $150 a month.

- **Flexibility and convenience** — A big overlooked factor with cord cutting is that nearly everything becomes on demand. You don't have to watch when the show is on — you watch when you want to do so. You don't have to watch the movie HBO is showing tonight — you pick one yourself. In some cases — such as with AMC's The Walking Dead, a big hit in my household — we watch it the day after it shows on cable, which doesn't bother us one bit. We just ignore the reviews until we've seen it.

- **No contracts** — All of the streaming services we use, except Amazon Instant Video, are on a month-to-month basis, and I can cancel or suspend them at any time with no consequence. Some U.S. sports packages require an annual payment, but most allow you to go month to month as well. Compare that to the silly contracts and conciliation rules cable companies impose on you!

- **Fewer things to go wrong** — Streaming video requires only internet, a streaming device and a TV or monitor. At its simplest, all you need is your computer. That's a great deal less complicated than the cables and set-top boxes required by cable setups. When we had Comcast cable, we had service outages nearly every month. We've never once had a problem with our streaming setup.

Cons:

- **Lost content** — The biggest con is the loss of some channels, especially live news and major sports. Some popular shows are only available after a delay, as I noted above, and this may matter to you. But honestly, considering the abysmal quality of most U.S. cable news, is that such a big deal? In any case, streaming offers are expanding rapidly, and I anticipate that content restrictions will fade just as fast.

- **Vulnerability to abuse of internet monopoly** — The cable giants are trying to combat cord cutting by chiseling us on the broadband internet side. Right now, for example, if I had a Comcast internet package, my typical streaming usage would incur significant additional broadband overage fees every month, which would cancel out the advantage of dropping cable. Fortunately, I have alternatives — Google Fiber is on its way to my town — so this isn't an issue. But it may be for you. I do predict, however, that the cable companies will ultimately lose the fight to extract excess profits via abuse of broadband markets, particularly with Google and Apple moving rapidly to enter the broadband market directly.

Conclusion

There's nothing stopping you from trying out cord cutting right now. Just get a streaming box or stick and check it out, and keep your cable until you're ready to decide. Even if you decide to stick with cable, a streaming option will still come in handy — after all, you can take it with you when you travel in the U.S. and view Netflix and other services anywhere you can get a suitable internet connection.

Give it a try — I promise you won't regret it. And remember … it's not just about the money … it's about what's right for all of us.

INCOME SECRET NO. 49:

Separate Your Landline Long-Distance Phone Carrier

The majority of households today subscribe to "bundle" services from telecommunication providers, which include phone, cable and internet. When considering a bundle, you should ask yourself: "Does bundling really save me money?"

Providers have built up — through their ads and sales strategies — the idea that you are better off subscribing to their bundle deals. But having all the components ordered together may not be saving you money, especially if you don't need all of them. Many of us also just pay the bill each month but don't pay close attention to what we are paying for. If you go over your bill in detail, you may find that you are being deceived into believing you are getting a "deal."

If you find you need to keep a landline in your home, instead of bundling phone services, consider separating them. There are several long-distance phone carriers that charge relatively cheaper rates for long-distance phone calls.

Here's how it works: These carriers charge about $0.03 to $0.04 per minute with six-second billing increments. There are no minimums or monthly fees.

If you were to call someone out of state and talk for over an hour, your bill could be as low as $5 or $6, including taxes and fees, for the month.

And if you do not talk to anyone in a month, your bill is $0.

A company that can offer such savings is Pioneer Telephone. Since 1994, Pioneer states that it has helped "…business and residential customers save on their phone bill. Over $1,003,206,851 in savings to date, and [they] are just getting started." For more details, visit PioneerTelephone.com.

Another strategy that you can consider to lower your phone expense is to go mobile and get rid of your landline altogether. The majority of mobile plans include unlimited calling and texting within the continental United States.

You can also use apps and computer-based software, such as WhatsApp and Skype. These applications allow you to phone local and international numbers at no cost.

In addition, there is the option to use a Voice over Internet Protocol (VoIP) provider, such as Vonage (see more at VonageForHome.com). A VoIP transmits phone calls using a digital connection.

The bottom line is, you can save yourself money each month by examining how you utilize your phone and what you use it for. Cut out what you don't need and take advantage of all the great options that cost close to nothing, if nothing at all.

INCOME SECRET NO. 50:

Get Paid to Clear Out Your Clutter

Over the course of just one year, it can be surprising to see how many items we can accumulate. We pick up things to make our life easier, or mementos from a trip or new experience. These wonderful items exist in almost every nook and cranny in our own homes.

Now is an excellent time to go through all of your belongings, decide what should be kept and what should be donated or discarded, and then get PAID.

Nowadays, you don't have to rely on simply dropping off to a donation center or dump, or even having those all-day garage sales.

In fact, if you have a smartphone or access to the internet, getting rid of unwanted things is easy. As the old adage says, someone's junk is someone else's treasure.

Here are some of the best free apps to help you clean the clutter and even make some money:

- **OfferUp** — This app and site allow you to browse local items by image, with thousands of new postings every day, and communicate with sellers entirely through in-app messaging. Simply take a photo, post the description and price, and get ready to take the best offer. People are selling everything from cars and grills to shoes and ocean kayaks.

- **LetGo** — This is another free app and website where you can sell (and buy) preowned stuff. It is very similar to OfferUp, but better organized by categories.

Now, for some of us, having a garage sale is an overwhelming amount of work — and in some communities, it is prohibited. So, another route you can take is donating the items to charity.

Although there are several national and local agencies that will gladly take your donations, it's always best to call first to make sure they are accepting donations, and in what form.

And don't forget, donations are tax deductible! Be sure to keep your receipts for tax purposes.

Recently, I came across a great app that will let you track and value your noncash charitable donations. The app, iDonatedIt, is dedicated to helping you get the most value possible from your charitable donations. This app is available on the Apple App Store.

When you're done, you'll have more room in your home and money in your pocket.